P9-CJC-069

DATE DUE

DEMCO 38-296

NAMIBIA

PROFILES • NATIONS OF CONTEMPORARY AFRICA
Larry W. Bowman, Series Editor

Namibia: The Nation After Independence,
Donald L. Sparks and December Green

*Guinea-Bissau: Power, Conflict, and Renewal
in a West African Nation,* Joshua B. Forrest

Zimbabwe: The Terrain of Contradictory Development,
Christine Sylvester

*Mauritius: Democracy and Development in
the Indian Ocean,* Larry W. Bowman

Niger: Personal Rule and Survival in the Sahel, Robert B. Charlick

*Equatorial Guinea: Colonialism, State Terror, and the Search
for Stability,* Ibrahim K. Sundiata

Mali: A Search for Direction, Pascal James Imperato

Tanzania: An African Experiment,
Second Edition, Revised and Updated, Rodger Yeager

Cameroon: Dependence and Independence, Mark W. DeLancey

*São Tomé and Príncipe: From Plantation Colony
to Microstate,* Tony Hodges and Malyn Newitt

Zambia: Between Two Worlds, Marcia M. Burdette

Ethiopia: Transition and Development in the Horn of Africa,
Mulatu Wubneh and Yohannis Abate

*The Central African Republic: The Continent's
Hidden Heart,* Thomas O'Toole

Mozambique: From Colonialism to Revolution, 1900–1982,
Allen Isaacman and Barbara Isaacman

NAMIBIA

The Nation After
Independence

Donald L. Sparks
and
December Green

Westview Press

BOULDER • SAN FRANCISCO • OXFORD

Profiles/Nations of Contemporary Africa

All photos courtesy John Liebenberg unless otherwise attributed. Maps courtesy U.S. Department of State.

Copyright © 1992 by Westview Press, Inc.

Published in 1992 in the United States of America by Westview Press, Inc., 5500 Central Avenue, Boulder, Colorado 80301-2847, and in the United Kingdom by Westview Press, 36 Lonsdale Road, Summertown, Oxford OX2 7EW

Library of Congress Cataloging-in-Publication Data
Sparks, Donald L.
  Namibia : the nation after independence / Donald L. Sparks and December Green.
    p. cm.—(Profiles. Nations of contemporary Africa)
  Includes bibliographical references and index.
  ISBN 0-8133-1023-7
  1. Namibia—Politics and government—1990– I. Green, December.
II. Title. III. Series.
DT1649.S64 1992
968.8104—dc20   91-38868
                                                                                  CIP

Printed and bound in the United States of America

The paper used in this publication meets the requirements of the American National Standard for Permanence of Paper for Printed Library Materials Z39.48-1984.

10   9   8   7   6   5   4   3   2   1

Under the sun
The earth is dry
By the fire
Alone I cry
All day long
The earth cries
For the rain to come
All night my heart
For my hunter to come
And take me away.

Oh! Listen to the wind
You woman there;
The time is coming
The rain is near
Listen to your heart
Your hunter is here.

—Anonymous
"The Song of the Rain"

Contents

List of Tables and Illustrations   ix
Acknowledgments   xi

Introduction   1

1   *Namibia's History*   5

    The Precolonial Era, *5*
    German Colonialism, *11*
    South African Colonialism, *14*
    Notes, *20*

2   *Namibian Politics*   23

    Efforts Toward Political Liberation: To 1960, *24*
    Efforts Toward Political Liberation:
      1960–1980s, *28*
    Toward a Solution, *39*
    The Solution: The Implementation of UN Resolution 435
      and Independence, *46*
    Regional Political Relations After Independence, *62*
    Postindependence International Political Linkages, *66*
    Notes, *69*

3   *The Economy*   73

    Major Economic Sectors and Resources, *74*
    Employment and Labor, *97*
    Economic Relations with South Africa, *101*
    Southern African Economic Relations, *108*
    International Economic Relations, *110*

Recent Economic Developments, *115*
Economic Prospects, *119*
Notes, *126*

4   Society and Culture   131

Peoples and Demographics, *131*
Religion, *138*
Role of Women, *141*
Education, *144*
Health, *147*
Literature, *151*
Sports, *152*
Notes, *153*

Conclusion   156

Notes, *161*

Appendix A: The Mandate for South West Africa
  of the League of Nations   163
Appendix B: Chronology of International Efforts   165
Appendix C: UN Security Council Resolution 435   167
Appendix D: UN Security Council Resolution 435
  as Supplemented   169
Appendix E: Protocol of Geneva   171
Appendix F: Tripartite Agreement   173
Appendix G: The Government at Independence   175
Appendix H: Goals of the SWAPO Women's Council   177
Selected Bibliography   178
Interviews   186
About the Book and Authors   187
Index   188

Tables and Illustrations

Tables

2.1   1989 election results   58

3.1   Structure of Namibia's GDP by sector of origin   74
3.2   Namibia's major minerals   77
3.3   Mining contribution to Namibian GDP   78
3.4   Value of Namibia's mineral exports   79
3.5   Namibia's major mines   80
3.6   Namibia's diamond production   83
3.7   Location of Namibia's manufacturing firms   90
3.8   Employment by economic activity   98
3.9   Namibia's debt   103
3.10 Customs and excise contributions to Namibia's
         central revenues   105
3.11 Merchandise imports and exports, 1920–1988   111
3.12 Namibia's trade balance   112
3.13 Namibia's direction of trade   113
3.14 Namibia's current account of the balance
         of payments   116
3.15 Namibia's gross domestic product, 1985–1989   117
3.16 Namibia's inflation   118

4.1   Namibia's population groups   132
4.2   Formal education/training estimates
         for the labor force   146

Maps

Namibia   xii
Vegetation and rainfall   2

3.1   Namibia's economic activity   75

4.1   Ethnic groups in Namibia   133

Photos

Post office workers repair telephone lines   31
Koevoet police enjoy a picnic on the banks
  of the Kunene River   35
Namibians sign one of many petitions   41
Pik Botha confers with Louis Piennar   42
Results of PLAN's March 1989 incursion   51
A bushman woman who planned to vote   55
Voting lines at Katutura   56
A Namibian registering to vote   57
President Sam Nujoma at the independence
  ceremonies   63
Windhoek's major street, formerly Kaiserstrasse   64
Mining uranium   85
Arandis houses workers for Rössing Uranium   86
Fishermen at Luderitz   93
Entrepreneurship in Katutura   100
Ovambo women in Oshakati celebrating
  independence   134
Herero woman in traditional dress   136
Windhoek retains much of its German colonial
  architectural heritage   152

Acknowledgments

Many people helped with this book. We are deeply indebted to our editor, Professor Larry Bowman, who was invaluable in all stages of this study. His patience and guidance maintained us.

We are in debt to a number of people who reviewed parts of earlier drafts or made helpful comments. Special thanks to Professor Faniel Tjingeate, Department of Economics, University of Namibia, Windhoek, Namibia; Dr. David R. Konkel, Office of Economic Analysis, U.S. Department of State, Washington, D.C.; Dr. Yoburt Shamapande, Office of the UN Council for Namibia, New York, N.Y.; Dr. Klaus Billand, United Nations Industrial Development Organization, Vienna, Austria; and M.R.V. Hodd, School of Oriental and African Studies, University of London. The photos from John Liebenberg, Namibia's finest photographer, helped to make the overall book more presentable. Thanks also to Edzard Ellerkmann who provided other photos.

We also acknowledge the generous support of the Citadel Development Foundation for helping to finance travel to Namibia.

Donald L. Sparks
December Green

NAMIBIA

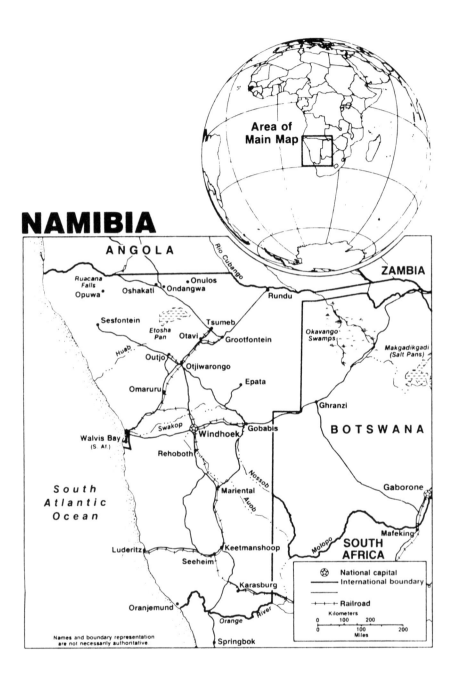

Area of Main Map

ANGOLA

ZAMBIA

Rio Cubango

Ruacana Falls
Opuwa
Oshakati
Onulos
Ondangwa
Rundu

Sesfontein
Etosha Pan
Tsumeb
Otavi
Grootfontein

Okavango Swamps

Makgadikgadi (Salt Pans)

Huab
Outjo
Otjiwarongo

Omaruru
Epata

Ghranzi

BOTSWANA

Swakop
Windhoek
Gobabis

Walvis Bay
(S. Af.)

Rehoboth

South Atlantic Ocean

Nossob

Gaborone

Mariental

Auob

Luderitz
Keetmanshoop

SOUTH AFRICA

Mafeking

Seeheim

Molopo

Karasburg

Oranjemund

Orange River

National capital
International boundary
Railroad

Kilometers
0   100   200
0   100   200
Miles

Names and boundary representation are not necessarily authoritative

Springbok

Introduction

On March 21, 1990, Namibia (formerly known as South West Africa) achieved independence after a century of colonial rule, first by Germany and then by South Africa. Since World War I the territory was considered almost a fifth province by South Africa, and the linkages between the two countries remain strong today even after Namibia's political independence. Namibia will face political, economic, and social challenges based on historical constraints over which it has limited control for change.

About the size of France, Namibia has been called a dry place located between two deserts. Except in the north, most of the country receives less than 400 millimeters of rain a year, and the average rainfall is 270 millimeters. Great variation in both rainfall and temperatures is found within the country. Rainfall increases from the coast inland; for example, Swakopmund—on the coast—receives less than 2 centimeters of rain annually, but Donkerhuk—about 150 kilometers inland—receives about 18 centimeters of rain. Regions in eastern Caprivi receive over 600 millimeters annually. However, because of the evaporation rate, the rainfall in much of Namibia is not particularly effective for agriculture. Further, the brief, heavy rain showers play an important role in soil erosion in many areas. Indeed, almost 95 percent of the country receives more than half of its annual rain in a four-month period. Namibia's agricultural zones correspond roughly to rainfall patterns. The country can be divided into three basic agricultural zones: (1) mixed, small-scale, and subsistence farming are found in the north; (2) small animal stock—karakul, other sheep, and goats—is found mostly in the center and south; (3) large animal stock, mostly beef, is found in the central and northern regions.

Although no perennial rivers are found within Namibia, four rivers help define its borders: the Kunene and Okavango with Angola, the Linyanti with Botswana, and the Orange with South Africa. Namibia is bounded on the south by South Africa, on the north by Angola, and

1

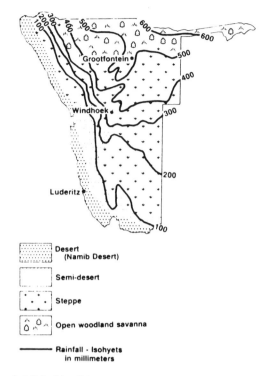

Vegetation and rainfall in Namibia

on the east by Botswana. A tiny part of Namibia—the 35 kilometer-wide Caprivi strip—just touches Zambia. The Namib Desert, from which the country receives its name, stretches some 1,300 kilometers along the entire Atlantic coast and is from 80 kilometers to 120 kilometers wide. Except for the two major ports of Walvis Bay (claimed by South Africa) and Luderitz, plus the town of Swakopmund, the coast is sparsely populated. Very few people live in the Kalahari Desert, in Namibia's far eastern region. Most of the country's 1.5 million people live in the north and in the high, arid region between the Kalahari and Namib deserts. This interior plateau, which covers just over half of the country's land area, has an average elevation of 1,097 meters. The largest ethnic group, the Ovambo, lives primarily in the far north and comprises about half of the country's total population. Most Namibians speak either Kwanyama (the major Ovambo language), Nama, or Herero. Although Afrikaans was the most widely used language in schools, government, and businesses, in an attempt to lessen its "South African connection," English was declared the country's official language.

The political and economic systems that dominated precolonial Namibia are no longer recognizable. The institutionalized racism of apartheid can be traced back to the beginnings of European penetration by missionaries and traders. As the riches of Namibia were made increasingly available to European merchants and settlers, Africans were pushed off their lands. Their status eroded to the point where they were crowded into European-created reserves and considered mere units of labor for European enterprises. Today about 40 percent of the country is communal land (which was formerly the "native homelands"). Whites own about 45 percent—most of the best ranging and agricultural land—and the state owns the rest. Africans did not accept the land divisions submissively: Resistance ranged from passive resistance to guerrilla war. This effort to free Namibia from German and later South African domination was also played out in the international arena as Namibian nationalists and their supporters worked with the United Nations and other international organizations. Although these efforts finally proved successful under a negotiated settlement to accept a UN-monitored transition to independence, Namibia now faces the huge task of over-coming the legacy of more than one hundred years of colonialism.

Namibia comes to independence with significant economic potential but with accompanying formidable challenges. It will face many obstacles to growth and development, including a lack of skilled workers, a low capital formation base, a small internal market, a limited manufacturing base, poor prospects for import substitution, and a potentially uneasy relationship with the Republic of South Africa—its economically powerful neighbor to the south.

Nevertheless, Namibia is blessed with one of the continent's best infrastructures. It is rich in natural resources, including some of the world's largest deposits of uranium and diamonds. Namibia has had over a decade in which to plan for independence. It has learned many lessons from its neighbors, and the postindependence government will have the opportunity to develop an economy that could become one of southern Africa's most successful.

Namibia has developed a constitutional democracy: a multiparty system that protects against abuses through a separation of powers among executive, legislative, and judicial branches of government. A Bill of Rights guarantees individual liberties without discrimination on the basis of race, religion, or gender. What is most surprising about the new system is that it is built on compromises by all those involved. Parties that were recently at war are now the majority parties in parliament and the government's loyal opposition. The South West African People's

Organization (SWAPO), which leads the government, has worked to incorporate representatives from many ethnic groups in its cabinet and to allay whites' fears of nationalization or revenge. Even the white, far–right-wing Action Christian National Party has called for everyone to put aside their differences and work in a spirit of conciliation.

1
Namibia's History

Although the history Namibia can be traced back thousands of years, most Namibian scholarship has focused almost exclusively on the colonial period.[1] In this chapter, we can only make a few tentative generalizations about the situation of some of the larger societies of the precolonial period before discussing the impact of German and South African colonialism on the entire territory.

THE PRECOLONIAL ERA

Precolonial Namibia was composed of many different societies with different political cultures and bases for economic organization. Several distinguishable ethnosocial organizations are found within the borders that demarcate Namibia today; other groups have members scattered over more than one state. For example, the Ovambo—the largest ethnic group—populate much of the area around the Namibian-Angolan border. Although none was as large as the epic empires of West Africa, Namibia developed large and highly centralized kingdoms, which ruled over sizable areas. Smaller societies based on the extended family were more common; yet for the most part these societies could hardly fall into the European stereotype of isolated, "primitive," subsistence communities. Rather, there was an interpenetration of these societies. Precolonial Namibia was traced by trading routes that tied together distinct groups within the territory and expanded beyond it as part of a huge regional network of long-distance trade.

In the far north the kingdoms comprising Ovambo based their wealth on a mix of pastoralism and sedentary agriculture. The Ovambo were also active in mining and marketing commodities such as copper, iron ore, and salt in the long-distance trade, which ran north into Angola and the Kalahari as well as to the south. The surplus afforded by the rich soils allowed for concentrations of relatively large populations and for complex political systems. The eight kingdoms (or clans) of the

5

Ovambo each had its own system of centralized authority based on hereditary succession but they all cooperated through a federal system. Clans often came into conflict over economic and legal issues such as access to land and water, cattle ownership, and extradition. Armed first with iron weapons and later with guns, Ovambo militaries were known for defending themselves behind the high walls that surrounded their villages. Historians suggest that the complex of Ovambo kingdoms was strongest in the seventeenth and eighteenth centuries.[2] Not only did agricultural production increase during this period but the kingdoms also built their wealth on a monopoly over trade in crucial commodities. Later, toward the end of the eighteenth century, as other groups moved north toward the Tsumeb area and into territories occupied by the Ovambo, it was rights to the copper mines rather than land that were in dispute.[3]

Located in the most northern reaches of Namibia and relatively inaccessible to Europeans coming from the south, the Ovambo were able to maintain their autonomy from European influence much longer than most other Africans in Namibia. Yet the Ovambo gradually became drawn into a trading relationship with the Europeans. The introduction of firearms in the 1860s and 1870s first allowed the clear domination of one clan over another. Through trade with the Europeans in the south, one clan (the Ondongas) obtained a large cache of arms. Because of this advantage, the Ondongas were able to dominate other clans for many years.

The Hereros were the other large population group in the precolonial period. They came into the territory at approximately the same time as the Ovambo, continued south into the central regions, and built their wealth on pastoralism. The Hereros gave their allegiance to a central authority but generally turned to a senior person in their own homestead or extended family. Although external disputes have been exaggerated by the Europeans, they did occur; as they were primarily pastoralists of huge herds of cattle, the need for large tracts of land and water rights occasionally brought the Hereros into conflict with other groups—especially the Nama, who lived in neighboring territories.

The external dispute that was most devastating to the Hereros involved the Europeans. Known for their large herds and relative self-sufficiency, the Hereros were generally uninterested in trading with the first Europeans who sought cattle and land. Consequently, the Hereros were only slowly pulled into the colonial economy that was controlled from the Cape in South Africa. They did eventually trade with the Europeans for a few necessities (such as guns and ammunition). The slow development of trade with the Europeans enabled the Hereros to maintain their own herds in large numbers until the 1870s and 1880s.

The first Europeans in Namibia came by ship on their way around South Africa to the East. The earliest solid evidence of a European presence is marked by a stone cross that bears the date 1484 and was erected by Portuguese travelers approximately one hundred miles north of Walvis Bay. There was little constant European presence in Namibia; rather, until the nineteenth century European involvement amounted to little more than an initial exploration of the coast north of the Cape by the Dutch East India Company in the 1650s. It was not until the eighteenth and nineteenth centuries that European interest in the area began to increase, with British, French, U.S., and Dutch whaling expeditions off the Namibian coast and a few individual travelers in the southernmost areas.

As late as 1800 the only part of Namibia well-known to Europeans was southern Namibia, referred to as *Namaland.* However, Hamburg and Bremen merchants soon made successful appeals to German politicians, and increasing numbers of Europeans were sent to Namibia to settle and seek their fortunes. In this early period of German interest, the three most important German actors in Namibia were the private companies, which sought the territory's resources and market; the government, which originally wanted a low profile and no military expense to protect these German nationals; and the missions, which in effect "opened up" the territory for colonization.

Germany was not the only country to send missionaries to Namibia; as early as 1802 the London Missionary Society was sending British, Scottish, Dutch, and German church people. By the 1840s, the Rhenish Mission Society and others had more than one objective in Namibia: In addition to evangelization, the missions began to engage in trade with Africans, directing it away from traditional routes to production for European consumption. In certain areas of Namibia, the missions soon totally dominated this African-European trade. Otijibingue became an important mission and trading post: It even had its own rifle factory and traded rifles and ammunition for ivory and cattle. Consequently, mission leaders became very powerful in these communities.[4] It was not unusual for leading missionaries such as Hugo Hahn to be treated as kings.[5] The missionaries taught obedience to authority and the joy of labor and laid the foundation for the integration of Africans into the European economy.

By the 1850s the influence of another group of Europeans— merchants—was felt increasingly in Namibia. Hundreds of Europeans were attracted by news of the territory's mineral resources and hoped to make their fortunes in mining. After an initial flurry of activity, surface ores were rapidly depleted. This slump contributed to the large-scale abandonment of mining in the 1860s. However, some entrepreneurs such as Charles Andersson stayed and made tremendous fortunes. The biggest prize went to F.A.E. Luderitz, a Bremen merchant who was granted a huge trading concession on the coast in 1883. He eventually purchased 3,200 square miles of the territory for approximately $3,000 and claimed the entire tract of land from the Orange River to latitude 26° south extending 20 miles inland.[6] That area became known as the diamond coast because diamonds were so abundant that they were often found loose in the sand. It is therefore easy to imagine why increasing numbers of Europeans came seeking their fortunes. As one indication of the volume of wealth exported to Europe, between 1908 and 1915 South West Africa exported 5.5 million carats in diamonds. This was an incredible boon to the German economy, which received R 6 million in taxes in the period.[7]

The first Europeans who sought the resources of the north were ivory merchants, who traded indirectly with the Ovambo through the Damara—another ethnic group living in central Namibia. Early European encroachment was closely surveyed by Ovambo kings, and these foreign merchants had to pay large duties to enter and exit the territory. It was not until the mid-nineteenth century that direct links were established between the Ovambo and the Europeans. By this time Portuguese merchants from Luanda had set up shop at the southern port of Mocamedes and were seeking ivory and slaves to work in coastal Angola and in the Portuguese-controlled "cocoa islands" of São Tomé and Príncipe. The Ovambo and others raided neighboring communities and rapidly thinned the elephant population to meet the European demand. As the demand for slaves subsided and ivory became more rare, cattle became the dominant item of trade. Gum, orchilla, and wax were of lesser importance but were also traded. Over time this trade became so important to the Portuguese that from 1859 to 1863 they made an unsuccessful attempt to control Ovamboland.[8]

Meanwhile, German and British merchants and missionaries from the Cape gradually penetrated the Ovambo economy. Consequently, for a brief period beginning in the 1880s, the Ovambo could exploit the rivalry between the Cape and the Portuguese as these groups vied with each other for control of the trade.[9] Yet this period of African control over participation in the European trade was short-lived. Without African participation the Europeans set the current boundaries of Namibia (at that time recognized by Europeans as South West Africa) and most of the rest of Africa at the Conference of Berlin in 1884–1885. Their decisions effectively divided the Ovambo clans between Angola and South West Africa. Yet for many years European penetration of the area was marginal. Other than the large German fort at Namutoni—which guarded the major trade route to the south—occasional Portuguese attempts to take Ovamboland, and the presence of small numbers of Finnish, Catholic, and Anglican missionaries, the kingdoms of Ovambo resisted European political (if not economic) dominance. Ovambo kings managed to maintain their independence until after World War I, when South Africans and the Portuguese took the area by force. More striking than political dominance was the growing European control over the Ovambo economies, a control that eventually contributed to the Ovambo's political decline. This decline was precipitated by a series of catastrophes (drought, floods, locusts, and a rinderpest epidemic in 1897 that destroyed more than 90 percent of Ovambo herds) that further drove the Ovambo into economic indebtedness and led to a greater loss of political autonomy.[10]

As Ovambo leaders became caught in a cycle of consumption of European luxuries followed by debt, demands on the population increased. Taxes were raised to pay these debts, and increasing numbers of Ovambo became indigent and had to seek contracts with Europeans as wage laborers in the south. By World War I, as many as ten thousand men a year were heading south as migrant laborers, and two thousand a year went north to Portuguese Angola.[11] This pattern has continued ever since.

It was also in the 1870s and 1880s that the Herero's relationship with the Europeans shifted. The Herero paramount leader, Samuel Maharero, invited the Cape administration to help remedy a long-standing economic dispute with the Nama, another pastoral society that lived in the southern and central territories. As pressures on the land, which were aggravated by the growing European presence, grew more intense, clashes between the Nama and other contenders for land (Europeans and Hereros) became more regular; the Nama were progressively being pushed off the land. Because they did not share European conceptions of individual ownership of land, they had no suspicions as they signed their rights to it away.

To add to the land pressures, by 1835 the Oorlams—a people of Khoi and European heritage—had moved from South Africa into the southern and central regions of the territory and had begun to dominate the Nama. Powerful Oorlam leaders such as Jager Afrikaner and his son Jonker arranged treaties with the Nama in which the Oorlams guaranteed protection against Herero expansion. The Nama's access to horses, guns, and Oorlam military leadership gave them a considerable advantage over other African competitors for land and water rights. However, in many ways the Nama were overwhelmed by the Oorlams. Upholding the terms of the treaties, the Oorlams and Nama succeeded in dominating areas once held by the Herero, further strengthening their position in southern and central Namibia by the mid-nineteenth century.

By the late nineteenth century, trade with the Cape became more regular, and the concept of private property was more widely accepted among the people of the southern and central territories. The traditional economy based on cattle gradually became less important, and as the Nama were increasingly drawn into the European-dominated trade, their self-sufficiency eroded. The Europeans were interested in trading for animal products. This demand for ivory, skins, feathers, and the like was so intense that by the mid-nineteenth century these resources were rapidly becoming depleted. As one analyst suggests, the Nama adopted much of the Oorlam identity, making the transition from a precapitalist, pastoral economy to a military economy based on raiding. Traditional trade routes and industries were being replaced by the focus on the Cape route, and a market was created for cheap European products— notably arms and liquor. The Oorlams had been instrumental in rerouting this focus of trade toward the Cape, although Europeans dominated the trade itself. With only a few traders and a captive market, the profits from this trade were enormous. Much of the trade was conducted on credit, and large amounts of merchandise were marked up 100–500 percent.[12]

Because of the adverse terms of trade, the Nama and Oorlams fell deeply into debt. The Hereros and other groups soon found themselves in similar straits, with similar political consequences. This situation was fundamentally destabilizing, as those in debt increasingly turned to raiding cattle to pay their accounts. Hostilities and casualties escalated by the mid- to late nineteenth century when the ownership of arms and ammunition was no longer the monopoly of a few. In effect, the Europeans had created a classic situation of divide and rule. Ironically, this period of anarchy actually facilitated colonization.[13] By this time the European presence had been virtually invited; the Hereros, Oorlams, and Nama all flirted with the idea of German protection. In terms of European opinion, the wars among Africans facilitated and rationalized the German takeover.

Yet formal colonization required one last push. Great Britain's growing interest in exploiting these resources seems to have been the last factor necessary for the once-hesitant German government to formally declare a protectorate over the entire territory, stretching from the Orange River to the southern boundary of Portuguese Angola. In 1884, in return for the German concession of the port of Walvis Bay and the surrounding area to the British Cape government, the British acknowledged German sovereignty over South West Africa. One of the first acts of the colonial administration was to secure domination of the economy and politics of the territory. The Germans would promote free trade in the territory and protect the lives and property of Europeans, and the German empire claimed jurisdiction over Africans as well as Europeans. Although African leaders ostensibly maintained authority over their own societies, all disputes between Germans and Africans were referred directly to German authorities.

GERMAN COLONIALISM

Thus, the Germans claimed authority over people they knew little about and developed plans for the territory. By the period of formal empire following the Conference of Berlin in the 1880s, Germany had decided to create a settler colony to secure what was by now considered its strategic possession in southern Africa. The German government actively encouraged Germans to emigrate to South West Africa and to establish a ranching economy in the prime central and southern lands. By 1902 large numbers of whites were immigrating, and African ranchers (especially the Hereros, but other groups as well) were soon being squeezed out as Germans, Afrikaners, and other whites sought larger and larger parcels of the best land. German economic policy clearly favored the Europeans, and laws were promulgated that restricted African rights to land and water to the rapidly shrinking "reserves" created during the late nineteenth century. Originally about 25 percent of the territory was set aside for African occupation, and the rest was set aside as crown land or game reserves or was open for European purchase. Although the land Africans were allowed to keep was clearly insufficient for their needs, the Germans gradually expropriated more and more African land and made it available to Europeans.

The "reservation" system was widely supported by the missions. In most cases the land comprising the reservation was held "in trust" by the missions for the Africans. As additional numbers of Europeans immigrated to South West Africa and took more African land, tensions between the Africans and Europeans escalated. The reservation system soon became recognized as an instrument for the alienation of land from Africans and the segregation of African and European communities. During the first two decades of formal colonization (1884–1903), colonial troops were engaged in continual wars against the Nama, Hereros and other groups. Increasing numbers of German soldiers had to be sent to the protectorate in the 1890s. A strong military was important to the larger German strategy for the territory. Land and cattle were regularly expropriated from the defeated groups; therefore, each defeat of a rebellion against German land and property policies meant more wealth for the Europeans.

The Herero-German War

All of these factors—including economic frustrations, the arbitrary colonial judicial system, and an all-pervasive German ethnocentrism and racism—contributed to an African-German war, which resulted in genocide. The Herero Rebellion of 1904 has been called the most bitter war in colonial history.[14] Although several sources of discontent existed for the Hereros at the time, the Herero attack followed a series of severe economic blows that were directly linked to German colonial policy. The January 1904 attack was a surprise to the Germans; their troops were already fighting another rebellion led by the Bondelswaarts in the south. The German administration in South West Africa, under the leadership of Governor Theodore Leutwein, was completely unprepared for the strike but believed diplomatic efforts could settle the problem. However, the Germans underestimated the depth of the problems to which the Hereros were reacting. They also were not prepared for African solidarity in support of the Herero rebellion. Africans, particularly the Nama, rallied behind the plan to overthrow the German administration and retake all expropriated lands. Africans were united by Herero leader Maharero's famous call to die together rather than by European cruelty: "All our patience with the Germans is of little avail, for each day they shoot someone dead for no reason at all. Hence I appeal to you, my brother, not to hold aloof from the uprising, but to make your voice heard so that all Africa may take up arms against the Germans. Let us die fighting rather than die as a result of maltreatment, imprisonment, or some other calamity. Tell all the Kapteins down there to rise and do battle."[15]

Analysts now maintain that the Hereros would have beaten the Germans handily had they fought according to European martial principles.[16] At the time of the attack, the Germans were outnumbered (the ratio was three to one in favor of the Hereros) and had focused their attention on the south. In addition, the Hereros had accumulated large quantities of weaponry and ammunition, the German settler population was dispersed, and transport and communication systems were weak. However, rather than attacking once they had surrounded the German settlement and colonial headquarters at Okahandja, the Hereros simply waited for the Germans to surrender. Meanwhile, the Germans waited for reinforcements and new military leadership. Once these arrived, the Germans easily put down the Herero attack. A new German military leadership under General Louis von Trotha was brought in to fight the war, resulting in a radical new approach. Governor Leutwein's ideas about mediation and diplomacy were no longer considered; rather, the objective of the war shifted from defense of the status quo to elimination of the enemy.

Under von Trotha, German colonial policy was distinguished by its brutality. After what traditionally would have been considered the defeat of the Hereros (their surrender at Waterberg in August 1904), von Trotha's men were instructed to continue annihilating the Herero people. Watering places were cemented, poisoned, or guarded. German soldiers were ordered to kill or drive out of the territory every Herero man, woman, or child—armed or not. The Herero population was pursued into the extremely harsh environment of the sandveld. German patrols continued to search for any stragglers. By the time von Trotha was instructed to make way for a new German policy of reconciliation, some 65,000 Hereros (approximately 80 percent of the population) were dead. The Hereros have never recovered from this slaughter; the population today is only 70,000.

For the few Hereros who survived the war and extermination campaign, the German policy of reconciliation offered little relief. According to the policy, all remaining Herero land was ceded to the German administration as reparation. Ten million more hectares of Herero land were confiscated as well as all the land of the Namas who participated in the rebellion.

Labor and Land

Another purpose was served by this German policy. In addition to a strong German desire for land, there was a great need for labor. The European expansion required manpower for construction and commercial, military, and administrative needs, and labor was in short supply. By confiscating their land, the Germans effectively rendered the Africans landless—removing the source of their livelihood and forcing them into the labor pool. However, despite the devastation wreaked on the population, the effects of the war were not enough to induce sufficient numbers of Africans to sell their labor.

This situation continued until the establishment of the 1907 Labor Code, which made wage labor mandatory. Other labor laws designed during this period forbade Africans to keep cattle without the permission of the colonial administration. The cumulative effect of such laws (as practiced in South Africa) was to make it impossible for these groups to continue their livelihood and thus to force Africans to sell their labor. Other laws to weaken African political organizations and social cohesion made it illegal for more than ten families or individual laborers to live on one piece of land. In addition, all African males over the age of eight had to carry a passbook (as was the case in South Africa itself), and all Africans without labor contracts could be considered vagrants and be liable to arrest. This barrage of regulations, plus the increasing numbers of Ovambo being pulled into the colonial economy as migrant laborers, effectively solved the problem of a labor shortage. From the European standpoint, the labor policy was a success; by World War I, approximately 90 percent of the male African population (excluding Ovamboland because of its distance from European centers) had been integrated into the colonial economy as unskilled laborers.[17]

Therefore, in the years just before World War I, the body of German regulations controlling Africans developed rapidly. Increasing numbers of Germans were immigrating and demanding land. In the years between the Herero genocide and World War I, the white population increased nearly threefold—from approximately 4,700 in 1903 to approximately 14,000 in 1913.[18] In stark contrast to the experience for blacks, this was a period of great economic success for most whites in South West Africa. Yet this success was threatened as South West Africa was brought into World War I.

SOUTH AFRICAN COLONIALISM

The conflict that tore at Europe ended fairly quickly in South West Africa. After some controversy within South Africa over whether it should come to the aid of the British, eventually South African armies under the leadership of Generals Jan Smuts and Louis Botha invaded German South West Africa. The South African armies outmanned and outmaneuvered the Germans in a few weeks. Botha took Windhoek and on behalf of the Allies set up an interim military administration in July 1915.

Toward the end of the war, expectations on the part of both blacks and whites grew rapidly. Yet again South West Africa's future was decided by Europeans. Ironically, many black South West Africans, urged on by South African propaganda and promises to restore liberties and freedom, viewed the white South Africans as their saviors. Toward the end of the war and coincident with the decision concerning South West Africa's future status, the most discriminatory German laws were relaxed somewhat, and South West Africans looked forward to a return to their precolonial status. This was not an unreasonable assumption because the Allies created publicity campaigns and published accounts of German atrocities committed in South West Africa.

However, black hopes for independence were disappointed. Indignation over German atrocities was part of a campaign by the Allies to rationalize their continued domination of colonies and to obtain control over territories won from the Germans.[19] During the war, the more benevolent South African policy contained unrest in the territory. After the war, favorable comparisons to the Germans (because of the horrible reports of German atrocities) strengthened South Africa's case with the British and other Allies for maintaining control over South West Africa.

In 1920 the League of Nations was persuaded by evidence provided by Europeans settled there that South West Africa was not prepared for independence. Consequently, the international community decided to grant the guardianship of South West Africa to South Africa under a system of mandates. The class "C" mandate, which was actually given to Great Britain but was to be administered on its behalf by South Africa, was undertaken with the stated aim of providing guardianship under a "sacred trust" to further the well-being of South West Africans and to aid in their political and economic development until the population was prepared to govern itself (see Appendix A). Despite the progressive language and paternalistically benevolent tone of Article 22 of the League of Nations Covenant, under a "C" classification South West Africa's status as a colony changed only in terms of who was going to be the foreign administering power. From the time of the assignment of the mandate until its independence, South West Africa was administered as an integral part of South Africa.[20]

With the support of the League of Nations, South Africa took full administrative and legislative control of South West Africa. All of the race discriminatory laws developed for South Africa were extended to South West Africa, with local modifications as necessary. Despite the fact that such laws were contrary to everything the covenant called for in terms of the promotion of material and moral well-being, the League of Nations' Permanent Mandates Commission could do (or was willing to do) little except occasionally criticize South African policy. This situation continued until after World War II, when the newly established United Nations and its Trusteeship Council called for the abolition of the mandate system. The Trusteeship Council was intent on reassessing South West Africa's preparedness for independence and wanted to replace the mandate with a widened possibility for international supervision through trusteeship status.

After World War II, the end of colonialism in much of Africa was foreseeable for the first time. The stated goal of trusteeship—the self-government or independence of all territories held in trust—was undeniable. In addition, the supervisory powers of the Trusteeship Commission were to be strengthened. The administering authorities would be subject to far greater scrutiny than had been the case under the mandate. Under the trusteeship, investigatory visits would become accepted and regular, and petitions from nationals of the trusteeship as well as examination and criticism of reports submitted by the administering authorities would occur more regularly.

Such activities were considered an intrusion, which South Africa rejected as unacceptable. Whether or not the mandate was only a thin veil for colonialism, it is clear that in South West Africa, South Africa had assumed the role of colonizer rather than benevolent guardian. South Africa followed and accelerated old German policies and frowned on any infringement of its authority. South Africa was the only mandatory power that totally disregarded the call to place the former League of Nations' mandated territory under UN trusteeship. Rather, South Africa provided meager evidence to support its claim in 1946 that according to the wishes of the South West African people, the territory would continue to be tied to South Africa as a mandate and South Africa would no longer submit reports to or allow petitions from South West Africa. Despite the Trusteeship Committee's rejection of this decision in a vote of 37 to 0 (with 9 abstentions), South Africa went ahead with its plans.

In essence, then, the policy pursued by South Africa was annexationist: White inhabitants of South West Africa were granted South African citizenship and the right to vote and were represented in the South African parliament. South West Africa's economy became even more tightly integrated into that of South Africa. Thus, by the end of World War II, South Africa had firmly replaced Germany as the reigning European colonial power in South West Africa.

Although the system of segregation had been established by the Germans before South Africa accepted the league's mandate, that system accelerated under South African tutelage. Even before 1948 and the development of the formal system of apartheid, white control over politics and the economy was guaranteed in many ways. In addition to laws restricting the political and socioeconomic rights of blacks, the system worked to undermine the souls of blacks, to teach subservience to whites, and generally to reinforce the barrage of laws set up by the Germans and elaborated on by the South Africans.

Whereas white South West Africans were represented in the parliamentary democracy that was established for them, blacks were allowed no meaningful form of self-government or participation in choice of leadership. The system of "native reserves," established in 1892, ostensibly granted blacks the right to run their own local affairs. However, the only aspects of the African systems that were allowed to operate with any measure of autonomy were those that were viewed as beneficial to the larger, overarching South African system. The precolonial African political systems were altered so radically by colonial rule that they were hardly recognizable. Because South Africa reserved the right to appoint and dismiss African leaders, these leaders lost their legitimacy with most of the population.

Even though whites in South West Africa had political rights in South Africa's system, crucial areas of South West Africa's government and economy—such as foreign policy, defense, "native affairs," and all of the modern infrastructure including mines, railroads, harbors, and the like—remained under direct South African control. The European power dominating the economy of South West Africa had changed from Germany to Great Britain (through South Africa), but this meant little to most blacks in South West Africa, because strikingly similar objectives were pursued by the both powers. For example, when the South African Land Ordinances of 1903 and 1912 were extended to South West Africa, all lands in the southern zone were converted to government property except those held in private title by settler (European) farmers or through concessions by companies. In effect, blacks in the southern zone lost any remaining rights to own land. Consequently, huge numbers of blacks were dislocated and forced into the reserves. Even the reserves were not secure; due to the European desire for more land, parts of the first reserves established by the Germans were expropriated for white use.

The reserves became notorious as increasingly overcrowded and poverty-stricken depositories for blacks. They were (and continue to be) located in South West Africa's most economically marginal lands; conditions were widely known as being poor. Although most reserves were located far from white population centers, some were within a distance that allowed blacks to commute to work in white areas. By 1922, mirroring the situation in South Africa, the reserves (excluding Ovambo) made up less than 10 percent of the total land area of South West Africa; in 1923, less than two of the 57 million hectares of land that comprise South West Africa were set aside for blacks.[21]

Thus, the increasing number of blacks forced onto the reserves was a direct outcome of land settlement schemes promoted first by Germany and later by South Africa, which encouraged whites (mostly Afrikaners from South Africa and others returning south from Angola) to buy farms in South West Africa. South Africa—as had Germany—encouraged whites to move to South West Africa by offering soft loans, the necessary infrastructure, and valuable ranching land (expropriated from blacks). Again, the immigration policy was considered by South Africa to be a success; the number of European settlers in South West Africa more than doubled—from 15,000 in 1913 to 31,200 in 1936.[22]

Further reminiscent of German policies in South West Africa, this policy opened up the land to whites and left more and more blacks with increasingly little option but to sell their labor and satisfy white demands. After 1919, but especially by 1930, South Africa had established firm control over labor in South West Africa. Although in the 1920s many white businesses depended on prison labor, this labor was insufficient for white needs on ranches, in the mines, and in white homes. Because of this demand, a labor recruiting organization was formed in 1925 to ensure sufficient labor, especially for the mines. By 1943 the South West Africa Native Labor Association (SWANLA) was a monopsony labor agent. With the mission of providing a constant and adequate supply of labor at the cheapest rates, SWANLA was crucial to the smooth functioning of the contract system. As the only body in South West Africa with the authority to offer blacks a job in the south, SWANLA could force blacks to sign a one-year contract in order to obtain a job in "white" South West Africa. Consequently, SWANLA and the contract system provided the institutional framework that made migrant labor a dominant feature of the South West African economy. With the rationale that the worker's situation was only temporary (the worker returned to his or her assigned reserve at the expiration of each contract), the employer made only the most minimal investment in housing and other social services (health, education, pensions) for the workers.

One of the most distinctive aspects of apartheid and the contract system was that it forbade the workers to bring their families. The vast majority of migrant laborers in South West Africa have traditionally been male. As with the situation of many black workers in South Africa, most workers in "white" South West Africa lived in a single-sex hostel or dormitory. They were paid "bachelor's wages"—a wage that is barely enough to maintain the workers and not enough for them to afford to return home.

In addition to the use of SWANLA and the contract system, the reserves were effectively converted into labor reservoirs through a variety of policies and laws (for example, the Pass Law of 1922 and the Vagrancy Law of 1920), which created the need for cash among blacks who were not previously integrated into the cash economy. The economic system created by South Africa ran efficiently; the labor recruiter worked in harmony with South African laws. One example of a labor-creating law was based on the old colonial policy of *corvee:* Any male resident of the reserves who had no apparent means of support or was considered idle faced being forced to volunteer his labor for state projects. Other laws, such as the Master and Servant Proclamation of 1920, clearly promoted the interests of the employer by forcing laborers to remain at their jobs without even minimal standards of pay or treatment. Another example of job discrimination was pay scales based on race. It was not unusual for a black worker to receive one-tenth of what a white employee was paid for the same job.

The response to this onslaught was worker dissatisfaction and unrest. However, in South West Africa trade unions for blacks were not just ignored by employers and the colonial administration; labor activists faced severe punishment.[23] The administration so clearly favored employers that strikes became a legal offense. Yet the repressive measures taken by the government to quell union activity were part of a larger goal: the transformation of South West Africa's economy into primarily a product, export-oriented, foreign-dominated economy. South West Africa was set up to provide minerals for South African and foreign industry. In return, the country would have to purchase virtually all its consumer needs from South Africa. Any imported goods would have to enter through South African ports, then travel north along South African roads or railways.

These are only a few examples of how the system of institutionalized racism operated in South West Africa and how it tied the country into a relationship of economic dependence on South Africa. After 1948 and the victory of the Nationalist party in South Africa, apartheid was formally imposed on South West Africa. The Nationalists swept into power decrying what they perceived as the sloppy application of the law, and they called for more comprehensive measures in order to guarantee white superiority. Although hardly a new concept in South West Africa, apartheid affirmed and promoted the development of the body of laws that structured the South African and South West African systems to cloak class exploitation in racist philosophy. South Africa no longer even made a pretense of administering South West Africa as a mandate; South West Africa was considered an integral part of South Africa, and the implementation of racist legislation was accelerated under the aegis of apartheid.

In the 1950s and 1960s, problems for blacks accelerated on two levels in South West Africa. First, blacks found their economic status continually eroding as the country was opened up for further exploitation by foreign capital. South Africa was willing to hand over the resources of the territory as a way of bonding it more closely with the Western industrialized countries. This policy was successful, as large numbers of European, South African, and U.S. firms flocked to South West Africa for tax breaks, minimal standards for treatment of labor, and other concessions. This influx benefited South Africa because an increased international economic interest in South Africa and South West Africa was effective in discouraging international pressures, especially sanctions.[24]

A second immediate effect of apartheid was the extension of South Africa's Bantustan system to the South West African reserves. A major component of the policy of separation of the races, the 1962 laws creating the Bantustans merely formalized the practice in the reserves. Building on past successes with policies of ethnic fragmentation, or "divide and rule," the Odendaal Commission Report of 1964 recommended that

South West Africa be divided into eleven ministates—one white and ten black. Every black person in South West Africa was assigned a homeland, regardless of whether he or she had ever laid eyes on the territory. Subsequently, 93 percent of South West Africa's population was crowded into ten black reserves totaling 40 percent of the country's land area. Approximately 7 percent of the population controlled the richest 43 percent of the territory. The remaining 17 percent of the land was demarcated as diamond fields, game reserves, or "unallocated government lands." In addition to its obvious economic interest, a crucial aim of this policy was to weaken black opposition by dividing 93 percent of the population into much smaller, more manageable ethnic groups and centering all political and economic decisions on ethnicity. Despite internal resistance and international disapproval, the Odendaal system of racial separation continued—although somewhat modified—until South West Africa's independence.

Thus, as much of the rest of Africa was finally gaining its independence, racial segregation continued for the South West African workers who left the reserves every year, traveled too far to commute home to their families, and had to be housed within "white" South West Africa. Housing for blacks living temporarily in white areas was handled in much the same manner as it was in South Africa under the Group Areas Act. Although on the books since 1923, the Group Areas Act became an increasingly significant form of influx control between 1948 and 1962, as the economy grew and more and more blacks came to white areas as migrant laborers. For black workers in large urban areas, specific quarters were established far from white neighborhoods. In addition to segregating residence, the Group Areas Act regulated a wide range of activities. Founded on the assumption that blacks were only temporary sojourners in white areas and were actually citizens of the reserves (and therefore had restricted rights in white South West Africa), this body of rules determined where blacks could shop, learn, worship, be entertained, and receive medical treatment. This act was a centerpiece of apartheid in South West Africa. Such circumstances could not go unaddressed forever.

NOTES

1. As is the case with many other parts of Africa, a comprehensive history of precolonial Namibia is only now being pieced together. Unfortunately, the documentation provided by Europeans has been largely ethnographic, with little exploration of oral or archaeological sources. These histories of Namibia have also been Eurocentric and patronizing, often distorting descriptions of blacks to serve political purposes. Even classics (such as Heinrich Vedder's *South West*

Africa in Early Times) are questionable in terms of accuracy because they rely almost solely on accounts by European missionaries, traders, and travelers. These studies commonly divide discussions of the various populations living in Namibia by ethnicity. This categorization schema can be criticized as an artificial creation that ultimately served as a tool in the not-uncommon policy of divide and rule. European histories of Africa have made much of tribal wars. However, as more recent histories have contended, conflicts among the various groups living in Namibia have more often been based on relations of production than on ethnic division.

Nevertheless, grouping people by ethnicity has now become a fairly widely accepted mode of distinction. Therefore, for the sake of clarity and utility, the discussion of precolonial Namibia in this book will be divided by ethnic group. Because this classificatory scheme has weaknesses as an analytic tool, in addition to ethnicity attention will be directed to the role that sociopolitical and economic forces played within and between each group.

2. Richard Gray, *The Cambridge History of Africa*, vol. 4 (Cambridge: Cambridge University Press, 1975), pp. 423–424.

3. Ibid., p. 424.

4. Gerhard Totemeyer and Vezera Kandetu et al., eds., *Namibia in Perspective* (Windhoek: Council of Churches of Namibia, 1987), p. 15; Gilbert I. Schrank, "German South West Africa: Social and Economic Aspects of Its History, 1884–1915" (Ph.D. diss., New York University, 1974), p. 17.

5. Brigitte Lau, "'Pre-colonial' Namibian Historiography: What Is to Be Done?" in Brian Wood ed., *Namibia, 1884–1984: Readings on Namibia's History and Society* (London: Namibia Support Committee, 1988), p. 95.

6. SWAPO Department of Information and Publicity, *To Be Born a Nation: The Liberation Struggle for Namibia* (London: Zed Press, 1981), p. 18.

7. Ibid.

8. Gervase Clarence-Smith, "The Angolan Connection in Namibian History," in Wood, *Namibia*, p. 172.

9. John E. Flint ed., *The Cambridge History of Africa*, vol. 5 (Cambridge: Cambridge University Press, 1976), pp. 231–232.

10. Gervase Clarence-Smith and Richard Moorsam, "Underdevelopment and Class Formation in Ovamboland, 1844–1917," in Wood, *Namibia*, p. 181.

11. Clarence-Smith, "The Angolan Connection in Namibian History," in Wood, *Namibia*, p. 172.

12. Arnold Valentin Wallenkampf, "The Herero Rebellion in SWA, 1904–1906: A Study of German Colonialism" (Ph.D. diss., University of California, Los Angeles, 1969), p. 165.

13. Brigitte Lau, *Southern and Central Namibia in Jonker Afrikaner's Time* (Windhoek: National Archives, 1987), p. 41.

14. Wallenkampf, "The Herero Rebellion in SWA, 1904–1906," p. xi.

15. Horst Drechsler, *The Struggle of the Herero and Nama Against German Imperialism, 1884–1915* (London: Zed Press, 1980), p. 143.

16. Ibid., p. 40.

17. Helmut Bley, *South-West Africa Under German Rule, 1894–1914* (Evanston: Northwestern University Press, 1971), p. 250.

18. Ibid., p. 73.

19. Andre du Pisani, *SWA/Namibia: The Politics of Continuity and Change* (Johannesburg: J. Ball Publishers, 1985), p. 8.

20. For more on this, see chapter 3. As late as 1989, South West Africa was often referred to as South Africa's "fifth province." Economic linkages reinforced this tie; South West Africa (or "South West," as white South Africa preferred to call it) was such an accepted part of South Africa that it was (and still is) included in the national South African weather report.

21. SWAPO, *To Be Born a Nation*, p. 61.

22. du Pisani, *SWA/Namibia*, p. 69.

23. See chapter 3.

24. Denis Herbstein and John Evenson, *The Devils Are Among Us* (London: Zed Press, 1989), p. 139.

2

Namibian Politics

In one form or another, all of Africa resisted the multifaceted assault of colonialism. One of the clearest lessons of African history is that the decolonization process depended to a great extent on the willingness of the colonial powers to accede to this resistance. Although the British were foresighted enough to allow their territories in West Africa to have a smooth transition to independence, the experience in Kenya and Zimbabwe was far less peaceful. Portugal is recognized as one of the most intractible powers in Africa, and it can be compared to South Africa in the latter's efforts to maintain control of South West Africa.

The South African government faced a long and sustained internal resistance in South West Africa. As was the case elsewhere in Africa, despite occasional incidents of violent resistance the movement in South West Africa was peaceful for many years. It was only after repeated violence by the colonial power that a large segment of the movement responded violently. This internal effort was at times hindered and at other times supported in various degrees by an external involvement—that of the international community. Perhaps in part because the international community had placed South West Africa under a South African mandate in the first place, that community (as represented by the United Nations) took an active, although not always positive interest in South West African affairs. It was the combination of these efforts, both internal and external, that ultimately led to the country's independence.

Although internal and external efforts sometimes seemed at odds with each other, it is necessary to discuss these efforts in conjunction with one another. For organizational purposes, we will divide the timeframe for this discussion of South West African politics at the 1960s—approximately the point at which the internal strategy shifted to include violence. Correspondingly, in the 1960s external efforts were increased as the composition of the United Nations was significantly altered—with important repercussions for South West Africa.

23

EFFORTS TOWARD
POLITICAL LIBERATION: TO 1960

Internal Resistance

There has always been African resistance to European domination in South West Africa. The Herero Rebellion of 1904 was just one of the most famous examples. Others include the Bondelswaarts Rebellion of 1922 (over, among other things, a dog tax); an antigovernment movement by the Rehobothers in the 1920s, which sought to preserve that group's autonomy; and a brave, seemingly final Ovambo clash with the South African administration in the 1930s. In the face of large-scale white immigration, pressures over land and labor, and a constitution that effectively ignored 90 percent of the population, black South West Africans adopted many different forms of resistance including nationalism. The resistance was positively influenced by two other forces—Christianity and pan-Africanism—which united blacks above the ethnic divisions emphasized by whites.

Many of the earliest political parties in South West Africa began as nonpolitical associations. Yet whether they were originally concerned with religious, cultural, economic, or social matters, by the 1920s many of these organizations had begun to focus on political issues. As with nascent political organizations in many other parts of the world, these first associations were small and often elitist and were usually dominated by strong personalities. These early parties were fraught with a number of difficulties, including ideological and ethnic divisions as well as organizational and financial problems. Only in the 1950s did the most successful of these parties deliberately set out to build a mass base of support. Two important sources of activism were the schools and the workplace.[1]

Education and Resistance. Issues of apartheid and education attracted students and faculty and contributed to the development of organized resistance in South West Africa. Drawing inspiration from the pan-Africanist movement of the 1910s and 1920s, the Universal Negro Improvement Association and other cultural associations led discussions and organization against institutionalized racism in South West African schools. As an example of how dire the educational situation was for blacks in South West Africa, it was not until 1948 that the first black student finished secondary school and matriculation. Only then did the first black teachers begin returning home from training in one of the few schools for blacks in South Africa. From this point on, student and faculty activism accelerated. Yet because so few blacks had the opportunity to attend school, these associations were by definition elitist; however, their aims were mass-based.

By the mid-1950s, the Southwest African Progressive Association (SWAPA) was established as an educational and cultural association. It was supported by religious associations, especially the African Methodist Episcopal (AME) church. With specific goals such as improving educational facilities for blacks, reforming the apartheid curriculum, and establishing independent schools, SWAPA worked to get more blacks into institutions of higher education in South Africa and elsewhere.[2] Because of their efforts to restore dignity and pride to blacks in South West Africa and in other oppressive situations around the world, such movements were tightly monitored by the colonial administration.

Labor and Resistance. The labor movement, which initially limited itself to economic issues, contributed to the development of political parties in South West Africa. Blacks in South West Africa had long reacted to economic discrimination by whites: the first efforts to organize labor originated in the 1890s when strikes and protests were conducted to condemn low wages and poor working conditions. However, most of these labor actions were quickly and ruthlessly put down by the government, which was—predictably—acting on behalf of employers. In the 1910s and 1920s there were several attempts to obtain legal recognition for unions; however, it was not until the 1950s that a labor movement solidified in South West Africa, and even then it was barely accepted by the government. The largest of the early labor organizations was the Ovamboland Peoples' Organization (OPO). At first the OPO was specifically an association of approximately two hundred Ovambo laborers who were working in Capetown and were disgusted with the terms of their contracts; however, the movement gradually pulled together workers (including non-Ovambo) throughout the territories. Although faced with organizational difficulties exacerbated by South African restrictions on labor action, workers presented their demands through letter writing and petitions, and strikes occurred sporadically. The first large strike, which was held at Luderitz in 1952, met with some success, and the workers gained a small raise in wages and amelioration of working conditions. This success contributed to the momentum for other campaigns, including a longer strike in 1953 that briefly virtually paralyzed the Luderitz lobster industry.

The labor movement faced several difficulties, the most formidable of which was a hostile employer-government reaction to labor activity. Police violence paralleled labor activism; during the 1953 strike, three workers were killed and several more were wounded. The risks for labor activists became increasingly severe as the South African administration developed laws to restrict all union activity. For example, the Terrorism Act included activities prejudicing any industry or causing financial loss to any person or to the state. Accordingly, workers who demanded higher wages or better working conditions were classified as terrorists. The penalties for contravention of this law were severe: The maximum sentence for such "offenses" was death.[3] Labor leaders were subject to constant harassment, and many, such as Andimba Toivo ya Toivo, were arrested and imprisoned. Toivo ya Toivo was sent to Robben Island (the desolate prison island off the Cape that is famous for holding Nelson Mandela and other leaders of the South African resistance) and was released in 1984, after sixteen years of imprisonment.

The South West African administration declared war on labor activism, and efforts were made to crush the movement through government crackdowns. Despite the risks, labor organizations such as OPO continued to operate. In fact, many argue that the repression only strengthened unity among all wings of the resistance.[4] The OPO eventually developed into the South West African People's Organization (SWAPO), which became well-known both internally and internationally and is now the dominant party in the nation's government.

As was suggested above, people involved in all forms of resistance in South West Africa were targets of the South African police. What was different about the OPO, and what eventually helped contribute to its transformation into a party based on multiethnic membership, was that it was not limited strictly to labor concerns but called for wider change. By the late 1950s, there were three main resistance movements in South West Africa: the OPO, the South West Africa National Union (SWANU), and the Herero Council. SWANU was the offspring of the educational association SWAPA. Led by an intellectual, Jariretendu Kozonguizi, SWANU's base of support drew from two institutions in South West Africa that accepted blacks: Augustineum College and Dobra Teachers Training School. Although many SWANU leaders were Herero, the group hoped to unite resistance above ethnicity and develop as an umbrella organization with a broad base of support. In fact, SWANU often quarrelled with the Herero Council, an ethnic organization composed of Herero traditional leaders. The Herero Council, a relatively conservative and elitist organization, was highly regarded by the resistance for its many years of petitioning against the colonial administration.

These three parties were part of a wider resistance movement that cooperated during the 1950s in a defiance campaign similar to that which was ongoing in South Africa. The campaign employed Gandhi's strategy of passive resistance and included boycotts of segregated facilities such as cinemas, buses, and bars as well as mass demonstrations and work absences. The most famous campaign in South West Africa, infamous because of the South African administration's response, was the defiance against forced removals from the Old Location.

The Old Location was the part of Windhoek set aside under apartheid for blacks. In 1959 the resistance swelled when the administration, pressed by whites who wanted this land, decided to remove all blacks from their homes there. The administration planned to resettle (forcibly if necessary) blacks to a new settlement on the outskirts of Windhoek known as Katutura ("the place where no one lives"). However, this decision was met with widespread resistance, not only because blacks were totally ignored in the decision-making process but also because the increased distance from town would mean a longer, more difficult commute and increases in transportation costs, which few blacks could afford. Concerns also included tremendous increases in rent and the fact that no freehold ownership would be allowed in Katutura. The final blow was the news that South Africa would continue its policy of divide and rule by segregating Katutura on the basis of ethnicity. Most of all, however, blacks rejected the forced resettlement because it underscored their official status as temporary guest workers in "white" South West Africa. The police response to the demonstrations at the Old Location drew international attention. In what are now known as the Windhoek Shootings, eleven people were killed by police and many more were wounded. The international response was shock and outrage; internally, the atrocity radicalized the population, as did the 1960 Sharpeville massacre in South Africa.

External Resistance

Although incidents such as Sharpeville and the Windhoek Shootings focused world attention on apartheid, the international community had long taken an interest in South West Africa in part because the international community bears some responsibility for the situation there because South Africa was originally asked by the League of Nations to administer South West Africa. Since World War II, the United Nations and other international bodies had taken an increasingly critical view of South Africa's failure to uphold the terms of the original mandate. Since that time, external pressures—whether in the form of an advisory opinion of the International Court of Justice, denunciations, or the diplomatic isolation of South Africa—have dominated the relationship between South Africa and the international community.

Much of the first international legal conflict involving South West Africa centered around the right of the United Nations to call for a trusteeship for the territory. In 1949, the UN General Assembly requested a decision from the International Court of Justice (ICJ) on (1) whether South Africa's rejection of the trusteeship for South West Africa had a legal basis; (2) whether South Africa still had obligations under the system of mandates and if so, exactly what those responsibilities were;

and (3) whether South Africa was recognized as having legal competence to modify the status of South West Africa and if not, what body had the right to decide South West Africa's future.[5]

The ICJ responded to this series of questions in 1950. The court advised that although South Africa still had responsibilities under the system of mandates, the United Nations, as successor to the League of Nations, had a role in the supervision of South Africa's administration of the mandate. Consequently, the ICJ found that South Africa was obligated to submit reports and petitions to the United Nations concerning its fulfillment of the responsibilities of the mandate. However, and most important for the inhabitants of South West Africa, the ICJ ruled that the international community did not have the legal competence to compel South Africa to place South West Africa under a trusteeship. On the final question of who had the competence to alter South West Africa's status, the ICJ ruled that neither the United Nations nor South Africa could unilaterally alter South West Africa's status from that of a mandate; rather, the status could only be altered through a cooperative decision between South Africa and the United Nations. This decision was a major disappointment for those who hoped to change South Africa's actions in South West Africa.

Throughout the 1950s, international action concerning South West Africa was marked by a series of frustrating, unsuccessful attempts to negotiate with South Africa over the status of the territory. As much of the rest of Africa was being decolonized, most of the international community hoped that South Africa would act in concert with other colonial powers and allow South West Africa a process of evolutionary, peaceful change. However, the South African response, which soon became routine, was that the international community had absolutely no right to interfere with South African activities in South West Africa. South Africa stubbornly maintained that its obligation was to the League of Nations, and because that body was no longer functioning, it had to explain itself to no one. By the mid-1950s, this stance had strengthened; South Africa refused even to cooperate in filing reports, facilitating petitions, or providing the United Nations with any information on South West Africa.

EFFORTS TOWARD POLITICAL LIBERATION: 1960–1980s

Internal Resistance

The Windhoek Shootings provided a turning point for the resistance, as from that point on the resistance movement began to seriously consider the possibility of responding to South African repression with violence.

As the OPO reorganized into SWAPO in 1959, it took the lead in moving toward armed resistance. After 1962 SWAPO decided that resistance would include violence as part of an overall strategy in seeking change. Because of their calls for a transformation of the apartheid system and support for their cause from the USSR, South Africa branded SWAPO and the other resistance groups not only as terrorist but also as Communist. Despite the clear statement of support for a democratic system based on elections, and despite international recognition of SWAPO by the United Nations and the Organization of African Unity as the rightful representative of the South West African people, SWAPO and other resistance movements enjoyed only quasi-legal status in South West Africa. Although the South African administration never actually banned the organizations, the barrage of laws and repressive measures taken against activists forced SWAPO members and members of other groups underground.

By this time there were some significant differences between SWAPO and the other leading resistance movements, especially in their attitudes toward the use of violence. SWAPO, SWANU, and the Herero Council agreed on the need for change; however, they disagreed on the best manner in which to pursue that change. For example, during the 1950s and early 1960s SWAPO devoted much of its efforts to petitioning the United Nations, whereas SWANU believed it was necessary to organize the South West African people for a more internally directed change. Further, the two groups differed on how South West Africa should be governed after South Africa ended its occupation. SWAPO, mindful of its appeal to workers and the Ovambo (the largest ethnic group in South West Africa), called for free elections based on one man, one vote. SWANU, aware of the likelihood that SWAPO would overwhelmingly win such an election, wanted a constitutional convention to bargain over the nation's future. SWANU and SWAPO also disagreed on the necessity for violent change. The Herero Council's position on all these issues was traditionalist: It sought to preserve precolonial systems and hierarchies. The Herero Council was a relatively conservative force that considered other resistance groups to be radicals. However, its participation was needed to secure Herero cooperation.

Given these differences, it is not surprising that although SWAPO and SWANU managed to build a coalition in the early 1960s in order to receive financial assistance from the OAU, this unity was short-lived. By 1971 there was another effort to unite opposition against South Africa's Bantustan policy. Led by Clemens Kapuuo, the resistance coalesced into the National Convention of South West Africa—a multiracial, multiethnic movement that included most parties in South West Africa (with significant white exceptions)—and worked to draft a constitution for an independent South West Africa. However, the convention fell apart for several reasons, especially after SWAPO and other more radical groups withdrew. Since that time, similar efforts have failed due to ethnic and ideological divisions.

Of all the groups, SWAPO was the most effectively organized and could rally the support of the largest segment of the population. Much of its support was Ovambo, but it could legitimately claim multiethnic representation. For these reasons SWAPO was recognized by the international community as the authentic representative of the South West African people. No other party closely rivaled its broad base of support. Nevertheless, SWAPO has had problems, which have included internal division.[6]

The War of Liberation

By the time it had decided to include a military strategy in its efforts, SWAPO had separated itself from the other parties and was clearly at the head of the resistance movement. Although its decision to adopt violence as one means of pressing for change was made in the early 1960s, it was not until 1968 with the apparent failure of a legal solution (when the International Court of Justice declined to pronounce on the issue of whether apartheid violated the mandate) that SWAPO began a full-fledged guerrilla offensive. The landscape of South West Africa clearly makes that area no place for a guerrilla war. The geography, which is mostly open and flat, left fighters highly vulnerable to air raids.

Yet the SWAPO army, known as the People's Liberation Army of Namibia (PLAN), could rely on the crucial advantage of having the support of much of the population. This was especially true in the north, where most of the fighting occurred and the population is primarily Ovambo. PLAN soldiers moved about rather freely there and were indistinguishable from the local population, which supported them with basic necessities and military intelligence. With this support, SWAPO successfully hid arms caches inside South West Africa. The civilian population regularly moved weapons throughout the country to assist SWAPO. Any study of guerrilla experiences elsewhere underscores the importance of this kind of support to the success of a movement.

The first battle staged by SWAPO forces occurred in 1966 in Ovamboland. Because it was composed of relatively small numbers of men and women, PLAN could only undertake small-scale encounters with South African and South West African forces. Generally the strategy was one of sabotage, ambush, and retreat. Attacks on electrical and communications installations as well as police stations were common. By 1969 PLAN was operating in many parts of the country (Ovambo,

Post office workers repair the telephone lines used by the locals. The poles had been blown up by PLAN forces.

Okavango, Kaokoland, Caprivi, and Grootfontein) and even claimed it was operating training bases inside South West Africa in what it considered the "semiliberated" parts of the north.

Many of the South West Africans who left in the mid-1970s to live in exile participated on a number of different levels in the effort to end South African domination of the country. It is estimated that approximately 10 percent of South West Africa's black population went into exile during these years: sixty-nine thousand to Angola and five thousand to Zambia and other countries that supported SWAPO. Those who left the country to join PLAN received training in African countries (Egypt, Ghana, Algeria, and Tanzania) and in Europe, the USSR, North Korea, and the People's Republic of China. Not all of those who left were soldiers; some were trained as medical personnel and teachers and in specialties other than military science. In its refugee and training camps in southern Africa, SWAPO developed a number of programs to provide medical care, education, political training, rural development, job training, child care, and sports programs. The SWAPO programs in South West Africa paralleled more extensive ones in Angola and Zambia. They were considered pilots for projects to be undertaken in an independent South West Africa. Many of the people were skilled, approximately 20 percent were women, and many were students. There are reports that entire classes with their teachers went over the border to Angola and into exile around the world.

By the late 1970s, the stage was set for more deadly clashes. Perhaps in response to the 1978 South African massacre of South West African refugees at Kassinga, SWAPO concentrated its efforts against South Africa. The mass exodus of the mid-1970s contributed to SWAPO's strength; although reliable estimates are hard to find, SWAPO maintains that its forces numbered in the thousands. Also, SWAPO had acquired increasingly sophisticated materiel. In addition to light weaponry, PLAN was using rockets, antiaircraft guns, bazookas, and mortars. PLAN's strategy was still one of sabotage, although the fighters had boldly moved south, often into what is known as "the white triangle"—the white population centers of Grootfontein, Tsumeb, and Otjiwarongo— and beyond, occasionally even into Windhoek and Swakopmund. SWAPO scored successful attacks on the important Ruacana electrical installation, railroad bridges and tracks, and even South African military bases.[7]

By 1979, contacts between SWAPO and the South African Defense Force (SADF) numbered almost one a day. A dramatic escalation of the conflict occurred just in the course of one year: The number of confrontations climbed from fewer than five hundred in 1978 to over nine hundred in 1979.[8] South Africa received another shock in 1980 when with the use of antiaircraft guns, SWAPO shot down a South African plane over southern Angola.[9] The war continued at this pace throughout the 1980s. The greatest military success for anti-South African forces, one that was influential in the later South African decision to pursue a negotiated solution in South West Africa, was the South African defeat at Cuito Cuanavale in 1987.

The anticolonial wars elsewhere in southern Africa, especially in Angola, have had a direct impact on events in South West Africa. SWAPO learned from the experiences of the liberation movements in Angola, Mozambique, Zimbabwe, and South Africa, and these movements provided varying degrees of moral and material support to SWAPO. In addition, the momentum of success against the Portuguese and later against the Rhodesians aided SWAPO's military campaign against colonial rule.

South African Response

Just as it had attempted to crush all earlier efforts, South Africa concentrated on countering the armed resistance. It moved swiftly to arrest a number of SWAPO leaders, including some members of PLAN. Many SWAPO activists arrested after the 1966 attacks were detained without trial for more than a year. They were tortured and later charged under the Terrorism Act of 1967, which condemned all those involved in SWAPO operations. This law was made retroactive to 1962 and clearly targeted SWAPO. Broad powers of arrest were provided by the Suppression of Communism Act of 1950, which gave the state the right to arrest an individual who was affiliated with any organization or publication considered to endanger state security or the maintenance of public order. Several more members of SWAPO were condemned to life imprisonment under these provisions. International condemnation and threats of punitive action persuaded South Africa to reduce the sentences of a few activists from life to twenty years. Emergency regulations imposed in 1972 permitted detention without trial from 2 to 111 days. As an immediate result of the police crackdown, 161 South West Africans were held without ever being charged with an offense.

The South African effort to diffuse SWAPO by removing its leadership, combined with a number of other factors, contributed to an acceleration of the war in the 1970s. In this period the South African Defense Force (SADF) began to steadily increase its numbers in South West Africa, replace the police as the law enforcement agency, and undertake counterinsurgency operations. In 1974, there were approximately fifteen thousand South African troops in South West Africa; this had doubled by 1979. One special branch of the SADF, the 32 Battalion, was operating virtually full time inside Angola. A twenty- to thirty-mile buffer zone was set up to control SWAPO movements on the border. The National Union for the Total Independence of Angola (UNITA) and South Africa cooperated to exert pressure simultaneously on SWAPO and the Angolan government.

As the military buildup continued, South African control over South West Africa became even more oppressive, and its war in Angola escalated. Soviet military assistance to the Angolan forces increased, providing the Angolans with surface-to-air missiles. Heavy fighting in Angola occurred in the early 1980s, including skirmishes between South African and Cuban forces for the first time since 1975.[11] Harsh punishment was exacted on any South West Africans who did not immediately report to the police any suspicious persons in "the war zone," which included virtually all of northern South West Africa (Ovambo, Caprivi, and Okavango). To enforce its rules, South Africa demanded and received the full cooperation of traditional authorities in South West Africa. As in the days of German colonialism, any traditional leader who failed to comply with directions was replaced. The SADF's aim was to seal off and systematically search any part of the war zone at will. This was accomplished by imposing a curfew on all of Ovamboland: It was well-known that anything that moved after 8 P.M. was likely to be shot without warning. Other examples of South African control over the area were the numerous checkpoints along all paved roads and the constant patrolling of rural areas by casspir, the armed personnel vehicles used by the SADF. The SADF's goal was to allow no entry into or exit from Ovambo without a permit.

As the war became more protracted and South Africa made border raids into Angola, the SADF sometimes became involved in confrontations with Cuban troops, who were in Angola at the request of the government to protect it from South African and UNITA attacks. South Africa increasingly turned to more lethal tactics. In violation of the Biological and Toxic Weapons Convention, the SADF began to use poison gas and other forms of chemical warfare in South West Africa and in southern Angola. As part of its "total strategy," South Africa staged one of the world's largest military occupations in South West Africa. In the 1980s, the proportion of South African soldiers to South West African adults was an amazing one to six.[12]

Two other campaigns were inaugurated by South Africa in the 1980s. One was the SADF's attempt to win the "hearts and minds" of South West Africans. Here, the SADF portrayed itself as a development agency, offering assistance and taking over the administration of schools and hospitals in the war zone. The other South African initiative involved recruiting blacks into the South African military. However, the number of blacks who voluntarily joined the "ethnic units" of the South West African Territorial Forces (SWATF) was always tiny—approximately 3 percent of the force. Much of the voluntary force was composed of San, who were used by the SADF as trackers. Forced into the poorest reserves, the San lived as they did hundreds of years ago but on increasingly marginal lands. Considered by other South West Africans to be apolitical, the San were easily manipulated by the South Africans for modest pay. Yet the San alone could not provide the number of recruits deemed necessary by South African strategists. Because of the small numbers of black volunteers, the force had to be built through conscription. In 1980, all South West African men became eligible for the draft. In response to this, an energetic anticonscription campaign forced reliance on SADF troops rather than on South West African conscripts.

Of the black volunteers, a select group began work as Special Forces, which includes the notorious Koevoet—"crowbar." Koevoet was a death squad trained in South Africa that was responsible for a widespread campaign of terror in the north. Officially a unit of the South African police, Koevoet staged "hunts" for SWAPO members and suspected supporters. South Africa placed no restrictions on Koevoet; Koevoet members had indemnity as agents of the SADF as long as they were acting "in good faith" in pursuit of "the suppression of communism." Koevoet members were known to dress as PLAN members and commit various atrocities in order to discredit SWAPO in the areas of its greatest

Koevoet police enjoy a morning picnic on the banks of the Kunene River. A box of hand grenades lies next to the child and picnic boxes.

support. The Special Forces was both widely feared and despised—a feeling summed up by its widely used nickname, *omakakunya*, or "blood-suckers and bone pickers."[13]

Thus, the violence continued—with sporadic lulls—throughout the 1980s. South Africa's activity in Angola continued into the late 1980s, despite UN condemnations of its illegal entry into Angola. In response to increased South African involvement, the Angolan government became more dependent on Cuban patrols in its southern regions. It was in southeastern Angola at Cuito Cuanavale (a town important for its air field and radar installation) where South Africa, UNITA, Cuban, and Popular Movement for the Independence of Angola (MPLA) forces met for what was to become a historic engagement. After four months of fighting and unusually high casualties, the SADF withdrew from the area in 1988. The battle for Cuito Cuanavale is considered a major success for the MPLA government, the Cubans, and SWAPO.[14]

International Initiatives

In international fora, the defiant, nonapologetic South African stance on South West Africa continued through the 1960s. The patience of those who had hoped for a negotiated change wore thin. As more African states became independent and joined the United Nations, General Assembly resolutions became increasingly critical of South Africa. In attempts to press South Africa to modify its position, increasingly assertive policies were considered. As every effort failed, relations between South Africa and the United Nations became further strained. South Africa twice refused to allow investigative visits by the UN Special Committee for Southwest Africa.

During this period the United Nations pursued a number of initiatives to try to remedy the worsening situation in South West Africa. The first of these was the move by two members, Ethiopia and Liberia, to once again submit the issue of South West Africa's status to arbitration. This time the question was whether South Africa was accountable to the United Nations for the administration of South West Africa and whether apartheid violated the terms of the mandate. On this question in 1966 the court reversed a 1962 decision and maintained that the ICJ did not have jurisdiction to hear the case. Based on the view that the applicants had no legal right to present the question, the decision sparked a tremendous controversy. Many attribute the decision to the composition of the court at the time, which was dominated by the representatives of conservative Western states.[15] South Africa hailed the decision as a vindication of its position, and South West African nationalist movements and their supporters were bitterly disappointed.

While waiting for the 1966 decision, the General Assembly began to coordinate a mandatory sanctions campaign to cut military assistance and oil supplies to South Africa. However, this campaign suffered a fate similar to that of the many other calls for sanctions against South Africa: The Western powers in the Security Council blocked it. Although there is wide disagreement about the use of sanctions as an instrument of change, the Western industrialized states have been the most consistent impediment to the sanctions campaigns. These states, which have economic and other interests in South Africa, maintain that sanctions do not work; yet many of these same states have a selective sanctions policy. The United States, for example, has pursued economic sanctions against Nicaragua, the USSR, and Cuba. With or without the support of Western states, the sanctions campaign has continued over the years. It would be difficult to measure and separate the effect of sanctions from that of other pressures on South Africa; yet it must be recognized that the effect of all international pressure has been a factor in South African decisions to "reform" and to negotiate the independence of South West Africa.

By 1966, the changed composition of the UN General Assembly made it possible to push through the unprecedented 1966 revocation of the mandate over South West Africa. The decision was important because it signified international unity and support for the goals of the South

West African nationalists, but it held little sway over South Africa, which rejected and ignored the revocation.

Spurred by this reaction, the United Nations continued its calls for pressure on South Africa. Once again South West Africa's supporters attempted to pursue the cause through legal channels—this time with some optimism, as by 1971 the composition of the court had changed considerably and was more representative of the UN's increased membership. The question this time was whether the court recognized the revocation of the mandate. In a significant shift, the court found that South Africa's occupation of South West Africa was illegal and called for South Africa's immediate withdrawal from the territory. The court then went even further and called for all UN members to recognize the illegality of this status and to refrain from giving South Africa any assistance that might help it continue its illegal occupation. This landmark decision in effect called for an end to all dealings (diplomatic, economic, social, cultural) with South Africa as concerned South West Africa. With the clearly stated position of the ICJ, the Security Council was again compelled to consider mandatory sanctions against South Africa. It was also during this period that the UN Fund for Namibia was created to help move the country toward independence. This time, as South Africa was outraged by the opinions of the court, the resistance and its supporters were ecstatic.

Although the 1971 decision was officially ignored by South Africa, South African Prime Minister John Vorster began seeking better relations with Africa and the international community. It was hardly the change the world demanded, but South Africa's policy did shift toward conducting a dialogue with the United Nations. One example of South Africa's conciliatory mood during this period was its allowing the United Nations to visit South Africa and South West Africa.[16]

Meanwhile, the United Nations began to set the framework for an independent South West Africa by revitalizing the UN Council for Namibia, a body created years earlier to promote a peaceful transition to independence. Under the new strategy, the council's powers and capabilities were enlarged. In this period the reference to the territory as Namibia took on clear political meaning and became widely used in the community that was supportive of the nationalist movement. The council assisted Namibians in exile and worked with other agencies to promote the interests of the territory on behalf of its people. The council played a crucial role in drawing world attention to events concerning the territory and in attracting the support and cooperation of UN members. Most important, in 1973 the United Nations recognized SWAPO as "the sole and authentic representative of the Namibian people."[17] Thus, the major goals of the council were to marshal support for independence and to build unity in the international bargaining group that was supportive of independence.

South Africa's Response

In disregard of the international community's desire to find a peaceful solution, South Africa made it clear through various means that it preferred its own "internal" settlement based on the 1964 Odendaal Commission recommendations. This revamped program to accelerate the implementation of apartheid in South West Africa was worked out at a conference held in a gymnasium in Windhoek—hence its name, Turnhalle. In effect, from the mid-1970s South Africa pursued a two-track policy, proceeding with its internal solution while continuing with UN-sponsored talks. As part of the proposed internal solution of 1975 and 1976, black leaders of the eleven reserves were invited to meetings with South West African whites to draft a new constitution. Based on the recommendations of the Odendaal Commission report, only ethnically based parties were allowed to participate in the meetings. Not surprisingly, more broadly based black political parties and opposition movements such as SWAPO and SWANU were excluded.

Although a wide range of issues was discussed, the Turnhalle Conference called for the separate development of ethnic homelands. It envisioned a government for independent South West Africa based on ethnic politics, or group rights. As mentioned earlier, the old system of reserves—now known as the homelands, or Bantustans—was one of the most central tenets of apartheid; it portrayed segregation as a positive concept that allows for separation by ethnicity in pursuit of "peaceful coexistence."

Under the plan devised at Turnhalle, a federal system would operate on three tiers: central-national, regional, and local. The first tier would be composed of a president, a council of ministers, and a national assembly. The third tier would represent local, municipal governments. However, the second tier is what distinguishes the constitution drafted at Turnhalle, which emphasized group, not individual, autonomy. It restricted political activity by ethnicity and stressed protection of minority rights. Thus, the crucial second tier of government was designed so that members of each of the government-determined eleven ethnic groups of South West Africa would elect their own representatives, who would then elect representatives to the first tier. At the first tier, any single ethnic group would have a veto over central governmental decisions. Further, each ethnic group was to administer government in its assigned homeland. The desired effect would again be that blacks would no longer be a unified block representing 93 percent of the population but would be broken down into significantly smaller (hence politically weaker) groups based on ethnic identity. Turnhalle's architects rationalized including the German, British, and Afrikaner ethnicities in one ethnic group.

The independence Turnhalle envisioned for South West Africa gave blacks rights to freehold property in certain areas of the country. At the second tier of government (within the reserves), black bureaucracies and middle classes with stakes in the system developed. This segment of the population would run the quasi-independent ministates and cooperate in maintaining the Turnhalle system. Under a policy at the second tier known as "own sources," each ethnic group would be responsible for raising revenues and providing services for its own constituency. Given the fact that the Turnhalle constitution allowed for no significant change in the economic structure, it is not surprising that the system would do nothing to remedy the tremendous inequalities that would be created among second-tier authorities. For example, in 1979–1980, of the R 129,960,000 paid in second-tier taxes, R 107,793,000 was spent on the white ethnic group. This left only R 22,167,000 to provide governmental services for more than 93 percent of the population divided into ten of the eleven ministates.[18]

TOWARD A SOLUTION

As much as South Africa hoped that the Turnhalle plan would satisfy demands for South West African self-determination, the overwhelming international and internal response was hostile. Although the United Nations was gratified by South Africa's acceptance of the concept of a political transition, it maintained that no legitimate negotiation or election could exclude SWAPO and other black opposition groups. Further, to ensure free and fair elections, some provision had to be made for international supervision of any proceedings. Finally, the United Nations argued that the strategy of dividing South West Africa into eleven quasi-independent ethnic states was untenable. In sum, the UN position was that South Africa and white South West Africans had to accept the concept of one person, one vote and the likelihood of black majority rule in South West Africa if there were ever to be a peaceful settlement in the country.

Unimpressed by South Africa's own internal solution, by the late 1970s the United Nations was again ready to pursue talks with South Africa. The Western members of the Security Council finally took the lead in making some effort to resolve the issue. The five members of what was to be known as the Contact Group (the United States, Great Britain, France, West Germany, and Canada) agreed in principle on the need to prevent the situation in southern Africa as a whole from escalating into a race war and also agreed that negotiations were necessary to promote stability and a peaceful transition of power. Yet, these countries often stood alone in opposition to the calls for sanctions and other diplomatic initiatives to force South Africa out of South West Africa. In the late 1970s, under increasing international pressure to impose sanctions on South Africa, this group finally took the initiative to persuade South Africa to compromise.[19]

This interest in mediation was motivated partly by the Contact Group's desire to avoid being forced into adopting sanctions. Most of the group's member-states were promoters of free trade who had large economic investments in South Africa and important trade links as well. For some members, another reason to oppose pressure on South Africa was because the country was generally pro-Western. Consequently, on three different occasions Great Britain and the United States vetoed mandatory economic sanctions against South Africa. France, which over the years had developed significant military relations with South Africa, vetoed sanctions twice. It was in the final days of détente and the aftermath of the disquieting South African response to the 1976 demonstrations at Soweto that in order to preserve any credibility in its opposition to apartheid, the Contact Group began to actively promote a diplomatic initiative.

In 1977 the Contact Group facilitated indirect talks between South Africa and SWAPO. Much of the early success of these negotiations was based on the shuttle diplomacy of Donald McHenry, deputy to Andrew Young, the U.S. ambassador to the United Nations. UN Security Council Resolutions 385 and 435 were used as the basis for negotiations. Resolution 385 called for a cease-fire and the withdrawal of all forces to bases. Further, it maintained that although South Africa should have a say in these contentious issues, the South African presence in South West Africa was illegal. Reaffirming its own legal responsibility over South West Africa, the United Nations called for a transfer of power to the people of South West Africa. Resolution 435 called for South West Africa's independence and respect for its territorial integrity as well as free elections based on universal suffrage.[20] UNTAG, the UN Transitional Assistance Group, would set up operations in South West Africa to ensure that the eventual electoral process would be free and fair. Yet despite initial agreement on the principles of Resolutions 385 and 435, many other contentious issues remained, such as: How soon would South African forces leave? Would they all go before the elections (SWAPO's position), or would substantial forces remain until a new government was seated (South Africa's position)? How soon should the elections be held: as soon as possible (South Africa's position), or with time for parties to organize (SWAPO's position)? What about control

Namibians sign one of the many petitions to South Africa to implement UN Resolution 435.

over Walvis Bay? Aware of the potential for problems, the Contact Group purposefully left much to be decided at the bargaining table and tacitly threatened South Africa with sanctions if it refused to at least take part in the negotiations.

By the end of the UN-sponsored sessions in 1978, both South Africa and SWAPO began to alter their positions in important areas. At the opening sessions, South Africa conceded in principle to most of the concepts contained in UN Resolutions 385 and 435 (see Appendix C). It agreed to the idea of an independent South West Africa, a phased withdrawal of the SADF, and plans for the transition under the direction of the secretary-general's special representative. South Africa even accepted the concept of elections based on one person, one vote. SWAPO also accepted all these provisions and agreed to postpone negotiations over the issue of Walvis Bay (perhaps the most contentious problem remaining). SWAPO was willing to continue talks even after the Kassinga massacre of May 1978.

Yet throughout the rest of 1978, South Africa made various attempts to halt the process and again brought up the issue of Walvis Bay. Most critically, at the end of the year South Africa contradicted virtually all the provisions agreed to in UN Resolution 385 and announced that it

During negotiations of UN Resolution 435, Pik Botha, at left (South African minister of foreign affairs), confers with Administrator-General Louis Piennar.

would go ahead with its own internal settlement and hold elections, as proposed at the Turnhalle Conference.

Thus, the Turnhalle elections were held in 1978 without international recognition and without the participation of SWAPO. South Africa openly supported one party, the Democratic Turnhalle Alliance (DTA), with administrative and financial assistance.[21] The DTA was created in 1977 when some participants in the Turnhalle Conference refused to accept the convention's strong pro-apartheid position. The Alliance, as it has come to be known, is composed of a number of small parties: the Bushman Alliance, the Labour Party of SWA, the Democratic Turnhalle Party of Namibia, the National Democratic Party, the Kavango Alliance Party, the Rehoboth Baster Association, the Republican Party, the Tswana Alliance, the SWA People's Democratic United Front, and the Caprivi Alliance Party. Its campaign was based on promises to eliminate petty apartheid; the party had South African backing and won the majority of seats in the 1978 election. This support was given partly because the DTA leadership recognized that change was coming and knew that the best way to protect white interests was to form a party that would draw some black (especially Herero) support away from SWAPO. In essence the DTA was, and in many ways still is, a party dominated by white

South West Africans, but it includes traditional black, anti-SWAPO elements. It was opposed by the many far right-wing white South West Africans who resist any conciliation with blacks and by the relatively few whites who support SWAPO.

The DTA attempted to portray itself as a progressive force with enlightened policies. It wanted to persuade the world of a fundamental change in government character and promised to do away with apartheid in South West Africa. However, it only did away with petty apartheid, or apartheid in some of its most obvious forms, such as desegregating some public facilities, modifying the Pass Laws (to facilitate the control of population movement), and repealing the Immorality and Mixed Marriages Act. A telling commentary on the DTA's real character was evidenced by its silence on desegregating more significant institutions such as schools, residential areas, hospitals, and the workplace—all of which remained segregated. Because whites continued to dominate the economy, because whites maintained dominance over politics and were represented in the South African parliament, and because South Africa continued to control crucial branches of the government (the police and military), the Turnhalle process was dismissed by the resistance and the international community as only adding complexity to the status quo.

The South African government was attracted to the DTA because of the prospect of presenting to the world an apparent multiethnic alternative to SWAPO. With the solid support of the South African government and no competitor that had any substantial recognition or support, the DTA easily dominated the 1978 proceedings. The effect of the elections was that South Africa now had in South West Africa a constituent assembly intent on protecting group rights and on ridding South West Africa of only the most obvious forms of petty apartheid while maintaining a warm relationship with South Africa.

Astonishingly, given South Africa's total disregard of all UN efforts, the Contact Group refused to perceive the 1978 elections as a failure of a conciliatory approach to South Africa and doggedly continued to pursue talks with South Africa. As it became clear to South Africa and the world that the Contact Group was unwilling ultimately to punish South African intransigence with sanctions, it was obvious that South Africa could continue to postpone a real solution interminably without risk.

Thus, South Africa went on with its internal settlement but at the same time continued talks through the Contact Group. Meanwhile, the international community scrambled to come up with increasingly creative ways to keep the talks going. For example, due to South African fears of SWAPO activities in Angola and Zambia during the implementation of UN Resolution 435, the United Nations suggested a demilitarized zone on South West Africa's borders that it would police. To further placate South Africa, the Contact Group worked hard to hold off the General Assembly's increasingly strident calls for sanctions. Yet South Africa continued with its plans for self-rule and made military attacks on Angola and Zambia at crucial moments in the negotiations, thereby effectively delaying any real progress.

In its efforts to gain international recognition of the DTA and the 1978 elections, South Africa pressed for a multilateral conference of all South West African parties, including SWAPO and the DTA. This conference was held in Geneva under UN auspices, and although the DTA succeeded in making its denunciations of SWAPO heard, in the minds of many listeners SWAPO remained the only legitimate representative of the Namibian people. At the conference the negotiators agreed to continue with the process outlined by UN Resolution 435, and, in seemingly a major breakthrough, South Africa accepted a timetable for South West Africa's independence, which was expected before the end of 1981.

However, South Africa equivocated again, about one year before the scheduled independence. By then South Africa had established a recognizable pattern of delay. Despite consistent, albeit weak UN condemnation of such actions, South Africa continued to toy with the negotiation process. For a time it seemed that the Contact Group's patience had worn thin, but in 1979 and 1980, respectively, Margaret Thatcher and Ronald Reagan were elected. South Africans celebrated the prospect of dealing with these conservative administrations, recognizing that they would substantially alter the Contact Group negotiations even more to the benefit of white South Africa.

No longer did the U.S. president pressure South Africa into accepting terms of agreement that were insensitive in any way to South African concerns. U.S. policy toward South Africa under Jimmy Carter was hardly severe; however, the policy of Constructive Engagement, developed by Reagan's Assistant Secretary of State for African Affairs, Chester Crocker, marked a significant departure from his predecessor's policy. The entire tone of the United States as a partner in the UN-sponsored negotiations was radically altered; in fact, the United States turned on the United Nations. According to one report, early in the first term a Reagan aide accused the UN Secretariat of being "Marxist."[22] Thus, given the new leadership of the Contact Group, all advances made during previous negotiations quickly disintegrated.

Both Crocker and his critics agreed that the U.S. policy of Constructive Engagement went beyond South Africa and affected the politics of all of southern Africa. Whereas the previous Western initiatives had been criticized for holding out neither carrot nor stick to South Africa, the policy offered by Crocker was criticized as all carrot.[23] In the early days of the policy, for example, the Reagan administration promised South Africa's foreign minister, Pik Botha, a relaxation of restrictions on the sale of arms. The United States reestablished an exchange of military attachés and renewed cooperation with South Africa in the critical areas of atomic energy and military intelligence. Further, P. W. Botha was the first head of state from an African country to be received by Reagan. The United States vetoed resolutions calling for mandatory sanctions and vetoed or abstained on calls to condemn SADF raids of neighboring states. In essence U.S. policy had clearly shifted: The Reagan administration had made a conscious move away from the UN's 435 process.

Crocker contended that the United States could win more influence with South Africa if it attempted to understand South Africa's concerns and interests. On the issue of independence for Namibia, the United States became the defender of South African interests. The many U.S.-backed demands that benefited South Africa included no deadline for negotiations (with the understanding that there would be no punishment if South Africa was reluctant to come to an agreement); guarantees to protect minority interests in advance of elections; and (what became the signature of the Reagan policy) the linkage formula, which tied Namibian independence and South African withdrawal from the territory to Cuban withdrawal from Angola. Once again negotiations were based on a view of southern Africa as a battleground between East and West. The linkage formula basically proposed that if the Cubans (who were there at the invitation of the Angolan government) withdrew from Angola, then South Africa would withdraw its troops from South West Africa and allow free and fair elections, resulting in South West Africa's independence.

Whereas the Reagan administration maintained that the United States could not expect South Africa to jeopardize its security interests, its linkage policy demonstrated that it had no similar appreciation of the Angolan government's insecurities. If, as critics have argued, this policy was all carrot and no stick, South Africa was happy to eat the carrot and continue to do as it pleased.[24] Others maintain that the Reagan administration failed to understand the issues in the region because it viewed southern Africa in East-West terms, taking a globalist approach.[25] Only through profound neglect of the regional factors at work did the Reagan administration blindly accept the South African contention that the problems of the region were due predominantly to "Communist adventurism." The administration's support of white-led change in South Africa was so solid that only by overriding a presidential veto in 1986 did the U.S. Congress manage to pass a weakened sanctions bill.

The Reagan administration argued that this policy was necessary to give the negotiating process a semblance of impartiality. It accepted the South African contention that the United Nations was biased toward SWAPO and against South Africa. Although the United Nations did find SWAPO to be the sole legitimate representative of the Namibian people, the UN Council for Namibia prepared Namibians to administer an independent Namibia, and some UN agencies provided humanitarian assistance to SWAPO, the United Nations made sustained efforts to appease South African fears and demonstrate its faith in the 435 process. Kurt Waldheim's replacement, Secretary-General Javier Perez de Cuellar, had little experience with SWAPO. Further, the United Nations sponsored talks among the various South West African groups (including the DTA) and even agreed to suspend assistance to SWAPO. Given these UN concessions and seeing no change in the U.S. stance, many criticized Reagan's policy as showing overt favoritism to the apartheid regime.[26]

Although some members of the Contact Group (especially Great Britain and West Germany) accepted Constructive Engagement and even formed policies mirroring it (for example, Great Britain's Positive Engagement), relatively few members of the Contact Group or the international community backed Crocker's proposal of linkage. The front line states most involved in the negotiation process unanimously opposed it. Nonetheless, after 1982 under U.S. leadership, linkage became the focus of negotiations. Once again, Namibia's independence was set aside for some "larger" issue. In effect, linkage held South West Africa hostage to events in Angola and gave South Africa a perfect excuse to ignore the terms of UN Resolutions 385 and 435. The larger issue that further complicated the negotiations was communism in southern Africa.

THE SOLUTION: THE IMPLEMENTATION OF UN RESOLUTION 435 AND INDEPENDENCE

Culminating Factors

Several circumstances help to explain why all parties, but especially South Africa, finally accepted a plan for South West Africa's independence. Chester Crocker is said to have suggested that the agreement was due to "the right alignment of local, regional, and international events like planets lining up for some rare astronomical happening."[27] Some argue that Constructive Engagement worked in the end. According to this logic, because the United States supported UNITA and was therefore hardly an impartial mediator, South Africa realized it was unlikely to get a better deal under any other (especially a Democratic) U.S. president.

However, analyst Gerald Bender suggests that the negotiations succeeded *despite* Constructive Engagement, not because of it. According to Bender, Crocker's policy prolonged the agony in southern Africa and gave South Africa the "green light" to intervene not only in Angola but in Mozambique and elsewhere. He observes that instead of reducing the instability in the region, this policy spurred a Cuban buildup in Angola (from fifteen thousand Cubans when Reagan was elected to fifty thousand when he left office).[28] In effect, linkage gave South Africa the opportunity to maintain control of South West Africa indefinitely without Western pressure.

If it was not Constructive Engagement, what factors ultimately led to the diplomatic breakthrough? In the mid- to late 1980s, if the West was not willing to exert pressure on South Africa, other actors were, and they became increasingly effective at it. As was suggested earlier, the war in Angola and South West Africa became increasingly costly for South Africa during this period. Recall that the SADF suffered heavy setbacks in 1987 and 1988 at Cuito Cuanavale. It is estimated that the war was costing South Africa $1 million a day. Additionally, the first signficant numbers of white casualties were mounting: The SADF admitted to the loss of fifty white soldiers and hundreds of black troops at Cuito Cuanavale.[29] Discontent was peaking inside South West Africa as well. In 1988, in addition to continual strikes, student boycotts, and demonstrations against conscription in South West Africa and South Africa, emotions ran high as the tenth anniversary of the massacre at Kassinga was commemorated. Two destructive bombings (one in the heart of downtown Windhoek) rocked South West Africa. These attacks contributed to the South African decision to send heavy reinforcements deep into the central and southern regions, parts of the country previously considered by the white government to be relatively stable.

To heighten the strain, by the late 1980s the South African economy was in trouble, with a declining standard of living among whites. The sanctions, so long dismissed as ineffective, actually proved influential. The withdrawal of U.S. banks from South Africa in 1985 and the 1986 U.S. Congressional passage of sanctions demonstrated that financial sanctions could take their toll, even in South Africa. For the first time in many years, economists began to talk about a loss of international economic confidence in South Africa, as a decline in monetary reserves became threatening. It is clear that its economic situation forced South Africa to become increasingly concerned about how pariah status might affect its prospects for securing future loans.

Finally, it is an important point that in the late 1980s, the changing relationship between the United States and the USSR caused all those who were capitalizing on the cold war to consider how long they could continue to do so. The Soviets wanted to distance themselves from their clients in the region in an effort to smooth the way for U.S.-Soviet agreement on issues considered to be far more important (for example, arms control, and economic relations between East and West). The USSR joined the negotiation process late, but its influence should not be overlooked. It took an active role and supported the United States as the mediator in the negotiations. By the late 1980s, all the players (with the possible exception of UNITA, which was simultaneously being promised U.S. assistance) were war weary and were willing to reduce the costs of the war. Angola was in economic shambles, unable to repay its $4.5 billion debt to the USSR and no longer able to pay Cuba its $1,000/day/soldier fee. Despite Fidel Castro's claims to the contrary there were reports that the Cubans were demoralized by what had become (by virtually all accounts) a war of attrition.[30]

The Agreement

In 1988, after the success at Cuito Cuanavale and spurred by the desire to pursue negotiations from a position of strength, the Soviets pressured Angola and Cuba to take seats at the negotiating table. Most telling, however, is the fact that seven years of Constructive Engagement was not enough to persuade South Africa to secure a political settlement. Perhaps *glasnost* and the prospects of an end to the cold war were needed to make a negotiated settlement more attractive to South Africa.

Despite its no-longer-covert support of a rebel group that posed a major threat to one of the crucial parties, the United States had replaced the Contact Group and stepped centerstage as mediator. Cold-war concerns continued to predominate, as South West Africa's independence depended more on what was going on in Angola than in the country itself. Astonishingly, SWAPO was excluded as a signatory to the treaty that arranged for the South African withdrawal. After weeks of talks, in August 1988, the parties agreed to what is now known as the Geneva Protocol. (See Appendix E.) Basically serving as an outline for the formal Brazzaville Accord, the protocol set target dates for the implementation of UN Resolution 435, the signing of the treaties themselves, and a cease-fire as well as South African and Cuban withdrawals from Angola and South West Africa. South Africa also agreed to the implementation of Resolution 435 and to free elections in South West Africa. Despite a last-minute South African threat to back out (probably made by the Botha government to quiet hardline criticism inside South Africa), the Brazzaville Accord was signed in New York in December 1988 (see Appendix F). Although it was not directly included in the tripartite agreement, SWAPO also accepted the cease-fire and the terms of the accord.

Under the terms of the accord, Cuba and Angola signed a separate treaty calling for the gradual withdrawal of Cuban troops. Three thousand Cuban soldiers would return home by April 1, 1989, when UN Resolution 435 was to go into effect. Cuban forces would continue to withdraw as a contingent of UN troops moved into South West Africa.[31] Throughout 1989 Cuba and South Africa would continue the cease-fire and move away from the Angolan-South West African border. By 1991 South Africa and Cuba were to have left South West Africa and Angola altogether. (The Security Council will verify that each side obeys the terms of the agreement.) The final component of the plan was the election process in South West Africa. Registration was held during the summer of 1989 for elections that were to be based on one person, one vote. In November 1989, a constituent assembly was elected by party to draw up a constitution and set the date for independence.

In many ways the Brazzaville Accord does not guarantee the long-sought-after stability in southern Africa. It is historic that all South West Africans can finally elect their own representatives. The SADF and Cuban withdrawals will contribute to a deescalation of the war in Angola, but that war is not over. U.S. support for UNITA poses perhaps the major obstacle to the final implementation of the accord. A UNITA threat to the MPLA risks interrupting the Cuban withdrawal and would give South Africa an excuse to move in. Another serious threat to the accord and the longevity of the settlement is the future of developments in South Africa.

Implementation and Elections

Although there were worldwide celebrations over the signature of the accord, many long-term observers of the proceedings watched with skepticism. Nevertheless, many analysts such as Randall Robinson were hopeful about its actual implementation.[32] South Africa had been known to back out at the eleventh hour, and several times in 1989 it seemed likely that the implementation of the agreement would fall apart. One very real threat to the success of the implementation was the constant accusations of fraud and intimidation traded by SWAPO and the DTA throughout the negotiation process.

The proceedings were threatened on the very weekend the first UN peacekeepers were to begin arriving in South West Africa. Although the details of events are still unclear, it appears there was a misunderstanding about the terms of the accord. The problem began when SWAPO moved approximately 1,700 PLAN troops into South West Africa during the last weekend of March 1989. According to SWAPO, its understanding of UN Resolution 435 was that once the implementation began, South West African exiles would be allowed to return home. (Because of budget cutbacks, UNTAG could not provide safe housing for the exiles.) SWAPO thought its only requirement was to make contact with UN officials in UN-monitored camps. However, this was not South Africa's understanding of the terms. South Africa intercepted intelligence reports on the SWAPO move across the border and interpreted it as a hostile action. With the tacit approval of the United Nations, the SADF attacked, and approximately 273 returnees and 23 South African soldiers were killed. The deaths have invited suspicion. One report suggested that many of those killed may already have been taken as prisoners and contrary to all international standards of treatment, that they had been shot in the head execution-style at close range.[33] Thus far there has been no official investigation of this occurrence. The issues of SWAPO's motivation to return to South West Africa before the United Nations was at full operating speed and why, if it was a simple matter of miscommunication, the United Nations was so inept at handling the situation have received some attention from analysts and the international community.

There is still no persuasive account of the events. On the one hand, it has been suggested that SWAPO came over the border just prior to the implementation of UN Resolution 435 to simulate a military victory that might help it in the upcoming elections. Others suggest that the decision to return was made by a lower-level SWAPO official without the knowledge of SWAPO leadership. Regardless of the reasoning behind the decision or the level at which it was made, South Africa quickly took advantage of the situation. South Africa called attention to itself as the injured party and threatened to call off the agreement altogether. On the other hand, SWAPO was not desperate for votes, and although a semblance of a military victory was appealing, surely its decision makers were aware that if South Africa used the occasion to reject the accord, only South West Africa and SWAPO would lose. Fortunately, quick UN diplomatic measures and pressure on South Africa forestalled what many observers believed was inevitable—another last-minute South African delay.

With this situation resolved, the 435 process began its first phase: voter registration. Yet long before the implementation of Resolution 435 and the campaign process began, it was clear that the elections would result in a race between SWAPO and one other party: the Democratic Turnhalle Alliance. Although several other, significantly smaller parties also vied for seats in the Constituent Assembly, only the DTA was considered to have any chance of challenging SWAPO for power.

The DTA platform for the 1989 campaign called for a Namibia free from outside interference; yet South African support always cast a shadow on the party's aspirations to international recognition. The DTA's conservative platform attracted much of the white community in Namibia,

The results of PLAN's late March 1989 incursion into Namibia: Many of SWAPO's best front-line operators were killed. These bodies were thrown into a mass grave near Oshakati on April 4, 1989.

which hoped for an upset. However, the DTA was well aware that if there were to be any upset, it would need to draw a significant percentage of the black vote. Consequently, the DTA attacked SWAPO as being Ovambo-dominated and portrayed itself as a moderate, multiethnic organization.

Meanwhile, SWAPO fought arduously against any suggestion that it did not seek to represent all of the people of Namibia. Despite constant DTA attacks, SWAPO had great appeal for the Ovambo (who made up approximately 60 percent of the voting population) and also nationwide. It was clearly the party with the widest recognition. After all its years of hardship, SWAPO finally reaped the benefits of its image as the leader in the liberation of Namibia. Given its history, SWAPO was able to make a convincing case for its desire to create a truly independent Namibia free from outside (namely South African) interference.

Yet even before the actual implementation of UN Resolution 435, SWAPO had begun to moderate its tone on economic policy and to call for reconciliation among all of the country's citizenry. For the first time, SWAPO began to talk less of nationalization and promised instead to respect private property. SWAPO manifestos urged whites to stay and work toward a better future. They promised a democratic constitution that would respect fundamental freedoms, and SWAPO leader Sam Nujoma changed his previous position when he suggested that Namibia would move to a one-party system "only if the people want it."[34]

Other problems throughout the period of registration and the campaign posed difficulties for the smooth implementation of UN Resolution 435. During the voter registration period (May–September 1989), the Commission for the Prevention and Combatting of Intimidation and Election Malpractices ("the O'Linn Commission") was plagued by accusations of fraud and intimidation. A total of 114 complaints was formally lodged (62 of those in the last month of registration), and the newspapers were filled with stories of abuse by all the major parties. In addition to accusations from all sides of UN bias and complaints about the peacekeepers' inefficiency, there were also physical attacks on UNTAG offices.

A constant problem was the outbreak of violence between DTA and SWAPO supporters at rallies. Death threats were made on Sam Nujoma and other leading members of SWAPO. Anton Lubowski, a lawyer well-known for defending black activists in South West Africa and South Africa and the highest ranking white official in SWAPO, was assassinated by unknown (reportedly white) assailants at his home in Windhoek in September 1989. This and similar murders in South Africa led to calls for an inquiry into the activities of white extremist vigilante groups such as the White Wolves. Of sixty such assassinations in South

Africa and South West Africa in recent years, there has been only one conviction.

Another controversy that arose during the implementation of UN Resolution 435 centered on the return home of South West African exiles. In an effort to return South West Africa to normalcy, part of the implementation of Resolution 435 called upon the United Nations to facilitate the arrival of approximately 41,000 exiles. However, this program, estimated to cost $9 million, was besieged by many problems. Approximately 300 former SWAPO supporters returned home in July and August, 1989, and received much attention because of allegations of human rights abuses committed in SWAPO camps in Angola and Zambia. They displayed scars and spoke of hundreds of others who died from SWAPO abuse. These returnees were accused by SWAPO of being collaborators hired by South Africa. An organization known as the Parent's Committee was specifically formed to charge SWAPO with the abuses. SWAPO denied mass ill-treatment and invited investigations of SWAPO camps in Angola and Zambia by the United Nations, the Red Cross, and Amnesty International. The UN investigations were unable to determine whether anyone was tortured or killed between 1977 and 1989. Although UN and other representatives visited Angola and Zambia in September 1989, they could not find persuasive evidence to either indict or clear SWAPO, but the charges created a continuing basis for concern. One of the early controversies for the new government will concern the compilation of a list of all Namibians who died or disappeared during the thirty-year war between SWAPO and the South Africans. This project will be as difficult to complete as it is contentious; there are literally thousands of unmarked graves of Namibians both inside and out of the country for which both sides are responsible.[35]

One final potential obstacle to UN Resolution 435 centered on Koevoet and its continued activities even after the 435 process had begun. Although all forces were supposed to be confined to bases, evidence suggests that Koevoet was still active in the northern regions of South West Africa. Casspirs (the armed personnel vehicles associated with Koevoet) were regularly reported to be on patrol. Because Koevoet is blamed for more than 80 percent of the violent deaths in the war zone, because of reports that its members regularly intimidated SWAPO supporters and interfered with the proceedings of UN Resolution 435, and because of UNTAG's inability to effectively monitor all Koevoet and police activities, the international community harshly criticized the South African–appointed administrator-general's seeming reluctance to effectively disband Koevoet.

In addition to more violent forms of intimidation, there was concern about more mundane matters such as election fraud. Complaints focused on election laws that allowed potentially ten thousand white South Africans (some of whose right to vote was dubious at best) to be bused in to vote. In addition, there were reports that false documents were being used by non-South West Africans crossing the Angolan border to register. There were long waits at registration points (apparently to discourage registration). Young blacks who could not provide proof of age were turned away. In many parts of the country, there has been no record of black births and deaths, thus, proof of age is difficult for many.

In early November 1989, a few days before the elections were to begin, one final incident threatened their disruption. South African Foreign Minister Pik Botha claimed that South African intelligence had intercepted messages indicating that some six hundred PLAN troops had illegally crossed the border. South Africa led an outcry against the supposed intervention and was embarrassed when UNTAG officials proved that the documents were false.[36] Yet despite such problems, the United Nations maintained that the registration and election process was successful. The voting process used a highly complex computerized system to prevent fraud and duplication. Although there were some concerns over the problems illiterate voters might have (confusion over party symbols, the use of a thumbprint as opposed to a signature), the process ran remarkably smoothly and voters were exceptionally patient.[37] In some places, polling stations ran out of ballots by 8 A.M. on the first day of voting.[38] By the end of the registration period, over 700,000 people had registered to vote. This far surpassed the original estimate of the total number of eligible voters. Most important, however, UN Special Representative Martti Ahtisaari was able to certify that the elections were free and fair. Ahtisaari commented that this was one of the best supervised registration processes anywhere.[39]

Thus, Namibians finally got the opportunity to vote over a five-day period (November 6–10, 1989). In all, the elections for seats in the 72-member constitutional assembly went fairly smoothly. The 701,000 voters cast their votes by party. The DTA proved to be the only real contender to SWAPO, although five smaller parties that spanned the political spectrum also drew a number of votes. (See Table 2.1.) The election results gave SWAPO a decisive but not overwhelming majority, with 57.3 percent of the votes. Consequently, through the system of proportional representation SWAPO holds 41 of the 72 assembly seats, and the DTA is second with 21 seats. The United Democratic Front (a Damara-dominated party) has four seats, the Action Christian National Party (white, extremely right wing) has three, and three other parties won one seat each. This rather narrow majority for SWAPO was surprising not only to SWAPO but to some analysts of Namibian politics, who

A bushman woman who planned to vote in the November 1989 elections.

had predicted a larger win for SWAPO. The question had been whether SWAPO would win a two-thirds majority, in which case it would have been able to dominate the constitution-writing process. As it was, SWAPO was forced to compromise with the DTA and other parties during what has been described as a surprisingly smooth period of coalition politics. Some suspicion still lingers between the parties, but, apparently the DTA, under the leadership of acting President Mishake Muyongo, has accepted its position as the loyal opposition. In that role, the DTA has taken steps to unite the opposition in hopes of gaining power in regional

Voting lines like these at Katutura extended for miles.

and local elections. For example, SWANU has split into leftist (Namibia National Front [NNF]) and rightist (Namibia Patriotic Front [NPF]) factions. The conservative, Herero-dominated NPF is already in coalition with the former Caprivi African National Union (CANU) and is seriously considering joining the DTA in order to more effectively contend with SWAPO.[40]

The Government

From the first days following the elections, all parties began to learn to work together. SWAPO needed to win seven votes in the new assembly to get its constitution adopted, and this required a concerted effort at conciliation by all involved. It is expected that the cooperative spirit that was demonstrated at the meetings of the Constituent Assembly will set the tone for Namibian politics, at least in the short term. Although SWAPO did not win the two-thirds majority it had hoped for, its numerical dominance of the assembly placed it in a position of leadership. The SWAPO leadership quickly facilitated cooperation. Not only did it moderate many of its policies to placate conservative elements within the assembly, it also reached out to include members from several ethnicities in its cabinet. The cabinet of sixteen ministers includes a large number of Hereros (many of whom voted for the DTA), coloreds, and whites. In fact, whites have been named to the key posts in finance and agriculture. Nujoma's first cabinet contains a great diversity of

A Namibian registering to vote gives his thumbprint as a signature.

experience and talent (see Appendix G). Although many of his ministers are long-time SWAPO members, others have little or no previous public political experience. For example, the minister of agriculture, fisheries, water and rural development and the minister of finance have broad experience in the private sector. On the other hand, Minister of Defense Peter Mueshihange was a founding member of the OPC. Minister of Education, Culture, and Sport Nahas Angula, Minister for Foreign Affairs Theo-Ben Gurirab, and Prime Minister Hage Geingob are just a few who spent many years in exile with SWAPO.

TABLE 2.1 1989 Election Results

Party	Popular Vote	Percentage	Number of Seats
ACN - Aksie Christelik Nasional	23,728	3.5	3
CDA - Christian Democratic Action for Social Justice	2,495	0.0	0
DTA - Democratic Turnhalle Alliance	191,532	28.6	21
FCN - Federal Convention of Namibia	10,452	1.6	1
NNDP - Namibia National Democratic Party	984	0.1	0
NNF - Namibia National Front	5,344	0.8	1
NPF - National Patriotic Front	10,693	1.6	1
SWAPO/D - South West African People's Party Democrats	3,161	0.5	0
SWAPO - South West African People's Party	384,567	57.3	41
UDF - United Democratic Party	37,874	5.6	4
Totals	670,830	99.6[a]	72

[a] Does not total 100 due to rounding.

Source: **Adapted from Joe Putz, Heidi von Egidy, and Perri Caplan,** *Namibia Handbook and Political Who's Who of Namibia* (Windhoek: Magus Company, 1990), p. 52.

The new government's Minister of Information and Broadcasting Hidipo Hamutenya is a second-generation supporter of SWAPO. Hamutenya's father was a founding member of the OPO, and Hidipo Hamutenya long served in exile as SWAPO's secretary for information and publicity. Another second-generation politician and hero of the movement is Hifikepunye Pohamba, the newly appointed minister of home affairs. Pohamba was arrested as a young man for his SWAPO affiliation. He was chained to a pole because there was no jail and whipped. He was arrested several other times while organizing in other parts of southern Africa. Pohamba held various important posts for SWAPO. One other cabinet minister noted for her bravery and long service to SWAPO in organizing health in the refugee camps is Dr. Libertine Amathila, the only female who is a full member of the cabinet. She was appointed minister of local government and housing.

More surprising (and disturbing for some) was the decision to name as the new chief of police a white policeman who served in the South African administration under General Piet Fouche. Also disquieting for some was the government's appointment of General Willie Meyer, former commanding officer of SWATF, to train Namibia's national army. According to SWAPO, the cabinet includes "patriotic" citizens of varying political orientations rather than a formal political coalition.[41] Yet although such moves may help to win the confidence of conservative elements, others watch these events warily. SWAPO has gone so far to address white and conservative fears that it has risked alienating some of its own constituency. There has been talk of a division being created within SWAPO, particularly among those who fear that the reconciliation is actually a cooptation and that the aspirations of those who have long waited for independence will be put aside as the new government seeks to placate whites and win international acceptance.

In terms of the specific provisions of the constitution, the republic is based on a unitary structure, and a multiparty system is guaranteed. It is a secular, democratic state with clear distinctions among the executive, legislative, and judicial branches of government. A president is directly elected every five years and holds executive authority. Following the constitution, the first president was to be elected on February 16, 1990, by a simple majority of the National Assembly. SWAPO leader Sam Nujoma was unanimously selected as the republic's first president. As an example of compromise, SWAPO accepted the DTA proposal to limit the presidency to two five-year terms. The presidential term will run for five years unless he or she dies, dissolves the legislature and is then obliged to step down, or is voted out of office by two-thirds of both houses of parliament.[42]

The president selects his or her cabinet from the members of parliament. Most important, the president makes the key appointment of prime minister, who will act as the president's deputy head of state and who has the power to declare war or martial law. The president may declare martial law, according to the constitution, "when a state of national defence involving another country exists or when civil war prevails in Namibia." However, the National Assembly must approve this action within an undetermined period of time. Similarly, the president may declare a state of emergency for all or part of Namibia "in time of war, national disaster or public emergency threatening the life of the nation or constitutional order," and such decrees must be approved by the parliament within thirty days. The president does not have powers of preventive detention without trial, and no secret court judgments are allowed; rather, preventive detention is allowable only under conditions of a state of emergency or martial law. Other presidential powers include the right to negotiate and sign international treaties, determine when parliament meets, dissolve parliament, pardon offenders, accredit ambassadors, and propose legislation. The president must approve all laws and may veto legislation, which can only be overridden by a two-thirds majority of both houses.[43]

The legislative branch is dominated by the Constituent Assembly, renamed the National Assembly after independence. The constitution creates a bicameral parliament composed of the National Assembly with seventy-eight members elected for five-year terms (seventy-two members elected through proportional representation plus six nonvoting members appointed by the president) and a National Council composed of two members elected by each regional council and serving six-year terms (through a single-member versus a proportional representation electoral system). All laws passed by the National Assembly are subject to review by this house, which may refer legislation back to the assembly. The constitution can only be changed by a two-thirds majority of both houses or a two-thirds majority through referendum. The National Assembly has the power to pass, amend, and revoke laws. It must approve the government's budget and taxation proposals and may call referenda "on matters of national concern."[44] The National Council has powers to review and delay the legislative process; however, it cannot be formed until regional elections are held. Regional and local elections are scheduled to be held after an independent Delimitation Commission divides the country into between nine and thirteen regions. Until then, the president has named regional representatives to fill the vacuum. These representatives are limited in their authority and connot make political decisions, but they can hear and investigate complaints against local administrations, publicize government policy at the grass-roots level, and seek solutions to local problems through the Cabinet.[45] In addition, there will be a Council of Traditional Leaders, whose powers are still to be determined.

The issue of how the boundaries will be redrawn is proving to be important. The November 1989 elections used the existing apartheid boundaries, and SWAPO won majorities in only eight of the twenty-three regions. As an indication that this is a working democracy that is deemed legitimate by the opposition parties, the DTA and others have already begun campaign plans for the regional and local elections, the outcome of which will prove critical in determining relative power bases. The DTA has made clear its desire to play the role of loyal opposition, and it will hold considerable power in the legislature.

In terms of the activities of the third branch of the government, the constitution allows for the creation of a strong and independent judiciary. Supreme Court judges and an ombudsman who has broad powers to investigate complaints are appointed by the president but act autonomously. The constitution includes a Bill of Rights that guarantees freedoms of religion, speech, press, movement, and assembly. Similarly, the Twelve Principles to Promote and Maintain the Welfare of the People contains a special section outlining children's and women's rights, and the rights of workers, pensioners, and the unemployed. Discrimination on the basis of race is a criminally punishable offense. Some of the legislation likely to pass will be the abolition of capital punishment and the creation of a nationwide program of affirmative action.

Again, it must be stressed that beyond simply establishing itself as a functioning government, reconciliation is clearly the dominant theme of the first administration. The process of reconciliation in Namibia is being led by the SWAPO-dominated government through a conscious policy of moderation. Contrary to what many had expected, there is little talk of retribution or nationalization, although one of the first tasks of the new authorities has been to remove and redress the abuses of the apartheid system. The new government has a huge job in taking apart the long and intricately established apartheid legal structure. Two examples of some of the earliest changes to be made are the exclusion of all racist language and a move toward English as the official language of Namibia. In an effort not to step on any toes it is the government's stated position that although anything that smacks of apartheid has to go, South African laws that do not offend anyone or any group and that continue to prove expedient will not be scrapped. Although the second-tier administrations that are tied to the homelands will be dismantled, the new government is attempting to find new appointments for these bureaucrats. Further, the government has promised not to eliminate many of the nearly fifty thousand civil servant positions, many of which were held by people who openly campaigned against SWAPO.[46]

Another example of the policy of reconciliation is reflected in the government's plans for a "development brigade" composed of former PLAN, South West African Territorial Forces and Koevoet members. These ex-soldiers will be retrained as farmers and construction workers at what were once military bases. In terms of defense policy, it is projected that the total strength of the new Namibian army will reach ten thousand soldiers. It will be a professional army trained by British and Kenyan army officers at bases in Namibia and abroad. The army is composed of former PLAN and SWATF members but at this time does not include women. There are currently no plans for an air force or a navy.[47] In addition, an international contingent representing Ghana, Nigeria, Pakistan, and India will remain for a brief period to assist in training the new police force. Some fifteen hundred former PLAN soldiers will serve as an auxiliary force and will cooperate with the Angolan government to ensure the security of the border. This new police force already has a challenge in the north, where crime has escalated; the situation is exacerbated by UNITA activities across the border with Angola.[48]

In sum, this constitution provides a basis for the country to become one of Africa's most democratic states. It represents a multiplicity of interests. Because of the speedy agreement on this constitution, the date set for independence was moved up. After more than one hundred years as a colony, Namibia finally attained its formal independence on March 21, 1990. During the midnight independence ceremonies staged at Windhoek's soccer stadium and attended by a crowd of twenty thousand (including seventy heads of state and government representatives), Namibia celebrated its first independence day as Sam Nujoma was sworn in as Namibia's president by the UN secretary-general.

REGIONAL POLITICAL RELATIONS
AFTER INDEPENDENCE

Although the relations between Namibia and the individual countries of southern Africa vary, Namibia will be welcomed into the fold of independent African states. For many years Namibia's neighbors (often referred to as the front line states) have awaited and supported its break from South African colonialism. These countries take special pleasure in Namibia's success and look forward to profitable political and economic links as Namibia joins the ranks of other southern African countries that have won their independence. However, Namibia will share another

Newly installed President Sam Nujoma delivers the opening speech at the independence ceremonies as South African President F. W. deKlerk looks on (March 21, 1990).

experience with the newly free in southern Africa—the looming economic and military presence of South Africa.

The states of southern Africa are in political solidarity on the despicable nature of apartheid, yet they disagree on the best way to conduct relations with their subimperial neighbor. These postures run the gamut from Malawi, which is the only black African state that diplomatically recognized the apartheid regime and refused even to criticize South Africa at international fora, to Angola, which has served as a base for the ANC and continues to fight a rebel movement financed by the United States and South Africa. In response, South Africa lavishes trade on its few friends and (as is evidenced in Angola and elsewhere) punishes its critics. South Africa has made it clear that any state harboring or suspected of harboring South African exiles is subject to military strike. Such strikes, often on residential areas in capital cities such as Gaborone, Botswana and Harare, Zimbabwe, were commonplace in the 1980s. And as is the case in Angola or Mozambique, South Africa successfully keeps its neighbors off balance by building and pouring support into rebel movements in these countries.

Although some states have been cowed by South Africa and others have only become more incensed by its misdeeds, Namibia's relationship with South Africa will be unique. Some of South Africa's most vocal

Vestiges of colonial rule: Windhoek's major street, Kaiserstrasse, intersecting with Goringstrasse (named after a German colonial governor). These signs were taken down on independence day. (Photo by Donald L. Sparks)

critics—especially Angola—provided materiel, sanctuary, and bases for SWAPO. The countries of southern Africa played crucial roles as intermediaries in the international negotiations to free Namibia. During the process, Angola was transformed from mediator to participant in the negotiations; it was pivotal in the final agreement that arranged a South African withdrawal from Namibia. The evolution of Angola's own civil war will affect Namibia's stability. As long as the issues in Angola remain unsettled, the new Nambian democracy is threatened. Additionally, disruptions associated with economic strains and political divisions within Namibia and SWAPO combined with continued war in southern Africa are worrisome. One analyst, Robert S. Jaster, has gone so far as to predict the possibility of a Renamoesque movement developing in northern Namibia, which would be supported by anti-Nujoma and anti-SWAPO elements.[49] Thus, the new government has much to consider in its first years.

Yet because of Namibia's new-found independence and its experience under direct South African rule, one might expect that it would be a vocal leader of the front line. However, independent Namibia has a SWAPO-led coalition government. It is a multiparty, multiethnic democracy that must respond to long-neglected interests as it moves out of an apartheid system. Meeting these demands will largely depend on the performance of Namibia's economy, which has long been dominated by foreigners (especially South Africa). Namibia is dependent on a smooth relationship with South Africa and also on development assistance from the West. It cannot risk a hostile relationship and certainly not a military confrontation with its neighbor to the south. All these factors must be considered in explaining the SWAPO-led government's moderate tone and when predicting Namibia's future course.

Following independence, the SWAPO-led government has begun to reduce its economic dependence on South Africa by joining the Southern African Development Coordination Conference (SADCC) and diversifying its links to other industrialized states. In the meantime, however, the government recognizes that it cannot afford to antagonize South Africa. This was made clear in late 1989 and again in early 1990 when Sam Nujoma asserted that although Namibia supported the struggle in South Africa, he would not allow his country to be used as a base for activities against any other government. At the same time, however, Nujoma has made it clear that Namibia would not cooperate in South African efforts to circumvent sanctions.

This moderate stance will be disconcerting for some because SWAPO has always worked closely with other antiapartheid movements in southern Africa. Reference was made earlier to the close ties between SWAPO and the MPLA. A special relationship has also existed between the African National Congress (ANC) and SWAPO. The liberation movements had much in common as the last nationalist forces fighting apartheid in southern Africa. The ties between Namibian and South African activists are deep; the Ovamboland People's Organization (the precursor of SWAPO) was founded by Namibian contract workers in Capetown. The Defiance Campaign of the 1950s closely paralleled the peaceful mass demonstrations, boycotts, strikes, and similar actions organized by the ANC for South Africa in the same period. Black Namibians sent to South Africa as students found well-established organizations that helped to focus their activism. Namibians sent to South Africa as political prisoners were often imprisoned with South African activists. In either environment, those opposed to the apartheid system operating in their countries shared experiences and ideas. It is not surprising that the leaders of the two opposition groups adopted similar strategies of resistance, including Gandhi's strategy of *satyagraha,* or passive resistance.

The parallels between the two liberation movements continued over the years. One crucial commonality was the shift in strategy from passive resistance to the adoption of limited violence in response to governmental attacks. Even the occurrences most salient in the reassessment of strategy (the Windhoek Shootings in Namibia and for South Africa, the Sharpeville massacre) happened within a year of each other. In the wake of these events (by the mid-1960s) the ANC and SWAPO developed military wings (the People's Liberation Army of Namibia and *Umkhonto we Sizwe*, respectively) and started separate but mutually supportive military activities against the apartheid regime.

Neither the ANC nor SWAPO was able to gain much assistance from Western nations. Consequently, both have had to rely heavily on the mostly moral but some important logistical and material support of African nations and on military assistance from the USSR and Eastern European countries. The mutual support of the ANC and SWAPO continues today; recently Nujoma met with leaders of the ANC and the Pan-Africanist Conference at a front-line summit in Gabarone.

The apartheid government of South Africa recognizes this relationship. In fact, one of the most frequently stated reasons for refusing to grant Namibia its independence has been the fear that a SWAPO government would turn "the fifth province" into a base for ANC guerrilla training and attacks. Yet given the new government's economic dependence on South Africa, it is unlikely that the country will be in a position to offer this kind of assistance to the ANC no matter how sympathetic a SWAPO-led government might be to ANC aspirations.

Because of Namibia's long struggle against apartheid, the SWAPO-led government will find it difficult to always play the pragmatist. The international community is waiting to see how the new government will conduct itself on this issue, and expectations are high. The issue of apartheid, whether in Namibia or South Africa, is an emotional one not only for SWAPO but for the country as a whole. Any SWAPO-led government will be extremely sensitive to accusations of selling out. For example, Nujoma has announced that Namibia will keep its vital trade links with South Africa, but there will be no diplomatic recognition of South Africa until there is significant reform. Thus, it can be expected that Namibia will adopt a position similar to that of Botswana or Swaziland: supportive of the struggle but from the sidelines and not as a leader, other than in a symbolic sense. Given the pressures from within, Namibia can be expected to concentrate its attentions at home, although it will play the role of a new democracy and call for similar change in South Africa.

POSTINDEPENDENCE
INTERNATIONAL POLITICAL LINKAGES

Namibia is preparing to take its place in international diplomacy. Minister of Foreign Affairs Theo-Ben Gurirab is developing a foreign service. At independence, nearly eighty countries had indicated the desire to establish diplomatic relations with the new state. The Western countries most active in Namibia are the United States, Germany, and Great Britain. These countries are primarily interested in Namibia for investment purposes and as a source of raw materials, especially minerals. Namibia's large deposits of uranium are particularly appealing. Japan and Canada share these countries' interest and can be expected to increase their economic activities in a stable, independent Namibia.

However, Western economic interests often translate into political interests. The West is pleased about the hard-earned but relatively and unexpectedly smooth transition to democracy in Namibia. U.S. Secretary of State James Baker has indicated his support for the democratic constitution of Namibia and has called it a model for all of Africa.[50] Further, as East-West antagonisms subside, cold-war thinking, which has long dominated policy toward southern Africa, is likely to diminish, which can only benefit the region. On the other hand, given the calls for Western support for the new democracies in Eastern Europe, Namibia can expect to be low on the list of assistance priorities. For example, given its history with Namibia, Germany was one country long expected to be at the forefront of a large group of donors. However, with German reunification that country will likely be distracted with what are for it far more important issues. And unfortunately for Namibia, other donors are not likely to fill Germany's place.

One group of Western states that is taking more interest in Namibia is the Nordic countries. Historically, through a connection fostered by their religious (primarily Lutheran) missions, these countries (Denmark, Finland, Norway, and Sweden) have been active in Namibian politics, and they demonstrated varying levels of support for the liberation movement in Namibia. Although they distanced themselves from the armed struggle, they extended humanitarian and development assistance. A Finn, Martti Ahtisaari, is the UN's special representative for Namibia, and he headed the UNTAG forces, many of which were also Finnish.

The USSR and its East European allies have provided limited support to SWAPO since the 1960s, primarily in the form of arms and some training (military and civilian). The East has less influence over SWAPO than it does over other groups such as the MPLA in Angola or the ANC. The primary influence of the USSR on Namibian politics is indirect through its influence on the MPLA. For many years the USSR policy for southern Africa was the mirror image of that of the United States: Each treated the area as an ideological battleground.

Under the leadership of Mikhail Gorbachev, the Soviet policy in southern Africa has been perceptibly altered. The USSR, represented by Soviet Deputy Foreign Minister Anatoly Adimishin, was instrumental in the negotiations leading to independence and was fully supportive of the mediating role played by the United States. In 1989, at the twenty-seventh Congress of the Communist party, the Soviets reemphasized their interest in cooperating with the West whenever possible to build confidence in East-West cooperation in matters of importance (such as arms control and trade). The solution of the Cuban-South African conflict is an early example of this interest, and it appears that the Soviets' preferred solution would involve a negotiated process to deescalate tensions. For now, the Soviets are emphasizing political rather than military solutions and are pressuring their allies to come to the bargaining table.

Several international organizations have supported the independence struggle and will be joined by independent Namibia. The United Nations has the closest ties to the new state. The General Assembly admitted Namibia as its 160th member on April 23, 1990. The UN Council for Namibia, which was founded by the General Assembly in 1967 to assist in preparations for independence, was formally dissolved in April 1990.[51]

The countries with the most obvious relationship to Namibia are the African states. Although the specifics of the relationship vary by country, all members of the Organization of African Unity (OAU) welcomed Namibia's independence, and some actively supported Namibia through the OAU's Liberation Committee. However, as the dominant economic and political relationships for many of these countries are with the developed countries (with the exception of the SADCC countries, which are particularly close to Namibia), interchange between Africa and Namibia is likely to be low-key for some time. As a member of the OAU, Namibia will have to conform to its policy of engaging in full diplomatic relations with South Africa only when a nonracial democratic system is established there. An issue likely to come up in OAU meetings is the future of Walvis Bay, the transfer of which will probably be supported by the body.

The Nonaligned Movement (NAM) is another international organization in which Namibia will take an active part. According to its manifesto, SWAPO regards itself as a founding member of NAM, and NAM consistently supported the liberation movement in Namibia. Namibia's SWAPO-led coalition government should have no problem with NAM objectives such as cooperation, solidarity, and noninterference in other countries' internal affairs. NAM's role in facilitating South-South cooperation will be especially important to Namibia.

Namibia will likely build on its relationship with Great Britain and several other states through membership in the Commonwealth. This association of independent states once linked to the United Kingdom welcomes Namibia, based on its former status as a mandate administered *on behalf of Great Britain* by South Africa. Namibia could benefit from the aid and other programs extended through membership in this multiracial body, which includes seven of the nine SADCC countries.

Although the new Namibian government will be working to set up a functioning administration, to pursue a reconciliation of its peoples, and to redress the abuses of the apartheid system, it will easily achieve recognition in the international community. Its independence was long anticipated, and the new government will be warmly received at international fora. More important, democratic Namibia will stand as an example of what can come about as the result of the finest efforts of international cooperation. Given the tumultuous changes of 1989 and 1990, however, Namibia has not and likely will not receive the attention that is its due, given its long struggle for a democratic, representative government. Now that this has been achieved, it is important that the international community not take this accomplishment for granted. Rather, the new democracy in Namibia faces many formidable challenges, and the support of the international community will be crucial in its success.

NOTES

1. The churches are described in detail in Chapter 4.

2. Andre du Pisani, *SWA/Namibia: The Politics of Continuity and Change* (Johannesburg: J. Ball Publishers, 1985), pp. 146–147.

3. Ibid., p. 68.

4. Gerhard Totemeyer and Vezera Kandetu et al., eds., *Namibia in Perspective* (Windhoek: Council of Churches of Namibia, 1987), p. 22.

5. du Pisani, *SWA/Namibia*, p. 130.

6. The most publicized schism began in the mid-1970s when members of SWAPO Youth, led by Andreas Shipanga, called for new leadership. SWAPO leadership demonstrated little tolerance for such criticism; eventually it accused the dissidents of collaborating with South Africa. The serious charge was that they had leaked intelligence to South Africa that facilitated the massacre of South West African refugees at Kassinga. Although Shipanga and his supporters maintained their innocence, they were arrested and imprisoned in Tanzania. After international pressure forced their release, Shipanga formed the SWAPO-Democrats, a party expressly opposed to SWAPO but with little mass support.

7. Peter Katjavivi, *A History of Resistance in Namibia* (London: James Curry, Ltd., 1988), p. 83.

8. R. H. Green, M. Kiljunen, and K. Kiljunen, eds., *Namibia, The Last Colony* (London: Longman 1981), pp. 159, 165.

9. *Sunday Times* (Johannesburg), February 10, 1980, cited in Katjavivi, *A History of Resistance in Namibia*, p. 87.

10. *New York Times*, June 27, 1980, p. 8

11. Robert S. Jaster, "The 1988 Peace Accords and the Future of Southwestern Africa" (Adelphi Papers No. 253, Autumn 1990), pp. 12–14.

12. A. T. Moleah, *Namibia: The Struggle for Liberation* (Wilmington, DE: Disa Press, 1983), p. 264.

13. Gavin Cawthra, *Brutal Force: The Apartheid War Machine* (London: International Defence and Aid Fund, 1986), p. 212, cited by Katjavivi, *A History of Resistance in Namibia*, p. 89.

14. Jaster, "The 1988 Peace Accords," pp. 18–19.

15. du Pisani, *SWA/Namibia*, p. 191.

16. The rapprochement soon became entangled in controversy after an early report by Dr. Alfred Escher, representative to the secretary-general, suggested that the United Nations support South Africa's "homelands" policy. Consequently, the General Assembly called an end to this round of talks. See du Pisani, *SWA/Namibia*, p. 219.

17. SWAPO Department of Information and Publicity, *To Be Born A Nation: The Liberation Struggle for Namibia* (London: Zed Press, 1981), p. 303.

18. "Suidwes Afrika/Namibie, 1980: Verslag van die Kommissie van Ondersoek na die Finansiele Verhoudintussen Sentrale, Verteen woordigende en Plaaslike Owerhede" (Windhoek, 1980), p. 129.

19. du Pisani, *SWA/Namibia*, p. 337.

20. UN Resolution 435 was supplemented in 1982; it was revised to call for elections of a Constituent Assembly and the adoption of a constitution that would determine the organization and powers of all levels of government and guarantee full freedoms, adult suffrage, fair representation of political parties, and similar rights.

21. The DTA was created from a split within the white Nationalist party that occurred when one member, Dirk Mudge, made an unsuccessful bid at party leadership. Mudge then formed the Republican party, which sought the cooperation of black and colored representatives at Turnhalle. Mudge maintained that it was in whites' interests to give in to some of the blacks' demands. For more on this, see Green, Kiljunen, and Kiljunen, eds., *Namibia*, pp. 152–153.

22. John Seiler, "South Africa in Namibia: Persistence, Misperception, and Ultimate Failure," *Journal of Modern African Studies* 20 (1982), p. 699.

23. Robert I. Rotberg, "Namibia and the Crisis of Constructive Engagement," in Gerald Bender, and James Coleman, et al., *African Crisis Areas* (Berkeley: University of California Press, 1985), p. 106.

24. Ibid., p. 107.

25. Howard E. Wolpe, "The Dangers of Globalism," in Bender and Coleman, *African Crisis Areas*, p. 285: Jaster, "The 1988 Peace Accords," p. 13.

26. This was the widespread view among the Africanist community. For example, see Rotberg, "Namibia and the Crisis of Constructive Engagement," in Bender and Coleman, *African Crisis Areas*, p. 108.

27. *Washington Post*, December 22, 1988, p. 3.

28. *New York Times*, December 15, 1988, p. 39. Just as it has affected Namibia, the cold war has affected politics in Angola. For many years, the United States supported the Portuguese for fear that the Angolan nationalist movements would welcome the Communists. With the Portuguese out of the picture in 1975, the cold-war focus switched to the contending rebel movements.

However, then-Secretary of State Henry Kissinger ignored this in his zeal to oust the Soviet- and Cuban-backed MPLA. In the heyday of deténte, he funneled aid covertly to UNITA. It was only the Clark Amendment of 1975 that effectively (and temporarily) put an end to covert U.S. assistance to UNITA.

As part of the Reagan doctrine to end "Soviet adventurism" and remove Marxist governments in the Third World, the Clark Amendment was repealed in 1985. In February 1986, the Reagan administration announced that it would renew military assistance to UNITA. That year UNITA received $15 million in U.S. military assistance, and the United States and South Africa formed a working partnership in southern Africa (by the mid-1980s, South Africa was spending approximately $200 million a year on UNITA). Meanwhile the numbers of Cuban troops escalated, as did military spending by Angola and the Soviets. Throughout the 1980s the East and West continued to pour military assistance into Angola.

29. John A. Evenson, "The Transition Timetable," *Africa Report* 65 (March–April 1989), p. 27.

30. Pamela Falk, "Cuba in Africa," *Foreign Affairs* 65 (1987), p. 1,095. Angolan casualties had been high for many years and the Soviets appeared to be willing to make one last effort before seeking a political settlement. U.S. officials maintain that the Soviets were spending approximately $1 billion a year in this period on Angola. With a buildup of 40,000 troops, the Cubans moved toward the Namibian frontier. In May 1988 at Cuito Cuanavale, the well-armed Cubans, aided by Angolan and SWAPO forces, successfully ran the SADF out of southwestern Angola. This display of dramatic increases in the numbers and sophistication of weaponry at the Namibian-Angolan border as well as the first significant number of white casualties contributed to a South African reassessment of its border strategy. South African public opinion soon began to show impatience with the war. For the first time the main Afrikaner church publicly questioned South Africa's military presence in Angola. Despite the rapid changes in 1989 and early 1990 and the apparent end of the cold war, the United States continued to give UNITA approximately $40 million a year in covert funds. However, Crocker recognized the potential problems that U.S. support for UNITA might pose for negotiations based on linkage. Concerned primarily with the essential ingredients for achieving a Cuban withdrawal and Namibian independence, Crocker rightfully surmised that strengthening UNITA could have spoiled his plans.

31. There was some controversy over the cost of the UNTAG program and the number of military and civilian monitors necessary. Once again Namibia's independence seemed to hinge on events elsewhere, as U.S. senators insisted on linking the U.S. contribution to the peacekeeping mission to continued support for UNITA. Although the United States has continued its support to UNITA, the overall UNTAG budget was cut dramatically—from a contingent of over 7,000 to a military component of 4,650 plus 1,000 civilian monitors. Despite cautions by the Third World that cuts in the peacekeeping operation would encourage South Africa to interfere in the elections, a vote was taken in the Security Council and a majority agreed on the cuts. The total cost of this aspect of the program was to have been approximately $700 million; it was cut to $450 million.

32. *Washington Post Weekly*, December 19–25, 1988, p. 18. For more on the negotiation process on the accord, see Charles W. Freeman, "The Angolan/Namibian Accords," *Foreign Affairs* 68 (3) (Summer 1989), pp. 126–141.

33. *Africa Confidential*, April 14, 1989, pp. 1–2.

34. Joe Putz, Heidi von Egidy, and Perri Caplan, *Political Who's Who of Namibia* (Windhoek: Magus Company, 1990), p. 264.

35. *Namibia Report*, Vol. 1 (6) (July 1990), p. 2

36. *The Economist*, November 4, 1989, p. 53.

37. *New York Times*, November 11, 1989, p. 3.

38. Ibid.

39. *New York Times*, November 12, 1989, p. 3.

40. *Namibia Report*, Vol. 1 (6), p. 3

41. Putz, et al., *Political Who's Who*, pp. 252–289.

42. *Namibia Report*, Vol. 1 (1) (February 1990), p. 2

43. Ibid., pp. 1–2.

44. Ibid., p. 2.

45. *Namibia Report*, Vol. 1 (5) (June 1990), p. 1

46. *Namibia Report*, Vol. 1 (1), p. 2; Collen Lowe Morna, "The Development Challenge," *Africa Report* (March/April 1990), p. 30; and *Africa Report*, "Opening a New Chapter" (May/June 1990), pp. 26–28.

47. *Namibia Report*, Vol. 1 (3) (April 1990), p. 3.

48. *Economist Intelligence Unit, Country Report*, No. 3 (1990), p. 16.

49. Jaster, "The 1988 Peace Accords" p. 68.

50. *Namibia Report*, Vol. 1 (5), p. 4

51. *Namibia Report*, Vol. 1 (3), p. 6 and (4) (May 1990), p. 3.

3

The Economy

Unlike many of its neighbors in southern Africa, Namibia comes to independence with significant economic potential. Yet like its neighbors at their respective times of independence, the new country faces formidable challenges. Namibia has one of the continent's best sets of infrastructures; the roads and railroads are excellent, for example. It is rich in natural resources, including some of the world's largest deposits of uranium and diamonds. Because of its location, it has potential as an export point for central African minerals and other exports for the North American and Western European markets. Namibia should be an attractive site for foreign investment and foreign economic assistance. Finally, Namibia has had over a decade to contemplate and plan for independence. It has learned many lessons from its neighbors, and the postindependence government has the opportunity to develop an economy that could become one of southern Africa's most successful.

The four overriding features of the Namibian economy will remain for some time: (1) its nearly total control by the Republic of South Africa; (2) its dependence on primary mineral resources; (3) its lack of industrial and manufacturing diversification; and (4) its dualistic economic structure, with a relatively rich, modern sector existing alongside an impoverished, traditional, subsistence sector and an economic division between the north (poor and underdeveloped) and south-central (relatively rich and developed) regions of the country.

Most of Namibia is arid, vast, and thinly populated. There is only enough rainfall to support sedentary agriculture in parts of the north, near the Angolan border. Although nearly two-thirds of the population depends either directly or indirectly on agriculture, it contributes little more than 10 percent of the gross domestic product (GDP) (see Table 3.1). Large-scale commercial agriculture is dominated by white settler ranches and is both capital- and technology-intensive, whereas black Namibian agriculture exists primarily on the subsistence level.

73

TABLE 3.1 Structure of Namibia's GDP by Sector of Origin (percentage of total GDP)

Sector	1980	1984	1986	1988	1989
Agriculture and fishing	11.5	8.5	7.8	12.5	11.3
Mining and quarrying	43.6	25.9	36.2	27.9	9.1
Manufacturing	3.9	5.2	4.5	4.8	4.8
Electricity and water	1.8	2.5	1.8	2.0	1.8
Construction	3.5	3.1	2.4	2.6	2.6
Wholesale/retail trade	11.5	13.0	11.2	11.9	2.3
Transport/communications	5.3	6.0	6.0	6.1	6.1
Finance/business services	5.4	7.8	6.3	7.0	7.2
Social/community services	1.3	2.1	2.0	1.9	2.0
General government	9.6	21.7	19.0	20.3	9.8
Other products	2.6	3.3	3.1	3.0	3.0

Totals may not equal 100 due to rounding.

Sources: United Nations Institute for Namibia, *Namibia: Perspectives for National Reconstruction and Development* (Lusaka: UNIN, 1986); Donald L. Sparks and Roger Murray, *Namibia's Future: The Economy at Independence* (EIU Special Report No.197) (London: Economist Intelligence Unit, 1985); Namibia Ministry of Finance, *Namibia/SWA Statistical/Economic Survey, 1989* (Windhoek, 1990); and Namibia Ministry of Finance, *Statistical/Economic Review: Namibia 1990* (Windhoek, 1991).

MAJOR ECONOMIC SECTORS AND RESOURCES

Namibia's economy contains a mixture of private and state enterprises (parastatals), and the state controls much of the key infrastructure (such as communications and transportation). In 1989 private business enterprises owned R 493.6 million in gross domestic fixed investment, compared with R 53.8 million for public corporations, R 19.5 million for parastatals, and R 238.3 million for general governmental departments.[1] Private domestic investment surpassed general government investment in both 1987 and 1988. Private investment had previously been less than that of the government.

Namibia does not have a well-developed manufacturing sector; it must import most of its manufactured goods, usually from South Africa. A United Nations Institute for Namibia (UNIN) report recently described Namibia as a "stereotype of the economy which produces what it does not use and uses what it does not produce."[2] In fact, Namibia exports about 90 percent of what it produces and imports about 90 percent of what it consumes. Namibia's manufacturing sector is small; it accounts for perhaps 5 percent of the GDP and 10 percent of the formal labor

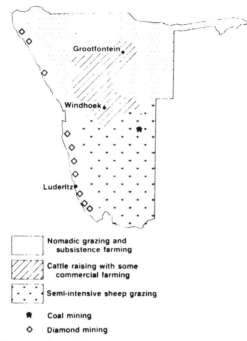

MAP 3.1 Namibia's economic activity.

force. Few Namibians have industrial skills, particularly at the managerial
and marketing levels; traditionally, these positions have been filled by
whites. Because of Namibia's small population and lack of manufacturing
resources (excluding minerals), the scope for local industrial and manufacturing development is limited, at least in the short term. The closeness
of and competition from large South African firms has greatly inhibited
local industrialization.

　　Although its overall economic resource base is somewhat limited,
Namibia does have considerable human and physical resources, which
will be necessary for economic growth and development. The challenge
for the new government is how to employ these resources in the most
effective way in order to achieve economic goals that will certainly
include (1) creating more employment opportunities and generating
higher incomes (especially for people in the north who have been
neglected in the past); (2) diversifying the economy with the eventual
goal of self-sustained growth; (3) developing export opportunities; and
(4) improving the basic social needs for Namibia's population, which
heretofore have been neglected.

Minerals and Mining

Namibia is Africa's fourth-largest nonfuels mineral producer. It is the world's leading producer of gem-quality diamonds, accounting for some 30 percent of world output. Namibia has the world's largest uranium mine and some of the largest known tin and lithium reserves. It is Africa's second-largest producer of lead, third-largest producer of cadmium, and fourth-largest source of zinc and copper.[3] A summary of Namibia's major minerals production from 1978 to 1988 is found in Table 3.2. Minerals typically make up 30 to 55 percent of the Gross Domestic Product and are the state's largest export, source of foreign exchange, and employer (see Tables 3.3 and 3.4). The proceeds from Namibia's mineral wealth, however, have not been shared equally among its population. In 1985 mining accounted for about half of private-sector economic activities. Taxes from minerals ranged from R 52.8 million in 1976 to R 203 million in 1986 and R 288.9 million in 1990.[4] However, revenues from mining as a percentage of total government revenues have declined since 1977, from providing over 60 percent of total taxes paid in Namibia to about 22 percent in 1990.[5]

Namibia's mining sector has maintained healthy profits since 1976, with a taxable profit of R 618 million for 1985. The major buyers of Namibia's minerals are Western Europe, Japan, and the United States. Mineral exports have grown in both real and relative terms since 1980. Total sales more than doubled, from R 1.138 billion in 1980 to R 2.671 billion in 1989. Minerals as a percentage of total exports remained about the same during that period, accounting for 79.8 percent of total exports in 1980 and 75.8 percent in 1989 (see Table 3.4).

Mining companies continued their investments in mineral explorations as Namibia approached and achieved independence. In 1987 these firms invested R 21 million, and increased that to R 39 million in 1988.[6] According to the Department of Economic Affairs in Windhoek, 229 new prospecting licenses were issued in 1988, up from 197 in 1987, and 1,670 new claims were registered, up from 580 in 1987. DeBeers invested R 225 million in expansion, and a number of smaller mines also increased capital investments.

Namibia's major minerals are *diamonds*, mined by Consolidated Diamond Mines (CDM), which is owned by DeBeers; *uranium*, mined by Rössing Uranium, Ltd. (RUL), which is owned by a consortium led by Rio Tinto Zinc (RTZ); and *base minerals*—principally copper and lead—owned by Gold Fields Namibia, Ltd. Tsumeb now forms the major operating division of Gold Fields Namibia, a virtual subsidiary of Gold Fields of South Africa. CDM (foreign owned) and RUL (primarily foreign owned but with a small percentage of Namibian government ownership)

TABLE 3.2 Namibia's Major Minerals: Production 1978 - 1988

Mineral	1978	1979	1980	1981	1982	1983	1984	1985	1986	1987	1988
Diamonds ('000 carats)	1,898	1,653	1,560	1,248	1,014	963	930	909.0	1,009.0	1,019.0	938.0
Uranium oxide (short tons)	3,500	4,980	5,250	5,160	4,910	4,079	4,079[a]	4,000.0[a]	4,000.0[a]	4,200.0[a]	3,600.0[a]
Copper (blister) ('000 tons)	46	43	40	40	50	54	49	47.6	42.3[a]	47.7	42.2
Lead (refined) ('000 tons)	40	42	43	42	41	35	29	38.5	39.5[a]	40.6	44.4
Zinc (concentrate) ('000 tons)	37	29	25	36	36	29	33	57.0	40.0[a]	37.6	34.2

[a] estimates

Sources: Adopted from Donald L. Sparks and Roger Murray, Namibia's Future: The Economy at Independence (EIU Special Report No. 197) (London: Economist Intelligence Unit, 1985); The Economist Intelligence Unit, Namibia, Botswana, Lesotho and Swaziland: Country Report, Second Quarter 1989 (London: Economist Intelligence Unit, 1990); Consolidated Gold Mines and DeBeers annual reports; and information supplied by the Chamber of Mines, Windhoek.

TABLE 3.3   Mining Contribution to Namibian GDP

	Total Economy (million Rand)	Private Sector (million Rand)	Mining (million Rand)	Mining as a Percent of the Total
1975	644.7	535.1	174.2	32.6
1976	757.8	634.0	215.1	33.9
1977	952.0	803.9	388.8	8.4
1978	1,140.2	962.2	531.3	55.2
1979	1,276.0	1,070.4	584.3	54.6
1980	1,410.6	1,167.6	630.0	54.0
1981	1,458.1	1,096.2	454.4	41.5
1982	1,665.0	1,192.8	456.6	39.0
1983	1,751.1	1,182.5	473.3	40.0
1984	1,952.5	1,308.5	510.4	39.0
1985	2,511.9	1,821.5	980.1	49.9

Source: Chamber of Mines, Windhoek, 1988.

contribute about 80 percent of the country's total mining revenues. Namibia's major mines are listed in Table 3.5.

The president of the local Chamber of Mines in Namibia has stressed that "the risky business of mining should be allowed to operate in an environment of free enterprise unimpeded by unreasonable controls, [as there] is no substitute for a prosperous privately managed and controlled mining sector."[7] The chamber believes that increased state involvement in mining would discourage future foreign private investment in that sector as well as in other areas of the economy. The chamber favors trade unions because it knows it has no choice, but it does not want the unions to engage in "irresponsible actions" (that is, political activities). There were no strikes in Namibia's mines during 1988, although in June 1988 there was a two-day "politically inspired stayaway." Namibia's mines have had a fairly low fatality and injury rate. For example, four miners were killed in 1986—the fewest ever—and thirty-six were injured.[8]

The new government will probably establish a comprehensive mechanism to monitor mineral extraction, but it will not push for nationalization. It will also likely introduce a new mining law rather than change the existing Mines, Works, and Minerals Ordinance of 1968. Controversy has surrounded mining activities for years. For example, in 1982 the Thirion Commission was established by South Africa's

TABLE 3.4 Value of Namibia's Mineral Exports (million Rand at current prices)

Mineral	1980	1981	1982	1983	1984	1985	1986	1987	1988	1989
Diamond exports	446.7	231.0	217.9	234.7	231.6	409.0	615.5	431.2	653.5	814.0
Other mineral exports	461.6	462.0	537.2	480.3	619.5	875.8	1,029.8	875.7	901.2	1,212.8
Total mineral exports	908.3	693.0	755.1	715.0	851.1	1,284.8	1,645.3	1,306.9	1,554.7	2,026.8
Total exports	1,138.0	946.7	1,009.2	941.3	1,101.1	1,593.4	1,994.0	1,796.4	2,140.9	2,671.6
Minerals as percent of total exports	79.8	69.4	74.8	75.9	77.3	80.6	82.5	72.7	72.6	75.8

Source: Adapted from Namibia Ministry of Finance, *Namibia/SWA Statistical and Economic Review, 1989* (Windhoek,1989).

TABLE 3.5 Namibia's Major Mines

Company	Major Shareholders	Type of Product	Date Established
Consolidated Diamond Mines (CDM)	DeBeers Consolidated Mines	Diamonds	1928
Kombat Mine	Tsumeb Corporation	Copper, lead, silver	1908
Navachab Gold Mine	Anglo American Corp., CDM, Metall Mining Corp.	Gold	1989
Otjhase Mine	Tsumeb Corp, Otjhase Mining Company	Copper, silver, gold, pyrite	1975
Peralin	Private	Marble	1962
Posh Pinah Mine	Iscor, Moly Copper	Zinc, lead, silver	1968
Rossing Uranium Mine	Rio Tinto Zinc Corp. (RTZ)	Uranium oxide	1976
Salt Company	Private	Salt	1936
SWA Lithium Mines	Utec	Lithium	1950
Tsumeb Mine	Gold Fields Namibia, Gold Fields S.A., RTZ Corp.	Copper, lead, silver, cadmium, arsenic	1900
Uis Tin Mine	Iscor	Tin	1924

Source: Chamber of Mines of Namibia information handout.

administrator-general to investigate irregularities in diamond mining and its taxation.[9] At the time, the administrator-general depended on the industry to supply it with all its data, and it had no way of verifying the accuracy of this information. Further disclosures to the commission in 1984 indicated that Namibia had little control over the industry and that DeBeers and CDM may have engaged in extensive transfer pricing. The Namibian official in charge of revenues receipts indicated during the inquiry that his department accepted the figures supplied by the Diamond Board of South West Africa (which consists of DeBeers and the Windhoek administration) and that the figures had not been audited. Namibia may have lost up to R 1 billion in taxable diamond sales and over R 500 million in state revenues in the early 1980s, although the exact amounts will never be known. CDM denied any "improper conduct" in the past.

The commission pointed to another practice—overmining. Evidence suggested that CDM overmined during the 1970s and that the life of the deposits had begun to decrease. CDM denied that it had engaged in transfer pricing or that its mining levels were inappropriate or damaging to the country's future economy: it cited its recent investments in off-shore exploration and recovery facilities. DeBeers' mining rights (which originated under the 1923 Halbscheid agreement with South Africa) do not expire until 2010, but the company is expected to enter into negotiations with the new government. DeBeers has been successful in a joint venture with Botswana (the Debswana diamond project), and this could serve as a model for Namibia.[10]

The new minister of mines, Andimba Toivo ya Toivo, announced just after independence that the nation's minerals must be developed for the benefit of the majority of Namibia's people and that minerals were the common property of all Namibians. Toivo went on to say, "Over the years, through the mining industry, Namibia has developed an abnormal degree of dependency on a foreign country. Such an economic dependency threatens the political aspirations of a sovereign state and cannot be allowed to continue."[11] The government realizes that it will need mining revenues and has instituted a general policy of creating a favorable climate for investment. There are no plans for nationalization.

The Ministry of Mines and Energy reviewed mining and petroleum regulations during 1990 and introduced new tax legislation for a "free and equitable return" to the nation.[12] In addition to this new tax system, the ministry wants to find ways to encourage new investment and exploration in an effort to diversify Namibia's mineral production and exports. Offshore oil exploration was suspended in 1974 when the United Nations imposed a ban on Namibia. The Kudu offshore gas field has reserves of between 5 and 50 million cubic feet. The ministry plans to launch a new petroleum code with licensing for offshore exploration for the Kudi gas field near the mouth of the Orange River. The Namibian parastatal, SWAKOR, will be revamped along more commercial lines in a manner similar to Angola's oil parastatal, Sonangol. Toivo has strongly criticized the large outflow of profits and dividends from foreign-owned mines.

Diamonds. Diamonds are the most important mineral in Namibia. They usually account for about 25 percent of the GDP and one-third of the country's exports. CDM, the diamond mining company, is the country's largest single employer. In Namibia, diamonds are not found underground as they typically are elsewhere in the world. Instead, they have been deposited at the mouth of the Orange River on the Atlantic Ocean, where over the centuries they have washed down from the Kimberley Fields of South Africa. Mining these diamonds presents different problems from mining those found inland. For example, these diamond mining operations must keep the ocean out and clear out vast amounts of sand. For every carat recovered, some twenty-three tons of sand must be removed from the shore.[13]

In 1989 DeBeers announced the development of a new mine at Elizabeth Bay, 30 kilometers south of Luderitz. It is expected to cost R 135 million and to produce 250,000 carats annually. The diamond stones there are reportedly 95 to 98 percent gem quality. DeBeers had previously begun a new R 90 million mine inland at Auchas on the north bank of the Orange River.[14]

In addition to diamonds, DeBeers also produces gold. The DeBeers gold mine near Karibib in central Namibia began operations in 1989. The open cast mine is expected to produce 1.8 tons of gold annually, with an estimated thirteen-year life based on initial reserves of 10.1 million tons. This mine has created about 200 new jobs.

CDM's marketing of Namibia's diamonds is complex and secretive. CDM sells its diamonds through the Diamond Producer's Association, which is partly owned by the South African government. The gems are then sold to a DeBeers company, the Diamond Trading Company, which organizes sales through the Central Selling Organization in London. CDM's diamond production declined in 1988, from 1,019,636 carats in 1987 to 938,275 carats (see Table 3.6). The average grade of diamond recovered was only 5.8 carats per 100 tons, compared with 7.6 carats in 1987 and 16.7 carats in 1976. Nevertheless, despite lower output in volume terms, the price level of diamonds increased. CDM recorded an R 115 million after-tax profit in 1988 compared with an after-tax profit of R 58 million in 1987.

TABLE 3.6 Namibia's Diamond Production

Year	Overburden Stripped (million tons)	Ore Treated (million tons)	Diamonds Produced (carats)	Ratio of Diamond to Waste	Average Grade of Ore Treated (carats/100 tons)
1950	2.88	0.85	377,595	1:49	44.75
1960	15.52	5.25	933,937	1:111	17.68
1970	30.59	10.27	1,509,263	1:135	14.36
1980	56.56	16.82	1,559,885	1:235	9.27
1981	37.70	12.54	1,247,960	1:201	9.95
1982	18.44	10.02	1,014,464	1:140	10.13
1983	17.18	9.59	962,752	1:139	10.04
1984	19.33	7.55	930,183	1:145	12.32
1985	20.54	8.18	909,530	1:158	11.12
1986	27.96	12.14	1,009,520	1:199	8.32
1987	32.19	13.44	1,019,636	1:224	7.59
1988	42.80	16.00	938,275	na	5.80

Sources: Adapted from Consolidated Diamond Mines and DeBeers annual reports, various years; Economist Intelligence Unit, Namibia, Botswana, Lesotho and Swaziland Country Report, No. 2, 1989 (London: EIU, 1989).

CDM ranks sixth in terms of production of near-gem and gem-quality diamonds worldwide. Production in 1990 was 750,115 carats, a decrease of 17 percent from 1989. Because CDM's diamonds are high gem-quality, Namibia remains important for the world diamond market. Although its exports are generally sent off in raw form, it is likely that Namibia will eventually mine and fully process its diamond output.

DeBeers has indicated that it would accept a 50–50 equity partnership with the new government in an arrangement similar to the Debswana joint venture in Botswana. Although the new government would probably not press for a higher equity ratio, even 50–50 participation would be significant in terms of potential earnings and foreign exchange during the next decade. In early 1991 DeBeers began operating a new mine near Oragjemund. Output is expected to reach 75,000 carats annually.

Uranium. Details of Namibia's uranium industry have been kept secret under the Nuclear Energy Act of 1982 and various other South African security regulations. The Rössing mine, located about 60 kilometers inland from Swakopmund, has been the world's largest uranium producer, with an average annual capacity of over 5,000 short tons. According to its general manager, it is currently operating at approximately 80 percent capacity.[15] Rössing is owned by the U.K.-based Rio Tinto Zinc (now called RTZ Corporation Ltd.) and other investors from South Africa, Canada, Germany, and France, and a small percentage (3 percent) is owned by the Namibian government. Importantly, the government controls 50 percent of the company's voting shares, which gives it an effective veto over the board of directors' decisions. As with diamonds, before independence Namibia had little control over the monitoring of its overseas uranium sales.

Rössing's output is sold on a long-term contract basis to European Community countries, Japan, and Taiwan, although RTZ will not disclose the identity of its buyers. In the early 1980s, the U.S. Department of Energy estimated that in addition to the United Kingdom, the major customers were France (which bought 11,000 tons of uranium oxide from 1981 to 1990), Japan (15,860 tons from 1984 to 1990), and the Federal Republic of Germany (10,600 tons from 1984 to 1990).[16] Although the world market for uranium has been slack for several years, demand now exceeds production, and when existing stockpiles are depleted by utilities—probably around the late 1990s—Rössing is likely to return to full production. The establishment of new uranium mines remains unlikely, however. Nevertheless, the feared results of the Greenhouse Effect may cause many (including environmentalists) to reconsider using nuclear energy.

Mining uranium. The 150-ton truck is hauling uranium and is checked by radiometric scanners before leaving the open pit for crushing. (Courtesy Rössing Uranium)

Directly after independence there were prospects for increased uranium sales, especially with the United States and others lifting sanctions. However, uranium prices have declined significantly because of slackened demand; also large quantities are now available from Eastern European suppliers. The spot price declined from $11.60 per pound in 1989 to $8.35 per pound in 1990.[17]

Despite lower production in 1988, Rössing Uranium's earnings increased over 1987 according to RTZ, which controls 46.5 percent equity in the company and provides management and technical services. Rössing's output in 1988 was probably about 3,600 short tons, down from perhaps 3,800 short tons in 1987. Rössing's net profits declined from R 245 million in 1988 to R 157 million in 1989. Its export earnings in 1987 were U.S. $336 million.[18] Rössing did secure a long-term contract

The town of Arandis houses workers for Rössing Uranium, one of Namibia's most important industries. (Courtesy Rössing Uranium)

from France in 1991 for 5,200 short tons, but deliveries will not start until 1995 and will continue until 2002.

During the year before independence, workers at Rössing, organized by the Mineworkers Union of Namibia, engaged in a dispute over wage-related issues and complained about alleged harassment of union members' activities. Rössing annouced a 15 percent across-the-board wage increase for 1990.

Base Metals. The vast majority—between 85 and 90 percent—of Namibia's base metal production comes from the mines at Tsumeb. The major metals produced there are copper and lead. The Tsumeb Corporation was consolidated in 1988 into a new company, Gold Fields Namibia, Ltd. Gold Fields of South Africa is the company's controlling shareholder, with 69 percent interest. The other major shareholder is the Rembrandt Group, also a South African concern. Some of the copper concentrates that are processed in Namibia are imported from South Africa. Namibia produces about 2 percent of Africa's copper.[19] It has about 670,000 tons of lead ore reserves, about 1.5 percent of the world's total (and perhaps 20 percent of Africa's total reserves). Lead has a number of uses after refining, including use in batteries, paints, cable coverings, ammunition, solder, and building construction.

Tsumeb's sales hit a record R 363 million in 1988, due primarily to improved world prices for base metals. These sales translated into an after-tax profit of R 58 million, up from R 20 million in 1987. Profits in 1989 reached R 55 million. The smelter at Tsumeb was only operating at about 50 percent capacity in the mid-1980s.[20] Tsumeb experienced several labor disputes in the late 1980s and a prolonged strike in 1987.

The prospects for discovering new minerals or for expansion are not bright, and there is only limited potential for increased local processing. Some minerals found in Namibia (concentrates that typically make up one-third to one-half of the mineral's total weight) are not processed locally because the local processing costs are higher than the transport costs. For example, uranium oxide is unlikely to be processed in Namibia because of the exceedingly high capital costs of creating a conversion and enrichment facility—especially without a domestic nuclear power industry.

Nevertheless, some minerals could be processed on site. There is potential for increased tin and zinc processing, which is currently being done in South Africa's Transvaal region. Virtually all of Namibia's copper and lead is refined at Tsumeb, and that facility has not been running near its full capacity. Although Namibia could process minerals from neighboring states, mineral processing facilities are capital-intensive and expansion would create few jobs. Additionally, these jobs tend to be technology-intensive and require foreign-trained managers and technicians. Finally, the quantities of other minerals produced in Namibia are generally too small to justify the investment of local processing facilities. If Namibia does expand the areas in which it has a natural advantage— for example, copper—it could develop important linkages through pipe and wire production, for lead in battery making, and for tin in tin can manufacturing. Tin can manufacturing, in turn, could result in increased local processing of fish and meat products. Mining is regulated under the 1969 Mines, Works, and Minerals Act, although a new minerals act will probably be introduced by the government. Despite SWAPO's calls for nationalization of mines before independence, there are no plans for massive state involvement in the mining sector.

Industry and Manufacturing

Namibia's industrial sector is export-oriented, and its products are mostly unprocessed minerals and fish. Despite their importance to the GDP, employment opportunities in these areas will remain limited. Industrial diversification of the economy will have to take place in labor-intensive, agro-based industries in rural areas—particularly in the north—and in the primary manufacturing industries in urban areas.

Namibia's manufacturing sector is small. Since 1920 its share of the GDP has never exceeded 6 percent of the total, and traditionally it contributes between 4 and 5 percent (see Table 3.1). In 1980 manufacturing contributed 3.9 percent of the total GDP, or R 56.5 million. By 1988–1989, manufacturing accounted for 4.8 percent of the GDP, or R 60.5 million (at 1980 constant prices).[21] In other Less Developed Countries (LDCs), manufacturing typically accounts for 10 percent of the GDP, and the manufacturing sector of most African countries has been increasing in recent years.[22] A number of reasons explain Namibia's small manufacturing sector: the lack of natural material inputs, limited markets and the remoteness of those markets, scarce water, high energy and transport costs, and the lack of a skilled workforce and an educated entrepreneurial class. Although these are important reasons, they do not totally explain the structure of the economy into which the manufacturing sector fits. That structure is also partly a result of South Africa's colonial policies, which created a dependency relationship in the manufacturing sector. Over the years of its rule, Namibia's industrial sector was deliberately designed to serve the economic interests of South Africa. For example, the larger South African industrial sector had unrestricted access to Namibia and often undercut prices whenever Namibian firms tried to produce a specific good. South African manufactured goods have been transported to Namibia through the parastatal, South African Railways & Harbour Corporation, at concessionary rates, thus also undercutting real and potential Namibian competition.

The manufacturing sector is based primarily on processing food products from fish and beef. Food products account for approximately 70 percent of all the goods produced in Namibia. Of that total, fish (pilchards and rock lobsters) contributes nearly 75 percent, meat products 20 percent, butter and cheese 2 percent, and other food products the remainder. Other industries include wood processing, textiles, furniture, and transport equipment. There are also a number of cottage industries and some manufacturers in the informal sector, although this sector was strongly discouraged from developing by the South African regime.

Namibia has experienced fluctuations in its food processing, which reflects the cyclical fluctuations in the supply of the major fish species, particularly pilchards. Overfishing of this stock in the late 1970s brought the fish canning industry to a virtual standstill; indeed, many processing plants were sold and shipped to Chile.[23] The stocks have recovered somewhat since then, and fish processing as a value-added activity should remain important to independent Namibia. Drought has affected the supply of cattle for beef processing.

Although the fish and meat processing plants are large and capital-intensive, about two-thirds of Namibia's manufacturing firms are small-scale, often employing only two or three people plus the owner. Namibia's informal sector has been limited and was forced into trade rather than manufacturing due to the restrictions on manufacturing in white areas. Informal manufacturing (including wood carvers, joiners, smiths, basket makers, potters, and others), however, does exist in the rural areas, particularly in the far north.

Namibia's 325 manufacturing firms are located primarily in or near the major population centers (see Table 3.7). There is little formal manufacturing in the north, where half of the population lives. Windhoek has the most firms (170), followed by Swakopmund with 25; these two cities account for nearly two-hirds of Namibia's manufacturing firms. No other city or town has more than 16 manufacturing entities. Except for the small artisanal and cottage industries, virtually all of the modern-sector manufacturing firms are owned by whites. The manufacturing sector does not provide significant employment for Namibia's formal economy. According to the First National Development Corporation (ENOK) in Windhoek, 5,787 people were employed in manufacturing industries in 1988. For companies under sole proprietorship, 1,193 men and 260 women were employed. Corporations employed 3,706 men and 628 women.[24]

Agriculture

Namibia's agricultural sector is divided between capital-intensive, large-scale, "modern" versus communal, subsistence, and poor "traditional" methods of production. Large-scale agriculture is usually found in the best farming areas of the country and typically accounts for some 10 percent of the GDP and of exports. It is owned and controlled primarily by white ranchers. Some 5,200 commercial farms are owned by about 4,500 individuals and businesses, but 48 percent of these are owned by absentee owners.[25] Redistribution of ownership of absentee-owned farmland will no doubt be a priority of the new, independent government. Livestock ranching contributes around 85 percent of all agricultural production, although this subsector has declined in recent years due to poor weather conditions and overgrazing. The major commercial crops are vegetables, sorghum, maize, and cotton.[26]

TABLE 3.7   Location of Namibia's Manufacturing Firms

Location (city or town)[a]	Number of Firms
Tsumeb	7
Otavi	5
Grootfontein	9
Otjiwarongo	9
Outjo	8
Okakarara	-
Khorixas	2
Omaruru	7
Swakopmund	25
Usakos	3
Karibib	4
Okahandja	16
Windhoek	170
Gobabis	8
Rehoboth	8
Mariental	3
Keetmanshoop	8
Karasburg	2
Luderitz	8
Gibeon	1
Other	22
TOTAL	325

[a] This survey listed no firms in Oshakati, although
at least three such firms should have been included.

Source: First National Development Corporation, Windhoek, 1989.

Agriculture plays an important role in the daily lives of most black Namibians, although the traditional agricultural sector generally only contributes 2–3 percent of the GDP. Black-owned cattle generally are not slaughtered for export but are consumed locally. Subsistence crops include beans, potatoes, and maize, and subsistence farmers occupy only 20 percent of the good ranching land. In the less arid north, planting and cattle herding were hampered severely by the liberation war. Approximately 120,000 heads of households are directly engaged in subsistence farming; when their dependents are included, well over half of the population is dependent on subsistence agriculture.

Agriculture will likely be a priority for the new government and foreign investors. Indeed, the day after independence the British multinational company, Lonhro, announced a major $150 million sugar-growing plan for the northern part of Namibia. Because of unfavorable growing conditions in Brazil, Namibia has become particularly attractive as an alternative site for Lonhro.[27] The establishment of agro-based industries to increase value-added activities and promote rural development will be important in an overall agricultural self-sufficiency program. Namibia is now in a position to import and export more freely, and it will not be tied—at least legally—to the South African market. The elimination of sanctions by the international community will also help Namibia's overall trade position.

With the help of the government, a number of the other subsectors should begin to develop. For example, irrigated orchards (mainly at the Hardap Dam and in the Otavi highlands) as well as specific areas in the far north will be well suited for fruit production. Currently the country loses value-added profits when it exports unprocessed karakul (baby lamb) pelts for auction in London. The new government may establish joint ventures so that these pelts can be exported as finished garments. Similarly, the new government may also gradually end exporting cattle on the hoof to South Africa in favor of expanding local meat processing facilities. Nearly half of marketed Namibian cattle and two-thirds of small stock are sent to South Africa If Namibia reduced this amount, it could increase its local processing and add to export potential. It already exports ten thousand tons of chilled and frozen beef annually. Botswana, which is in a similar position, has been able to diversify its foreign markets. Nevertheless, Namibia remains at the mercy of adverse climatic conditions over which it has virtually no control. According to a United Nations Industrial Development Organization (UNIDO) study, "In stock-rearing, overall rancher strategy has been to maximize production by stocking pastures to the full during a good rainfall sequence, then offloading surplus stock in large numbers during drought. Such a policy leaves them at the mercy of market gluts and low prices, which their oversupply worsens. It also risks ecological damage."[28]

At independence parts of Namibia faced their worst droughts in over thirty years. Farmers in Ovamboland had to travel up to 40 kilometers for water for their livestock. Although most of the southern region was not as heavily affected, much of the north suffered greatly.[29] The United Nations organized an interagency task force composed of the Food and Agriculture Organization, the World Food Programme, the UN Children's Fund, and the UN Development Program to offer help to drought-stricken areas.

Land tenure reform remains a potentially explosive issue. A national conference on land and rural development was to be held soon after independence under the auspices of the prime minister's office. By mid-1991 the government had allocated over R 6 million to purchase land on a willing buyer–willing seller basis.

Fisheries and Marine Resources

Traditionally, marine fishing has been Namibia's third-most-important economic sector, after mining and agriculture. If properly managed, fisheries are an important self-renewing resource, and they are one of Namibia's most important prospects for economic development. Minister of Agriculture, Fisheries, Water, and Rural Development Gerhard Hanekom suggests that the fishing industry could contribute up to 50 percent of the country's annual budget revenues.[30] Fisheries contribute as much as 20 percent of exports and are one of the major segments of the industrial sector. Namibians generally do not eat pelagic fish; instead, fish is used to produce fish meal for cattle or fertilizers, and some is tinned for export. The Benguela Current off Namibia's coast produces a rich fisheries area, and some of the world's largest stocks of pilchards (sardines), anchovies, tuna, maasbanker, and mackerel are found in these waters; in the mid-1979s, Namibia was the world's largest producer of canned pilchards.

Large-scale, capital-intensive operations based out of Walvis Bay began to expand during the 1950s and 1960s. However, overfishing by South African and, to a lesser degree, other foreign trawlers in the late 1970s dramatically reduced pilchards, which are traditionally the most important catch. In 1969 some 676,000 tons of pilchards were caught, but in 1980 only 10,247 tons were caught. As a result of conservation efforts, pilchard catches have recovered somewhat, and in 1987 around 62,000 tons were caught—still drastically below the 1960s and early 1970s levels.[31] With the decline of the pilchard stock, deep sea trawler fishing has become the major force in the marine fisheries industry. Virtually all of the industry (including processing, fleet repair and maintenance facilities, and the general infrastructure) is located in Walvis Bay and to a lesser extent in Luderitz, both of which are on Namibia's remote and desolate coast. Rock lobster processing, seal pelt preserving, and seaweed processing are located in Luderitz, and nearly everything else is at Walvis Bay—South Africa's port enclave. The local fishing fleet consists of around 60 vessels and can only use about 15 percent of the available fisheries. Nearly all of the rock lobster caught at Luderitz is shipped to Japan.

Namibia's fisheries and offshore resources show potential for industrial contribution to the overall economy. The new government will have to make several important changes in this sector, however. According to a 1986 study completed by the United Nations Institute for Namibia, after independence the fisheries sector will need to (1) establish a national fishery administration; (2) declare an exclusive economic zone (EEZ); (3) introduce and enforce strict resource management regulations; (4)

Fishermen at Luderitz, along Namibia's southern coast.

salvage remaining vessels, processing plants, and equipment from damage through misuse; (5) provide sufficient amounts of fish for food at low cost to the Namibian population; (6) negotiate preliminary and temporary agreements with foreign fishing companies on fishing of surplus resources and possibly on joint ventures in processing; (7) train personnel for the entire fisheries sector; and (8) start the preparatory phases of programs to develop the national fisheries sector.[32]

Namibia's fisheries licensing arrangements are likely to change. The new government declared a two hundred–mile EEZ in May 1990 and has applied for membership in the seventeen-member International Commission for Southeast Atlantic Fisheries (ICSEAF).[33] Other members of ICSEAF include South Africa, the USSR, and several East and West European states. Membership, quota limitations, and subsequent enforcement will be critical if Namibia is to control the currently uncontrolled foreign trawler operations in its two hundred–mile zone. Although all members of ICSEAF have agreed to halt fishing in Namibia's waters, Soviet and Spanish vessels were still operating offshore after independence. The new government has begun a comprehensive fish stock assessment in its two hundred–mile EEZ with help from Norway and Iceland. The United States agreed to help monitor the zone because Namibia has only one patrol vessel and one research vessel for the entire zone. According to the director of sea fisheries, it will cost Namibia about R 15 million annually to monitor its EEZ. The Norwegian government has supplied a research vessel under UN Food and Agriculture Organization auspices to survey the fish stocks in Namibia's EEZ.[34] South Africa's Department of Environmental Affairs has refused to turn over Namibia's only research vessel, the *Benguela*, until Namibia begins negotiations with South Africa over fishing rights along Walvis Bay and the twelve off-shore islands. However, Minister of Agriculture, Fisheries, Water, and Rural Development Gerhard Hanekom has maintained that ownership of the vessel is "non-negotiable."[35]

Energy and Water

Both energy and water supplies will be vital for independent Namibia's development efforts. They share some common characteristics: Energy and water needs will be most pressing in the north, and the sources for energy generation and water for irrigation are located in the north. Industrial expansion is most likely to take place in the north. Virtually all of Namibia's coal and petroleum has been imported from (or at least through) South Africa. The South West Africa Water and Electricity Corporation has been responsible for the bulk sales to Namibia's major consumers, and the pricing has been set by the South African Electricity Supply Commission. Pricing and allocation decisions thus have been made by these two bodies for the benefit of the country's mining industry. These arrangements will no doubt change soon.

Namibia's energy use is skewed by population group, economic activity, and economic sector. Over 50 percent of all energy is consumed directly by the mining industry.[36] Most of the country's energy goes to the major cities and not to the north, where over 50 percent of the population resides. About one-fifth of total energy consumption comes from charcoal, which is the only source of energy for most of the rural population. This could lead to further deforestation problems in the future. According to a UNIN study, in 1980 Namibia's total consumption of energy by manufacturing activities (excluding fish processing) included 45,000 tons of coal, 400 tons of gasoline, 1,700 tons of diesel, and 125 million kilowatt hours (kwh) of electricity. The construction and services sectors used around 11 percent of Namibia's commercial energy—67,000 tons of coal, 100 tons of gasoline, 1,200 tons of diesel, and 230 million kwh of electricity.[37] Rural electrification is a priority in the government's development efforts. Currently only a few rural households (including most white-owned farms) are hooked up to the national grid. Indeed, until now rural electricity expansion has been a low priority.

Namibia's power generation has changed radically since 1980. Prior to 1982 about 70 percent of all electricity was produced from coal-fired generation stations. In 1983, after the completion of the Ruacana station located along the Angolan border, hydroelectricity could potentially produce about 53 percent of the country's electricity needs, coal-fired stations 42 percent, and oil-fired stations 12 percent. The new government has begun talks with the Angolan government on repairing hydroelectric installations in Angola, which should help the Ruacana station generate at full capacity year-round instead of only during the flood season, which is presently the case.[38]

Namibia and Angola signed an agreement in 1991 to develop energy sources from the Cunene River. Namibia is considering building a new hydroelectric facility downstream from the existing dam at Ruacana. Although with the major hydroelectric dam at Ruacana Falls and its 240-megawatt capacity Namibia is virtually self-sufficient in short-term energy needs, it will likely want to increase its energy development for both export and potential increased domestic demand. In fact, during the 1970s U.S. firms undertook considerable offshore oil exploration under the auspices of the Southern Oil Exploration Corporation, a South African parastatal. In 1974 a Texaco-Chevron consortium found methane gas at the Kudu fields about 150 kilometers from the mouth of the Orange River, although there has been no additional exploration because of the uncertain political situation in the entire region. Oil experts predict that the Kudu fields could be the most promising offshore gas deposits in southern Africa, with a potential output of 300 cubic meters per day for twenty years.[39] Several exploration projects were approved by government-issued permits to begin in 1991–1992, and over forty companies have bought preliminary data surveys. A Taiwanese company, Overseas Petroleum Investment Corporation, began exploration in the 260,000-kilometer^2 concession it acquired from the Etosha Petroleum Company in 1988.

Water supplies in Namibia, which is basically a desert nation, are precarious at best. Except for the Namib Desert there is a good deal of underground water in the country; however, because of large amounts of dissolved rock particles, much of this water is virtually unusable. Fortunately, however, water is less of a problem in the northern part of the country. Since 1980, water demand from the mining industry has slackened, although urban household and agricultural demand has increased by about 10 percent. Mining demand for water has decreased since 1980 because of several mine closures and the reduced demand from Rössing, which traditionally uses around 80 percent of all the mining industry's water.[40] The major consumers of water today are urban areas (47 percent), mines (34 percent), and rural communities (17 percent). Namibia has had some success in water recycling. For example, Windhoek's reclamation plant can recycle nearly 25 percent of the capital's water needs.

Transportation

Namibia is blessed with one of the more advanced transportation infrastructures in southern Africa, particularly compared with Angola or Mozambique. Nevertheless, although the transportation network is good, it was designed with the almost-exclusive purpose of linking Namibia and its unprocessed minerals and agricultural products to South Africa, either through the rail lines or through Walvis Bay. South Africa saw no need to establish significant transport links from Namibia to Angola, Botswana, Zambia, or Zimbabwe. Further, except for expansion for military purposes in the late 1970s and early 1980s, there has been virtually no attempt to broaden the transport network throughout Namibia in an integrated fashion.

With the transport link, Namibia "provides the most expeditious outlet for the central African copperbelt to North America and Western Europe, much closer than, say, Dar es Salaam or South Africa."[41] Further, the containerized port of Walvis Bay is more attractive than Lobito or Luanda. The average turnaround time at Walvis Bay is forty-eight hours, the average boat time is six hours in port, and imports can be cleared and on the trucks in four hours if necessary.

Railroads. Namibia has a network of 2,340 kilometers of 1,065-millimeter-gauge single-track railways. The major lines run north-south from the mineral areas of Tsumeb through Windhoek to the border town of Ariamsvlei. The major east-west line goes from Okahandja to Swakopmund–Walvis Bay. There are two "spur" lines, one to Luderitz on the coast and the other to Gobabis east toward the Botswana border. Diesel locomotives power the trains, which in 1983 carried approximately 4.4 million tons of cargo—mostly imports from South Africa. The railroad has fifty passenger coaches, which carry about half a million passengers annually.[42] A new parastatal, Transnamib Limited, was created in July 1988, which took over the South African Railway's assets in Namibia. This has increased the fixed capital stock for the emerging government as well as strengthened Namibia's rail transportation system.

Roads. Namibia's road network also runs basically north-south, with a few important branch roads running east-west; in fact, the major highways virtually parallel the railroads. Namibia had some 4,438 kilometers of tarred roads and 38,000 kilometers of gravel roads in 1987.[43] Combined with earth and sand tracks, Namibia has a total of over 60,000 kilometers of mapped roads. The road system was designed to benefit the mining interests, white commercial farmers, and the military and to expedite transport with South Africa. After independence, the government has been pressed to build more feeder roads in the rural areas, as about two-thirds of the country's roads are in the "white" areas. Public transport is poor, and pressure to expand it has increased after independence.

Ports. Namibia has two natural harbors, Walvis Bay and Luderitz. Walvis Bay is the country's only deep-water port and is controlled by South African Transport Services, a South African parastatal.[44] It handles about 95 percent of all seaborne cargo—about 750,000 tons of petroleum products and 750,000 tons of dry cargo annually. The harbor was deepened several times in the 1980s, and it now has a channel depth of 12.8 meters. S.A. Transport Services employs about 2,000 workers (100 whites, 200 high-wage blacks, and 1,700 black manual workers). Walvis Bay is a modern, containerized port adapted for "Ro-ro" (roll-on, roll-off) services. Luderitz, which was once a fairly prosperous port that handled diamonds, has been in a state of decline for over twenty years. It is not as deep as Walvis Bay and is less accessible to the major population centers and mining areas. It now survives on the rock lobster and fisheries industries.

Air transport. Namibia has 110 registered airfields, three of which (Strijdom 48 kilometers east of Windhoek, Walvis Bay, and Keetmanshoop) can handle wide-bodied jets. Of the remaining runways, eight are paved and many of the others are gravel. Scheduled internal flights operate from Eros (Windhoek's domestic airport), Keetmanshoop, Luderitz, Walvis Bay, Tsumeb, Grootfontein, and Swakopmund. Although prior to independence only South African Airways served Namibia's international connections and Namib Air its internal ones, there is now at least weekly air service to Botswana, Zimbabwe, and Zambia. At independence, Namib Air announced the opening of direct flights to New York and Frankfurt.

EMPLOYMENT AND LABOR

Namibia has a relatively high dependency ratio of 49.4 percent (that is, nearly 500 out of every 1,000 people are under the age of 18).[45] This ratio varies from region to region but is most highly concentrated in the rural areas. Namibia's economically active population (excluding the jobless, retired people, students, housewives, and preschool children) is low in both absolute and relative terms. On a country-wide average, only 200 to 400 people per 1,000 could be categorized as "economically active." Namibia thus has a total labor force of perhaps 600,000 to 800,000 people. Of these, about 50 percent are employed in small-scale agriculture (see Table 3.8).

South Africa's apartheid ensured discrimination against blacks in the labor market. South Africa developed a contract labor system whereby workers were recruited from the rural areas to work on the large, white

TABLE 3.8 Employment by Economic Activity

Activity	Percent of Total Employment
Small-scale agriculture	50.3
Large-scale agriculture	11.8
Fishing and fish processing	1.6
Mining	4.7
Manufacturing and public utilities	2.6
Construction	3.2
Transportation and communication	2.6
Commerce and finance	5.2
Government	6.3
Domestic services	7.3
Other	4.4

Sources: Reginald H. Green, Manpower Estimates and Development Implications for Namibia (Lusaka: UNIN, 1978); and W. van Ginneken, Incomes and Wages in Namibia (Geneva: International Labour Office, 1985).

commercial farms or in the modern urban economic sectors. The authorities ensured that such labor was controlled to guarantee that supply always exceeded the demand. This migrant labor was believed to be an expendable commodity, and the migrants were not integrated into the wider society. In many cases they were not even allowed to live with their families. As in South Africa, dependents were forced to stay behind in their respective "homelands" (Bantu Reserves). Black workers have generally remained in the semi- or unskilled areas, and whites hold the vast majority of skilled jobs. There is a wide range of pay between the races, with average monthly wages for whites at R 2,000, black skilled at R 600 and black unskilled at R 200.[46] Small-scale subsistence agriculture (which provides only 2 to 3 percent of the state's GDP) is the occupation of most black Namibians—perhaps one-half of the total population.

About 25 percent are low-paid contract or migrant workers employed in the mines, on large-scale commercial farms, and in the fishing and manufacturing industries.

With independence, many blacks moved into leadership positions in government. Prior to independence, many whites were fearful of their future in the new government. However, there was no mass exodus of public servants from Namibia at independence. Only two hundred civil servants were officially classsified as seconded from South Africa. In May 1990, Prime Minister Hage Geingob tabled the Public Service Commission Bill, which would have increased affirmative action in the government sector with the ultimate goal of a more balanced structure for the civil service. According to Hidipo Hamutenya, minister of information, there are around 47,000 state employees, and "virtually the entire top echelon of the civil service and parastatals is white and male. The blacks are largely employed in jobs such as drivers and cleaners."[47]

Employment in Namibian industry can be grouped in the following categories: highly mechanized, artisan workshops, and cottage workshops.[48] The highly mechanized are usually the larger establishments (employing at least twenty people) whose output is usually exported. Output from these firms includes mineral processing, fish and meat packaging, beverages, and chemicals. Most of the technological or managerial expertise remains with whites. Recently blacks have been given limited supervisory positions, but most black workers remain in unskilled jobs. Artisan workshops generally serve the local market and employ fewer than twenty people each. These establishments include bakeries, butcheries, and building material producers. There has been a recent trend to train more blacks for jobs in these firms. Nevertheless, blacks are generally excluded from management, although many are employed as clerks and low-position personnel officers. Cottage workshops generally produce goods for the rural and tourist markets using traditional skills and local inputs. These activities include woodcarving, basketware, pottery, and illicit beer brewing. Skills have generally been handed down to family members, and wages are often low.

Trade unions have played an important role in Namibia's labor scene. Even before South Africa gained control of Namibia from the Germans, workers engaged in strikes and other industrial actions. Strikes have occurred continually since 1916. Perhaps the most important strike occurred in December 1971 through January 1972 when over 13,500 mostly migrant workers struck against the Pass Laws and the criminal indenture system of migrant labor. Nevertheless, early attempts to form formal trade unions did not succeed, as the South African regime removed the leaders. Some early efforts did work; for example, a branch

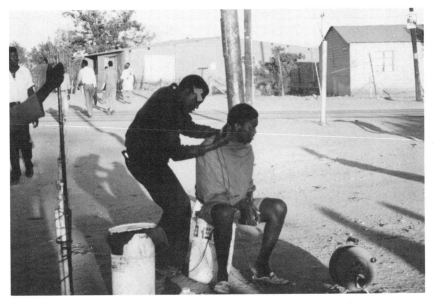

Entrepreneurship in Katutura: Note that the razor is powered by an electric generator. (Photo by December Green)

of the Industrial and Commercial Union of Africa existed in Luderitz as early as 1920. It was not until the 1950s that organized unions, mostly based on fish canneries located in Walvis Bay and Luderitz, were established. A number of strikes were launched in the early 1950s, with brutal police retaliation. The Ovambo People's Congress (OPC) was formed by Namibian workers in Cape Town in 1957 under the leadership of Herman Toivo ya Toivo. The Ovamboland People's Organization emerged from this. OPC and OPO were both basically union-oriented organizations that wanted to reform the contract labor system. OPO membership spread throughout Namibia.

Since the mid-1980s there has been a tremendous amount of union activity. Many trade unions did not officially register, and many disbanded almost as fast as they were created. Most unions are affiliated with political parties; there are those that support SWAPO, those that support other parties, or the older, traditional trade unions. In 1989 eighteen unions were registered with the Department of Civic Affairs and Manpower under the Wage and Industrial Conciliation Ordinance, including the Automobile and Metal Workers; Drivers, Transport, and Allied Workers; Food Products and Associated Workers; Government Staff Association; Independent Mineworkers Union; Metal and Allied Namibian Workers; Mineworkers Union of Namibia; Namibia Building Workers;

Namibia Wholesale and Retail Workers; Namibian Food and Allied Workers Union; Namibian National Teachers Union; Namibian Transport and Allied Workers Union; SWA Municipal Staff Association; SWA Mineworkers Union; and Transport Corporation Workers Union of Namibia.[49]

Perhaps the two most important labor unions are the Mineworkers Union of Namibia (MUN) and the National Union of Namibian Workers (NUNW). The 12,590-member MUN is determined to see changes in the mining industry. Its 1989 annual report criticized the mining companies for low wages, forced overtime, unsafe conditions, poor housing, and discrimination in training and promotion. Although Rössing and CDM had minimum wages of R 3.00–R 4.00 per hour, most companies paid R 2.00, and some paid R .40 per hour. Tsumeb Corporation Limited (TCL) was the most heavily criticized, as it was late to recognize MUN. NUNW is trying to consolidate with the unions affiliated with it.

ECONOMIC RELATIONS WITH SOUTH AFRICA

Namibia's future relationship with South Africa will be primarily economic, at least initially. Namibia has been and continues to be economically dominated by the Republic of South Africa. Because South Africa has maintained complete control of the economy, there has been little opportunity to develop autonomous local institutions in virtually any economic sector. Over the years, South Africa deliberately pursued measures designed to force Namibia into a dependent relationship. This relationship continues and extends into the most vital parts of Namibia's economy. Because Namibia was long considered an integral part of the Republic of South Africa, it faces difficulties in expanding or altering its economic linkages immediately after independence. Its economy has been geared almost exclusively toward South Africa. For example, Namibia is a member of the Common Currency Area (and thus uses the South African Rand as currency) and the Southern African Customs Union; South Africa thus has total control over Namibian monetary and custom-tariff affairs. Its economy is open: Exports exceed 60 percent of the GDP, and at least one-third of the GDP goes abroad—mostly to South Africa. Three-quarters of Namibia's imports are South African, and South Africa traditionally is Namibia's major customer. Virtually all of Namibia's trade goes through South Africa.

Perhaps the most important question facing the new government is what economic influence South Africa will likely retain or try to retain. Such influence is determined by a number of important economic linkages including monetary, debt, trade, transportation, the EEZ, and perhaps most important, the relationship with Walvis Bay and the twelve off-shore islands. In the future Namibia may try to alter some of these linkages, but many cannot be changed.

Monetary

The Common Currency Area includes Namibia, South Africa, Lesotho, and Swaziland; Botswana used the South African Rand until it established the Bank of Botswana and issued its own currency in 1976. Lesotho and Swaziland both have their own currencies, but the Rand is also legal tender and is freely interchangeable. The 1974 agreement between South Africa and other area members (to which Namibia was not a party) gives both Lesotho and Swaziland a share of the profits from the interest of Rand notes those countries have in circulation. South Africa holds the official foreign exchange reserves of the members and determines how to invest them. It also sets the exchange rates.

As a member of the Common Currency Area, Namibia depends on the South African Reserve Bank (South Africa's equivalent to the U.S. Federal Reserve System—its central bank) for monetary control and uses the Rand as its legal tender. Minister of Finance Otto Herrigel indicated on April 23, 1990, that Namibia would like to establish a central bank on June 1, 1990, and its own currency by March 1992, although it would use the Rand until a new currency is issued.[50] The International Monetary Fund is helping the new government develop its currency system.

Namibia has a number of choices.[51] It could create a new currency area—perhaps composed of Botswana, Lesotho, and Swaziland—whose members would share a common currency and a joint central bank. The currency could be linked to a basket of major currencies, with the Rand probably playing a major role as it is the major external economic partner of all the states potentially included. Such a system would have a number of advantages, such as facilitating trade and investment among members and providing economies of scale in operations of the monetary system (one system would be less expensive to operate than four independent ones). Unfortunately, there is little trading among the four countries, because they produce similar goods. Such a scheme would require an enormous amount of political goodwill and coordination. An independent central bank will give Namibia control over its monetary policies. One of the country's leading economists believes that "it doesn't appear that an independent Namibia will be able to afford its own currency [and] for some time it will have to use the Rand. . . . Nevertheless, a new currency would not deter South African or other investors from this country, since the same thing happened in Botswana."[52]

According to the United Nations Development Programme (UNDP), "If Namibia remains a member of the Rand [sic] Monetary Area, the

TABLE 3.9 Namibia's Debt (million Rands)

Nature of Debt	March 1988	March 1989
Foreign loans	160.0	141.0
Term bonds	na	115.0
Credits from South Africa		
Stock loans	569 .0	534.0
Other loans	68.0	101.0
Development bonds	1.5	1.3
Total	789.5	892.3

Source: United Nations Development Programme, Report of the Reconnaissance Mission to Namibia (New York: UNDP, 1989).

constant danger likely to face it is not that of periodic influxes of resources from its big southern neighbor, but that of capital outflows to the Republic. In 1978, there was a massive flight of capital from the territory to the Republic, and since the beginning of last year there is evidence of some capital flight, though not on the 1978 scale."[53] Representatives of the two major banks, First National (formerly Barclays) and Standard, admit that money continues to leave the country. Other sources in Windhoek maintain that the liquidity position of the two banks has been affected and that they have insufficient cash reserves and deposits.[54] Demand deposits have continued to increase, from R 244.2 million in 1985 to R 816.4 million in 1989.[55]

Debt and Finance

Namibia does not have massive foreign debt compared with many other LDCs. According to a 1989 UNDP survey, Namibia's total foreign debt in 1989 was R 892.3 million, of which R 141 million was foreign loans and R 534 was stock loans held by South Africa (see Table 3.9). Since 1981 South Africa has been a continual source of public finance for Namibia. Its contribution to the country's public revenues collected rose from R 40 million in 1981 (or 12 percent of total revenues collected) to R 499.6 million in 1987 (or about 30 percent of total revenues collected). South Africa contributed R 308 million in 1988 and R 317 million in 1989. Pretoria reduced its financial contribution for 1990 to R 141.9 million.[56] The new government will probably ask the International Monetary Fund (IMF) or others for support when these payments end. According to economists at the University of Namibia, in 1988 Namibia's public debt stood at R 900 million, amounting to almost 50 percent of that year's government budget of R 1,946 million and almost one-third of the GDP.[57]

The finance minister predicted that Namibia's first year of independence would show a budget deficit of about R 500 million. This deficit would result from, among other things, increased public expenditures on the infrastructure, housing, and education. Namibia will probably be able to finance its budget deficit domestically and will not have to resort to external borrowing, at least for the short term. Indeed, Namibia's government revenue was healthy at independence, due largely to over R 80 million from mining and other taxes plus larger-than-expected general sales tax revenues.[58]

Trade and Transportation

South Africa maintains that membership in the Southern African Customs Union (SACU) allows the member to benefit from customs duties on a large amount of trade, as each member is "rebated" an amount that is supposed to equal what it would have received had it maintained its own customs authority. However, in Namibia's case much of the indirect tax paid in the country is included in the pretax GDP, paid to South Africa in the import bill, and then returned by South Africa under SACU auspices as a transfer payment. Customs and excise payments to Namibia have nevertheless increased from R 47.6 million in 1979 (or 14.4 percent of total revenue collected) to R 447.8 million (amounting to 22.7 percent of all revenues collected) in 1990 (see Table 3.10). For 1983 and 1984 about half of the total revenues collected were from customs and excise duties. According to Great Britain's Overseas Development Institute, these revenues were perhaps double what Namibia could collect independently because of the compensation payments built into the complex SACU revenue-sharing formula.[59] With regard to the Customs Union, a professor of economics at the University of Namibia suggests that, "we should identify the negative aspects and negotiate them with South Africa."[60] In fact, Minister of Trade and Industry Ben Amathila announced that Namibia had formalized its membership in the Customs Union and that "Namibia may call for a re-negotiation of certain paragraphs."[61]

TABLE 3.10   Customs and Excise Contribution to Namibia's Central Revenues

Year[a]	Total Revenue Collected (million R)	Customs and Excise Collected (million R)	Customs and Excise (percent of total)
1979	330.5	47.6	14.4
1980	337.8	44.5	13.2
1981	331.8	41.5	12.5
1982	650.0	257.9	39.7
1983	438.5	250.0	57.0
1984	513.0	250.0	48.7
1985	625.6	250.0	39.9
1986	881.9	300.0	34.0
1987	1,100.2	350.0	31.8
1988	1,212.8	350.0	28.8
1989	1,477.5	394.2	26.7
1990	1,971.5	447.8	22.7

[a]Financial year ends March 31.

Sources: Adapted from Namibia Ministry of Finance, Statistical Economic Review, SWA/Namibia 1987 (Windhoek, 1988); and Namibia Ministry of Finance, Statistical/Economic Review: Namibia 1990 (Windhoek, 1991).

Namibia sells 25 percent of its exports to South Africa and buys about 75 percent of its imports from the republic. For primarily political reasons, Namibia's trade relationship with South Africa will change— probably slowly. Over time Namibia's imports will likely become more costly because of transport costs as alternative sources to South Africa are developed. Further, locally produced goods as substitutes for South African manufactures will be more expensive than their South African competition, which will cause problems for many poor Namibians. There will also be problems in diversifying Namibia's export markets. For example, there is no ready alternative market for cattle sold on the hoof to South Africa. Virtually all foreign trade now transits South Africa, which controls all points of entry and exit. Namibia is the world's only coastal state that is virtually economically landlocked. For the immediate future, South Africa will remain the major trade partner and will have a virtual stranglehold over Namibia's transport system.

Walvis Bay, the Off-Shore Islands, and the Two Hundred-Mile Exclusive Economic Zone

The enclave of Walvis Bay was never part of the original German colony of South West Africa but was administered as part of the Cape Colony and, after World War I, by the Union of South African government on behalf of the United Kingdom as a League of Nations mandate. The Class C mandate did not include the enclave or the twelve off-shore islands. Nevertheless, from 1922 Windhoek administered Walvis Bay as if it were an integral part of the mandate. South Africa recognized the strategic importance of Walvis Bay and during Contact Group negotiations in 1977, transferred the enclave back to Cape Province, with the eligible (white) voters reregistered with the parliamentary constituency of Greenpoint. In 1988 South Africa spent around R 22 million in additional military facilities in the enclave.[62] In April 1989, South Africa established border posts at Walvis Bay to further maintain the distinction between Namibia and South Africa.[63]

Although UN Resolution 435 does not deal directly with the issue, Resolution 432 of July 1978 declared, "The territorial integrity and unity of Namibia must be assured through the reintegration of Walvis Bay within its territory" and that South Africa "must not use Walvis Bay in any manner prejudicial to the independence of Namibia or the viability of its economy." Prior to independence, the OAU reaffirmed that "Walvis Bay and the off-shore islands constitute an integral part of the territory."[64] At independence, South Africa did not cede the enclave to Namibia, although rumors circulated widely throughout Windhoek that South Africa would indeed relinquish control at independence. Upon his departure from the independence day events in Windhoek, South African President de Klerk told reporters that he had not discussed the issue with President Nujoma. He went on to stress that South Africa would not alter the legal status of Walvis Bay as "sovereign territory of South Africa."[65] It is in South Africa's economic interest to continue to operate the port and not jeopardize the enclave's economy.

The 969-sq-kilometer enclave is vital for Namibia. The port handles perhaps 95 percent of the country's seaborne trade. Virtually all of Namibia's petroleum products and other bulk items as well as a variety of consumer goods go through the port. Copper from Tsumeb and uranium from Rössing are the major exports that transit the port. The twelve off-shore islands, with exotic names such as Plumpudding and Penguin, are also claimed by South Africa and have economic potential. These islands contain large amounts of guano used for fertilizer, which is exported. Additionally, each of the twelve islands is entitled to a 200-mile exclusive economic zone surrounding it, and there are potential mineral resources under the continental shelf.

South Africa may use the enclave as a way to exert pressure to influence the new government. Most likely the two governments will come to terms whereby Namibia can continue to use the port. In any event, South Africa's continued ownership or occupation of Walvis Bay amounts to "an economic sword of Damocles over the future of any new Namibian government."[66]

Given South Africa's virtual stranglehold over its transport network, Namibia will likely consider alternatives to Walvis Bay, of which there are none in the short to medium term. Although Namibia has a long coastline, it has few natural harbors. The long-term alternatives include Luderitz in the south and Swakopmund adjacent to Walvis Bay. Luderitz has a small, rocky, shallow port with only limited ability to handle general cargo. Because the port is so shallow, large ships have to load and off-load their cargo at outer anchorages. The ocean bottom is rocky, and deepening the port would be almost prohibitively expensive. Its remote location is also a disadvantage. Swakopmund was developed by the Germans before World War I as an alternative to the British enclave at Walvis Bay. At one point it could handle two vessels of up to 10,000 tons apiece. When South Africa occupied German South West Africa during the war, the limited port facilities were abandoned in favor of the better port at Walvis Bay some 35 kilometers to the south. Swakopmund is on the main rail line. However, although it is sheltered and has a short and deep access channel, it quickly fills due to massive siltation. According to a UN study, reviving the port would require almost continual dredging, and an artificial breakwater would need to be built to deflect the current borne silt. The port would need modern roll-on, roll-off facilities. A UN Economic Commission for Africa (ECA)–commissioned study concluded that such improvements and maintenance make the site unrealistic.[67]

Besides Luderitz and Swakopmund, there are three other alternatives. Henties Bay, 80 kilometers north of Swakopmund, is so shallow that it offers no protection from the prevailing wind and ocean swell; it is also far from a rail link. Cape Cross, home of one of the world's largest seal colonies, is nearly 130 kilometers north of Swakopmund. It provides a reasonable natural site for port development, but it would require building a link to the major rail line, which is extremely expensive. Additionally, there are environmental constraints at Cape Cross due to the seal colony. Third, Mowe Bay, which is located 435 kilometers north of Walvis Bay, was surveyed during the 1970s, but it can be ruled out because of its remote distance and considerable silting problems. None of these locations is a realistic alternative as a major port for Namibia.

Transport officials from Namibia and Angola have begun talks to launch a transport route from northern Namibia to the southern Angolan port of Namibe. The project, which could be financed by the World Bank, would be a rail and road link to this underutilized port.[68] The only other viable transport alternative would be the trans-Kalahari rail link through Botswana to central Africa. That route could link through Zambia and go on to Tanzania, for example. As Namibia considers alternatives to South Africa as discussed later in this chapter, it has been suggested that Namibia should not "underestimate the road transport . . . because the country . . . must look for the long term. South Africa will not always be ruled by a white government [and Namibia] shouldn't destroy all our links now, as we will need them in the long run."[69]

SOUTHERN AFRICAN ECONOMIC RELATIONS

Namibia has developed few economic linkages with any of its neighbors other than South Africa. There is some informal trade with Angola, Botswana and Zambia. Exact data are not available, but this trade cannot constitute more than 1–2 percent of Namibia's total foreign trade. There are no major surface road or rail links among the three countries, although there are numerous gravel roads. The major link with Botswana, from Gobabis to Mamuno, is a poor gravel road. This link is important because through Botswana, Namibia could have transport linkages with all of central-southern Africa.

Because of its close physical proximity and the strong political ties between SWAPO and Luanda's central government, Angola is targeted as a potential major trade partner. Potential areas of expansion include tourism on Angola's part and basic consumer goods from Namibia. Angola's state-owned Overseas Business Corporation has established an office in Windhoek. Transportation and joint industrial ventures are longer-term areas of potential cooperation.

Namibia will no doubt try to cooperate with regional states in its effort to distance itself politically and economically from South Africa. Unfortunately, subregional economic development in southern Africa has been limited because most of the states share many of the same problems and have similar needs. They produce similar goods, which makes increased trade almost impossible. Trade among African countries remains low relative to intra-trade in Asia and Latin America; Africa's intra-trade as a percentage of total exports is about 9 percent, and Latin America's and South and South East Asia's averages 20 percent.[70] This low level of trade among African states can be attributed partly to their respective low levels of industrialization. Many countries have engaged in import substitution. This has: "led to the protection of industries which cannot be deemed essential from the point of view of the economy as a whole; failed to establish linkages between sectors and thus to turn manufacturing industry into an engine of growth and technological transformation; often been associated with foreign control and unduly capital intensive technologies; and tended over time to aggravate rather than alleviate the balance of payments constraints."[71]

Regional cooperation could, at least in theory, help to remove one of the major constraints facing Namibia: its small market size. Such economic cooperation could take the forms of joint investment, planning, management, production, marketing, and trade. Namibia has joined two subregional organizations: the Southern African Development Co-ordination Conference (SADCC) and the Preferential Trade Area for Eastern and Southern African States (PTA).

SADCC was established in 1979 by nine states in the region with the ultimate goal of lessening their economic dependence on South Africa by promoting greater economic, financial, and commercial linkages among themselves. It is not a traditional economic regional grouping as it does not advocate a free-trade area or common market. Instead, it is a project-focused program with the goal of encouraging projects of value to two or more members. Its major areas of cooperation are transportation, communications, industry, food policy, and trade. One member-state is assigned the major coordination effort for each activity. Such cooperation takes the form of coordinated sector planning, resulting in less waste and duplication. Although it is too early to assess, SADCC *appears* to offer Namibia an alternative to South Africa in the areas of transportation, trade, and perhaps communications, but only at great expense and over the long term. On March 21, 1990, Namibia became the tenth member of SADCC and hosted the SADCC summit in February 1991.

The PTA was established in 1980 and came into force in 1983 in accordance with the Organization of African Unity's *Lagos Plan of Action*. The major goal for its eighteen member-states is to increase intraregional trade and at the same time lessen trade with South Africa by gradually reducing and eventually eliminating tariffs and nontariff barriers to member trade. It plans to move gradually toward a common market. The PTA includes both very large economies, such as Zimbabwe, and very small ones, such as Botswana. The smaller members have expressed concern over membership because of fears that the larger states would outcompete them because of their potential economies of scale. It is unclear what tangible economic benefit Namibia will receive from PTA, at least in the medium term. In any event, membership will be at least somewhat beneficial for Namibia, as it will be granted Most Favored Nation (MFN) status with all PTA members.

There are other avenues of regional cooperation. For example, Namibia is located in a strategic area vis-à-vis the major markets for central and southern African minerals. Walvis Bay is the closest modern, containerized port to Western Europe and the United States in Africa, and minerals that are now being transported from other regional ports such as Dar es Salaam, Maputo, Durban, or Port Elizabeth could be shipped through Namibia. Such a move would require building either a better road link or a trans-Kalahari rail link through Botswana. The rail link—although almost prohibitively expensive—would provide direct access to Namibia's coal deposits in the Kalahari region and could act as a growth pole for industrialization. It would result in significant time and freight savings for products originating in central Africa. This link— either road or rail—would be complicated by South Africa's continued control of Walvis Bay. Additionally, Lonhro is planning a study on the feasibility of a rail link between the mines at Tsumeb and the southern Zambian railhead at Sesheke on the border at Caprivi. Transport industry sources in Namibia maintain that products are regularly being sent across the Zambezi for transport to Walvis Bay.[72]

INTERNATIONAL ECONOMIC RELATIONS

Foreign trade is very important to Namibia's economy. Merchandise imports and exports are vital (see Table 3.11 and 3.12). For example, merchandise exports and imports account for over half of the country's GDP. Namibia has generally had a healthy trade balance in terms of merchandise exports and imports. During the early 1980s, it had small merchandise trade deficits—in 1981 (−R 120 million), 1982 (−R 99 million), 1983 (−R 66 million), and 1984 (−R 56 million). By 1985 Namibia achieved positive merchandise trade balances—R 355 million in 1985, R 547 million in 1986 and R 97 million in 1987. Using 1980 constant Rand prices, Namibia had an R 327 million balance in 1985, R 450 million in 1986, R 4 million in 1987, and R 180 million in 1988. Namibia's trade balance in 1989 was R 332 million.

International Trade

Namibia's major trade partners are South Africa and the Western industrial countries. This will likely remain so long after independence. As Table 3.13 shows, half of its exports are to Switzerland and South Africa; Germany, the United States, and Japan make up 30 percent of the rest. The connection with Switzerland is so great because most diamonds are exported through Switzerland for sale by the Central Selling Organization (CSO) in London. South Africa is by far Namibia's largest supplier, providing it with around three-quarters of all its imports. West Germany, the United States, and Switzerland are the other suppliers to Namibia, and the four countries provide virtually all of Namibia's

TABLE 3.11 Merchandise Imports and Exports, 1920 -1988 (Rand at current prices)

Year	Merchandise Exports (R million)	Merchandise Imports (R million)	Merchandise Exports (% of GDP)	Merchandise Imports (% of GDP)
1920	10.6	-9.8	84.8	78.4
1930	5.1	-5.4	54.8	58.0
1940	7.2	-4.6	68.6	43.8
1950	41.2	-27.7	72.5	48.8
1960	88.0	-76.5	82.2	71.0
1970	196.8	-131.4	58.3	39.0
1980	1,138.0	-888.4	78.8	61.5
1981	946.7	-1,066.6	62.8	70.8
1982	1,009.2	-1,108.3	60.0	66.0
1983	941.3	-1,007.7	52.9	56.6
1984	1,101.1	-1,157.7	55.9	58.8
1985	1,593.5	-1,238.4	62.4	48.5
1986	1,993.1	-1,446.9	68.0	49.4
1987	1,809.8	-1,712.9	57.8	54.7
1988	2,140.9	-2,076.6	63.5	61.6
1989	2,671.6	-2,339.6	61.7	59.1

Source: Adapted from Namibia Ministry of Finance, Statistical/Economic Review 1988 (Windhoek, 1989).

imports. International trade will improve because sanctions against Namibia (launched against South Africa) have been lifted.

As Namibia slowly begins to diversify its trade linkages, both as a result of geopolitical motives and its diversified domestic industrialization, it will consider membership in a range of international groupings, including the Lome Convention and General Agreement on Tariffs and Trade (GATT). Namibia could apply for associate membership in the European Economic Community (EEC) through the Lome Convention. In September 1989 the European Community's Council of Ministers agreed to ask Namibia to sign Lome IV at independence.[73] The convention is an agreement of cooperation between EEC and African, Caribbean, and Pacific States (ACP) that allows certain products to enter the EEC on a duty-free basis. The convention also provides financial, technical, and industrial cooperation. Namibia could benefit from membership in GATT through the Generalized System of Preferences (GSP).

Namibia has become a formal member of the fourth Lome Convention, and it has access to a new market for its processed beef products, as it has an initial quota of ten thousand tons. Because of the high prices offered by South Africa for Namibian beef on the hoof, Namibia's

TABLE 3.12 Namibia's Trade Balance (current prices in million Rands)

	1980	1981	1982	1983	1984	1985	1986	1987	1988	1989
Merchandise exports	1,138.0	946.7	1,009.2	941.3	1,101.1	1,593.5	1,993.1	1,809.8	2,140.9	2,671.6
Merchandise imports	-884.4	-1,066.6	-1,108.3	-1,007.7	-1,157.7	-1,238.4	-1,446.9	-1,712.9	-2,076.6	-2,339.6
Trade balance	253.6	-119.9	-99.1	-66.4	-56.6	355.1	546.2	96.9	64.3	332.0

Sources: **Adapted from Namibia Ministry of Finance, *Statistical Economic Review, SWA/Namibia 1987* (Windhoek 1988); and Namibia Ministry of Finance, *Statistical Economic Review: Namibia 1990* (Windhoek 1991).**

TABLE 3.13 Namibia's Direction of Trade (1988)

Major Destinations of Exports (as a percentage of total)		Major Origins of Imports (as a percentage of total)	
Switzerland	30	South Africa	75
South Africa	20	West Germany	10
West Germany	15	United States	5
Japan	10	Switzerland	5
United States	5		

Source: Economist Intelligence Unit, Namibia, Botswana, Lesotho, Swaziland: Country Report, No. 1, 1990 (London: EIU, 1990).
Reprinted with permission.

processing industry operates under capacity. There may be opportunities to expand beef exports to neighboring states.

International Development Assistance

Namibia will need support from the international community if its economic development efforts are to succeed. Indeed, Namibia has sought some $270 million annually in concessionary aid pledges for 1990–1993, with a total need of $810 million. Namibia has been accepted for membership in the important international and regional financial institutions such as the World Bank, the International Monetary Fund, and the African Development Bank. It can expect prompt program and project support. The United Nations Development Programme made $12 million available in a trust fund to be used primarily for training and technical assistance during Namibia's first year of independence.[74]

Official development assistance (ODA) to Namibia was restricted prior to independence due to the political situation. In 1987, for example, ODA amounted to perhaps 1.3 percent of the GDP. Bilateral donors funneled their aid through UN agencies or private voluntary organizations (PVOs). Although Namibia's per capita income exceeds the cutoff point for World Bank concessional loans, Namibia could gain "concessional status" as Zimbabwe did at its independence. Namibia is also ineligible for least developed country (LLDC) status from the donor community. LLDC status is important, as those countries receive a higher proportion of grant and concessionary loans than other aid recipients.

In June 1990 a donors' pledging conference was held in New York. Namibia presented its needs to a number of bilateral and multilateral donor agencies. During the conference the donors pledged $696 million in assistance for the period 1990–1993. Around $531 million of this amount is bilateral. Although this total falls short of the $810 million discussed above, President Sam Nujoma declared the conference a "resounding success" and Finance Minister Otto Herrigel indicated that the amount of pledges was "more than we expected."[75] The UN agencies pledged $42 million, and other multilateral agencies pledged $123. Germany will be the largest donor at $186 million, followed by the Scandinavian countries with a total of $184 million. President Nujoma asked the United Nations to grant LLDC status to Namibia during his speech to the General Assembly in 1990.

Namibia would benefit from Lome IV; Botswana, which is smaller and richer than Namibia, received ECU 32 million under Lome IV. Namibia could gain a beef quota from the EC worth over R 15 million annually (nine thousand tons of beef). Also under Lome IV, Namibia should be eligible for over $30 million in official development assistance. The European parliament promised $11.4 million for the new nation's first year of independence.

Namibia will need help in a number of areas. For example, education in agriculture and industrial training will be vital for years after independence. Namibia will also need help to devise appropriate agro-industries to diversify its agricultural base, both for domestic consumption and for export. Irrigation schemes in the north would appear most appropriate for rapid crop diversification. After different crops have been successfully introduced, the value-added profits should be local. Further, Namibia will need appropriate technology in a range of economic sectors and manufacturing branches. It will need help especially with small-scale, labor-intensive enterprises.

Namibia will need other types of technical assistance and project support from traditional multilateral and bilateral donor agencies. Because of its historical relations and its current strong ties (many Germans are still living there), Namibia can expect continuing help from the Federal Republic of Germany in a number of key areas, including medical training and supplies and other health services, housing, and transportation. Agriculture and fisheries will also be priorities for German aid. West Germany provided nearly $60 million in bilateral assistance during the first year of independence, according to the German secretary of state for economic cooperation.[76] Great Britain has promised assistance in English-language training, help with the police and army, and aid in a number of economic development spheres. Norway pledged over $100 million for development projects in 1990–1991, and other Nordic countries may make similar levels of aid available. The Soviet Union has announced plans to help in fisheries and fish processing industries. The Soviets believe it will take perhaps $500 million to create a national fleet of sixty seiners and two hundred trawlers.[77] As the United States was so heavily involved in the independence process, it is viewed as having a vested interest in seeing the new nation begin a viable economy. The United States agreed to provide around $10 million in official development assistance in 1991.[78] During the first year of independence, the United States signed four agreements on economic and technical cooperation for Namibia. These agreements were signed by Presidents Nujoma and Bush during Nujoma's visit to the United States in June 1990. One provided for Peace Corps volunteers to work in a number of areas, including agriculture, education, health, and rural development. The United States agreed to help finance small-scale businesses. Another agreement calls for preferential duty-free access to the U.S. market for over four thousand products under GATT and an agreement with the U.S. Overseas Private Investment Corporation (OPIC), which provides risk insurance for U.S. businesses operating in Namibia. The United States granted duty-free trade benefits under the Generalized System of Preferences (GSP) in January 1991. The GSP will allow over four thousand items into the United States duty-free and should stimulate trade between the two countries. During the June 1990 donors' pledging conference, President Nujoma repeated his wish that Namibia not develop a dependency syndrome on economic aid, which he believes is detrimental and is characteristic of many other developing countries.[79]

RECENT ECONOMIC DEVELOPMENTS

Namibia's economy expanded during the four years before independence. The economy is slowly recovering from the depressed conditions of the late 1970s and early 1980s. Finance Minister Otto Herrigel has suggested that these depressed conditions were the result of tight fiscal and monetary policies, the low rate of public investment, a persistent inflation rate, and difficult export markets.[80] Other causes included a worldwide recession in the early 1980s, the collapse of the pilchard stocks, decreased demand for base metals, and general political uncertainty. From 1982 to 1987 the country's balance of payments was positive, with a record R 560.6 million recorded in 1986. Namibia experienced a balance of payments deficit of R 153.4 million in 1988 (see Table 3.14). Because of a higher-than-expected trade surplus, the current account on the balance of payments recovered to a surplus of R 60 million in 1990.

During 1989, real Gross Domestic Product (GDP expressed in 1980 constant prices) grew by 0.2 percent, down from 1.7 percent in 1988, 3.0 percent in 1987, and 3.2 percent in 1986 (see Table 3.15). The economy's stagnation in 1988–1989 was due primarily to a 7 percent

TABLE 3.14 Namibia's Current Account of the Balance of Payments (current prices in million Rands)

	1980	1981	1982	1983	1984	1985	1986	1987	1988	1989
Merchandise exports	1,138.0	946.7	1,009.2	941.3	1,101.1	1,549.4	1,994.0	1,796.4	2,140.9	2,671.6
Merchandise imports	-901.9	-1,082.5	-1,124.5	-1,024.4	-1,176.4	-1,272.2	-1,552.4	-1,882.4	-2,076.6	-2,339.6
Trade Balance	236.1	-135.8	-115.3	-83.1	-75.3	277.2	441.6	86.0	64.3	332.0
Net payments for nonfactor services	-167.4	-173.1	-185.3	-192.8	-200.8	-262.7	-319.7	-384.7	-364.7	-392.5
Net factor payments	-152.8	-102.7	-132.7	-76.4	-112.6	-297.7	-319.7	-196.7	-399.8	-372.2
Net transfer receipts	71.2	342.6	466.4	518.6	541.4	583.2	758.4	616.4	546.8	531.4
Balance on Current Account	-12.9	-69.0	33.1	166.3	152.7	345.0	560.6	9.0	-153.4	98.7

Sources: Adapted from Namibia Ministry of Finance, *Statistical Economic Review, SWA/Namibia 1987* (Windhoek 1988); and Namibia Ministry of Finance, *Statistical/Economic Review: Namibia 1990* (Windhoek, 1991).

TABLE 3.15 Namibia's Gross Domestic Product 1985 -1989
(GDP at constant 1980 prices in million Rands)

Year	GDP	Growth Rate (real GDP in percent)
1985	2,540	-0.1
1986	2,927	3.2
1987	3,084	3.0
1988	3,767	1.7
1989	4,500[a]	0.2

[a]estimate.

Source: Economist Intelligence Unit, Namibia, Botswana, Lesotho, Swaziland. Country Report: No. 3, 1990 (London: EIU, 1990).

drop in the real value of the mining industry. Indeed, nonmining output achieved a real growth rate of 3.6 percent in 1989, up from 2.1 percent the year before. According to the UNDP, Namibia's GDP was expected to rise by 6 percent in 1990–1991, and by between 3.5 and 4.5 percent during the next few years, just enough increase to cover the expected rises in population.

Economic growth actually declined by 2 percent in 1990. Namibia's negative economic growth rate in 1990 was due to weaker prices for its mineral exports on the world markets; the withdrawl of South African Defense Forces, which represented a major source of spending, especially in the north; the withdrawl of UNTAG; lower productivity; and the South African recession. The annual inflation rate declined from 15 percent in 1989 to 12 percent in 1990.

In 1988 the agricultural sector's 2.3 percent growth could not match that of 1987 when it recorded a significant 29 percent increase due primarily to better cattle and small-stock marketing and increased productivity. The fishing industry, however, made an upturn with a growth rate of 26 percent over 1987. This was due to improvements in the pelagic fish catches (resulting from a 25 percent increase in pilchard landings—66,000 tons—and a 24-fold increase in anchovy catches—376,100 tons). The mining industry in 1988 grew by about one percent, after a 2 percent decline in 1987 (if diamonds are excluded, the mining industry actually declined by some 6.5 percent in 1987). After six years of depressed building activity, construction grew by a remarkable 6

TABLE 3.16 Namibia's Inflation

Year	Index^a	Percentage Change
1980	100.0	15.1
1981	104.9	4.9
1982	119.2	13.6
1983	130.4	9.4
1984	146.3	12.2
1985	188.7	29.1
1986	210.5	11.6
1987	217.3	3.2
1988	258.6	19.0
1989	296.3	14.6

^{a}1988 = 100.0

Source: Namibia Ministry of Finance, Statistical/Economic Review: Namibia 1990 (Windhoek, 1991).

percent in 1988 following a dramatic increase in building investment in late 1987.[81]

Private consumption expenditures only grew by one percent in 1988, following a surge of more than 8 percent in 1987. The reasons for this decline were a slower rise in personal disposable income as well as higher inflation and interest rates. Nevertheless, demand for consumer goods remained strong in 1988, as shown by high levels of consumer bank credits. Namibia "imports" inflation from South Africa, as the majority of its merchandise imports originate in the republic; higher prices in South Africa are passed along to Namibia. For example, in 1986 the price of imported commodities increased by around 21 percent, although this rate declined to 13.7 percent in 1987 and 13.3 percent in 1988. Domestic inflation was 19 percent in 1988 but declined to 14.6 percent in 1989 (see Table 3.16).

The first postindependence budget proposed by the finance minister called for expenditures of R 2.57 billion, up from R 2.36 billion the previous year. The largest expenditures were targeted for education (R 469 million) and health and social services (R 352 million).[82] The increased spending for health and education is a bit misleading, as much of the increase results from transferring budget spending from previous local authorities to the national government. Defense spending was reduced by some R 3 million, to R 1,232 million. Finance Minister Herrigel estimated revenues at R 2.36 billion, leaving a budget deficit of R 210 million for 1991. Around R 542 million was expected to come from South Africa's share of customs and excise receipts from the Southern African Customs Union. Government spending for 1990–1991 was R 2,576 million, an increase of 5 percent over the previous year's spending. In real terms it represented a decline in spending, given an inflation rate of about 12 percent. The budget deficit will be financed by loans rather than increased personal taxes, according to the Ministry of Finance.

ECONOMIC PROSPECTS

Since 1970, the economic policies SWAPO said it would pursue at independence have made a radical shift. Before 1988, when it appeared that independence was far in the future, SWAPO took an extremely radical stand on the economic issues. This rhetoric was no doubt intended for domestic as well as international audiences. SWAPO adopted the same rhetoric that was being used by other newly independent African countries, especially Tanzania and Zambia—countries that espoused their own forms of socialism. As many of SWAPO's few leading economic technocrats were living in these countries, their policies are easily understood. Further, the leading source of economic training and planning for Namibia, the United Nations Institute for Namibia, located in Lusaka, housed some of the world's leading radical economists. During this period, SWAPO's economic policy statements contained much rhetoric but few specific, realistic policies.

SWAPO's radical positions on many economic issues were stated in the comprehensive study *Namibia: Perspectives for National Reconstruction and Development* published by UNIN in 1986. During late 1988 and early 1989, when it became apparent that independence might become certain, SWAPO began to change its rhetoric. It published an important policy statement, "Namibia's Economic Prospects Brighten Up," in which it withdrew its previous calls for massive nationalization and heavy state involvement in the economy.[83] This was followed by a presentation by Hage Geingob, a member of SWAPO's politburo and director of UNIN, to a Business International conference, "Southern Africa: What Namibian Independence Will Mean for Business," held in London in April 1989. During this conference it became clear that SWAPO had considerably changed its rhetoric.

SWAPO changed its positions in a number of important areas prior to independence.[84] The most important ones follow.

1. General Economic Relations with South Africa. Before 1988, SWAPO maintained that Namibia would sever all relations with the South African racist regime. The new government, however, is coming to terms with its relationship with South Africa. For the short term the new government is making few changes, except there has been and will continue to be a departure of some key South African parastatal and mid-level government personnel.

2. Membership in the Southern African Customs Union and the Rand Monetary Zone. Prior to 1988, SWAPO maintained that the country's industrial structure was highly vulnerable to South Africa and that industrialization had been inhibited by hostile colonial policies and a captive market for the South African industrial sector. Namibia was coopted, SWAPO maintained, without its consent into the Southern African Customs Union and the Rand Monetary Zone. The implication was that Namibia would withdraw from the union directly after independence. However, for the short term, Namibia will benefit by remaining in the customs union and, to a lesser extent, the monetary area. Namibia will eventually establish its own central bank and place its currency on par with either the Rand or one of a group of major currencies.

3. The Private Sector. In the 1970s, SWAPO wanted to bring all the major means of production and exchange into the ownership of the people. Private ownership of productive assets would have been allowed only within a national planning framework consistent with the interests of the people. Further, the nationalization of land, natural resources, finance, public services, and transport would have given the state the formal and economic means to pursue a transformation toward socialism. Just prior to elections, however, SWAPO declared that "although SWAPO believes in the 'superiority of the socialist system,' it will, in the immediate future, opt for a mixed economy comprising state, cooperative and joint-venture enterprises plus a 'significant role' for private-sector undertakings."[85] For the immediate future and in the medium term, SWAPO will have no choice but to allow and possibly at times encourage private domestic and foreign ownership due primarily to low capital formation by the local black population.

In February 1991 over one thousand delegates attended the Private Sector Investor Conference in Windhoek. During that conference the trade and industry minister remarked, "The Constitution of our country prescribes our economic order. Article 98 . . . spells out our economic system. The article reads in part, 'The economic order of Namibia shall be based on the principle of a mixed economy with the objective of securing economic growth, prosperity and a life of human dignity for all Namibians.' The government is, therefore, committed to a mixed market economy based on social responsibility and the private sector as a pivot of our recovery and growth."[86]

4. *Nationalization of Farms and Land.* Although there was widespread belief that a SWAPO government would immediately nationalize Namibia's white-owned farms, the new government has maintained that "there is to be no 'wholesale nationalization' of the mines, ranches, and other productive sectors in the foreseeable future. Fair and adequate compensation will be paid where state acquisition of private property is considered necessary."[87] In July 1990, President Nujoma addressed the land issue when he spoke to the National Assembly. He stressed that he is "determined to see that a substantial amount of land is made available to those who badly need it. Within the framework of the law which this Assembly must enact as soon as possible, my government will see to it that some of the families in overgrazed and overcrowded areas are moved into some of the present under-utilised commercial farms."[88] Except for land owned by absentees, there will probably be little expropriation. The new government is likely to move slowly in this area because of the strong influence of current property owners. The government plans to address land issues in a national conference on land distribution to be headed by Minister of Lands, Resettlement, and Rehabilitation Marco Hausiku. Many options exist for Namibia, including, for example, creating a special fund to promote land settlement, as was done in Zimbabwe.

5. *The Mining Industry.* Namibia's most important sector is mining. SWAPO previously maintained that "the aim, therefore, is not just for the mineral resources of Namibia to belong to the nation, but also for mines to be publicly owned and operated. . . . Ownership and control of Namibia's mineral resources will belong entirely to the independent Namibian state. . . . The government should be entirely responsible for the rational use of mineral resources."[89] The new government maintains, however, that the mining sector must be integrated into the economy and that there is a proper and significant role for foreign and domestic private companies.[90] For the medium and long terms, Namibia will likely revise the tax regimes of the mining industry, mandate more jobs and job training for local employees, launch a code of conduct, and establish a parastatal mining organization that at first will have little relevance.

6. *Fisheries.* In 1976 SWAPO maintained that "the state sector should become dominant in Namibian fisheries."[91] It has recently suggested, however, that the new "government will declare the usual 200 nautical mile exclusive economic zone. . . . As with mining and agriculture, SWAPO's ownership and control policy in fisheries envisages a mixture of a state fishery sector in the form of a national fishing company, and . . . local private companies as well as worker's cooperatives."[92]

7. *Walvis Bay.* Prior to independence SWAPO was clear on its position regarding Walvis Bay: It supported UN Security Council Resolution 432 of 1978, which declared, "The territorial integrity and unity of Namibia must be assured through the reintegration of Walvis Bay." Although Namibia has strong claims to Walvis Bay under international law, if South Africa remains adamant the republic will retain control. Most likely, at least for the medium term, the government will call for some sort of "free port" arrangement or try otherwise to come to terms with South Africa. In fact, there has been speculation that Namibia might welcome South Africa's management of the port for the short term to ensure efficiency and maintain investor confidence.

8. *The Role of the State in the Economy.* Perhaps the most important issue in the economy is the proper role of the state. In 1980, SWAPO believed that "a national planning system in Namibia will be expected to express and assume the overall authority of the state. . . . A strong public sector should provide the state with the economic strength it requires to ensure that the economy remains in the hands and under the direction of the people of Namibia."[93] Just prior to independence, however, SWAPO "acknowledged the superiority of the socialist system especially with regard to ownership and control. . . . However, in the immediate future, a SWAPO government will, for reasons including colonial legacies, manpower constraints, etc., opt for a mixed economy."[94] Because of the many constraints already discussed, the SWAPO-dominated government will have to move slowly in its long-term wish to increase state involvement in Namibia's economy.

9. *Foreign Involvement in the Economy.* The Foreign Investment Act of 1990 was passed unanimously in December 1990. It provides a liberal basis for foreign involvement in the economy. For example, there are no provisions for mandatory Namibian equity in business firms (except in the area of natural resources); investors have access to foreign exchange and protection from nationalization; and profits from products sold outside Namibia may be kept in foreign currencies elsewhere. The finance minister remarked, "The Investment Act will be applied in a flexible manner because our objective is to facilitate and encourage investment rather than put obstacles in its way."[95]

The new government's wish to give economic payoffs to the northern part of the country will put a strain on the government's budget. The government wants to expand health, education, and housing services to Ovamboland, an area neglected by the South African regime. There are perhaps 750,000 people in the north who currently have little human services support. Programs to change this will be expensive, and they could take up much of the new government's budget. The new government will also be pressured to offer jobs to its supporters. Given the current unemployment rate of perhaps 15 percent (in the formal sector), Namibia will need around fifty thousand jobs—a small number in comparison with employment generation in neighboring states (such as Zaire or Zimbabwe) but large for a country with a total population of under two million people.

For the long term, the country's fundamental strategic goals will likely include rapid economic growth, economic independence, employment expansion, more equitable income distribution, a more integrated national economy, and the abolishment of the colonial structure and attributes of the economy. Namibia will not achieve all of these goals during the next generation. However, its chances of achieving some of these goals are good, especially in light of an orderly and successful transition period and aftermath.

Namibia was faced with a number of long-term realities at independence. The country's resource-based industries will be the cornerstone for long-term industrial expansion and will be geared primarily toward the export market, although new, non-South African markets will have to be developed. These domestic resources will be vital for agro-business, which will be composed primarily of fish and beef processing and will form the basis for developing new agro-industries. The domestic market will remain small; due to income redistribution, some internal demand should increase, although employment potential will not increase dramatically. General economic expansion, particularly in the resources-based industries, will be limited due to the lack of trained manpower.

Namibia will find it essential to integrate industry and manufacturing with the broader, resources-based economy. There are six major sectoral areas the new government may be expected to gradually—and for the long term—integrate into the nation's economy: crops, minerals, livestock, fishing, tourism, and energy and water.

Crops

Minister of Agriculture, Fisheries, Water, and Rural Development Gerhard Hanekom announced just after his appointment that he "wanted to make Namibia totally independent on [sic] vegetables and food supplies."[96] He added that his goal would be difficult because Namibia imports as much as two-thirds of its cereal and a large percentage of its other foodstuffs from South Africa. The northern areas of Namibia, particularly Kavango, are targets for new agricultural development projects.

Grain milling would offer opportunities in food processing, and vegetable oil production shows potential. Other oilseeds would likely include cotton, ground nuts, sunflower and soya. Cotton could be produced with irrigation, and with sufficient production Namibia could launch a modest textile industry. Namibia could easily satisfy domestic demand, but it may not be able to sell all of its output and would have to seek export markets for its textiles. The garment manufacturing strategy of the cotton industry is highly labor-intensive, and it could easily be diversified into small-shop production. Agricultural growth and development would support and encourage expanding other industries such as feeds, tools, fencing wire and posts, protective clothing, and fertilizer (using the guano deposits on the off-shore islands).

Minerals

Unless new mineral deposits are discovered, there is little room for major long-term expansion of Namibia's mineral industry. According to a senior Namibian economist, "We're not sure how long the diamonds, for example, will remain. In the not too distant future CDM will have to cease its production. . . . due to depletion of reserves."[97] Further, there has been too little investment in human capital by South Africa. Also, virtually no new mines have been established since the early 1970s due primarily to political considerations, as large companies were reluctant to invest.

Unfortunately, few final products are made only of copper, lead, or zinc—minerals of which Namibia has generous reserves. The complexity and cost of processing uranium beyond the yellow cake stage are prohibitive. Diamond cutting and polishing could develop into a small industry if CDM is forced to give up some of its control of those processes.

Several minerals such as ferro alloy and zinc could develop into potential local processing industries. Although Namibia has abundant deposits of iron ore, coal, and limestone, the likelihood of establishing a steel mill is low because of a lack of capacity demand and of nearby competition (that is, South Africa). A fertilizer industry based on lime, sulphur, and natural gas could be developed. Salt production would be an appropriate industry to expand for export because domestic demand (for food additives, meat and fish processing, and the like) is unlikely to increase dramatically, even over the long term. Namibia has high-quality salt at its coast, and there are several potential uses: for simple export, as a construction input (for example, the roads of Swakopmund are made with salt), and for chemicals.

Livestock

There are opportunities to further develop meat ranching and related industries. Leather products have potential increased employment opportunities in the rural areas. The industry is now underdeveloped because most hides and skins go directly to South Africa for tanning. Namibia could produce around five thousand tons of cattle leather and one thousand tons of goat and sheep leather annually. Leather products are suitable for rural artisanal production on ranches or in subsistence farming communities and could be manufactured for local demand and exports.[98]

Fishing

Given the historical aversion to fish as a source of protein in Namibia's traditional diets, marketing will pose a serious problem for domestic expansion. Nevertheless, even if domestic demand does not increase significantly, there is room for export and the related linkage industries.[99] A Spanish multinational fishing company, Pescanova Industries, announced that it is planning to invest R 64 million in Namibia's fishing industry (this will be the second-largest nonmining investment). The investment will be in a processing factory in Luderitz, which will employ five hundred Namibians. Fishing officials predict that related investment could increase to R 80 million by 1992. The Soviet Union has also expressed interest in establishing a joint venture with the new government, particularly in fish processing and technical training.[100]

Tourism

Namibia has impressive tourism and outdoor recreation potential, although because of the country's remoteness there will probably never be a market for mass tourism. About 8 percent of the country's land mass is devoted to nature conservation areas. The largest are the Namib–Naukluft Park (located along the coast and inland near Walvis Bay), Etosha Game Reserve (in the north-central part of the country), and the Skeleton Coast Park (along the remote northern coast). Although most visitors to Namibia's tourist attractions are local, about one-third are divided almost equally between South Africans and other nationalities.

Energy and Water

Increased use of energy and water will be necessary for the economy's growth and development. These industries will be highly capital-intensive and would require substantial state or foreign support. Although they are capital-intensive, because of their scale they would require considerable amounts of labor. Each has the potential for small-scale production, (solar energy production and labor-intensive, small-scale bore wells).

Should Namibia institute appropriate economic policies that encourage the required foreign investment and expertise and that allow a significant domestic private sector to operate, it will have a good chance of gradually integrating its resources into a broad-based economy. Its long-term economic prospects could be among the brightest in the region.

NOTES

1. See Namibia Ministry of Finance, *Statistical/Economic Review: Namibia 1990* (Windhoek: Ministry of Finance, 1990). Please note that South African Rand (abbreviated as R) will be used throughout this study. Unless noted otherwise, figures will be in current terms. The exchange rate for the South African Rand per U.S. Dollar from 1970 to 1990 is as follows.

1970:	.72	1985:	2.19
1975:	.74	1986:	2.27
1980:	.78	1987:	2.04
1981:	.87	1988:	2.26
1982:	1.08	1989:	2.70
1983:	1.11	1990:	2.76
1984:	1.44		

(*Source:* South African Reserve Bank).

2. United Nations Institute for Namibia, *Namibia: Perspectives for National Reconstruction and Development* (Lusaka: United Nations Institute for Namibia, 1986), p. 76.

3. W.C.J. van Rensburg and D. A. Pretorius, *South Africa's Strategic Minerals* (Johannesburg: Valiant Publishers, 1877), p. 18; and D. L. Sparks and R. Murray, *Nambia's Future: The Economy at Independence* (London: Economist Intelligence Unit, Special Report No. 197, 1985), p. 36.

4. Namibia Ministry of Finance, *Statistical/Economic Review*, p. 4; and Economist Intelligence Unit, *Namibia, Botswana, Lesotho, Swaziland: Country Report*, No. 3 (1990), pp. 25–26.

5. Namibia Ministry of Finance, *Statistical/Economic Review*, p. 4.

6. Namibia Ministry of Finance, *Statistical/Economic Review*, p. 5; and Economist Intelligence Unit, *Namibia, Botswana, Lesotho, Swaziland*, pp. 25–26.

7. Interview with H.A.R. Meiring, chairperson, Namibian Chamber of Mines, in Swakopmund, January 1990.

8. Ibid.

9. See Republic of South Africa, South West Africa Administrator-General Thirion Commission of Inquiry.

10. *DeBeers Annual Report 1988* (Kimberley: DeBeers Consolidated Mines, Ltd., 1988), p. 4.

11. *The Namibian* (March 22, 1990), p. 5.

12. *Namibian Report*, I (6) (July 1990), p. 5.

13. For details about the mining industry, see Roger Murray, *The Mineral Industry of Namibia: Perspective for Independence* (London: Commonwealth Secretariat, 1978).

14. *DeBeers Annual Report 1988* p. 4; and *Namibia Report*, p. 5.

15. Interview with Steve Kessler, general manager, and Brett Hone, superintendent industrial and public relations, Rössing Uranium, in Arandis, March 21, 1990.

16. Interview with Steve Kessler, March 21, 1990.

17. *Namibia Brief*, No. 13 (Windhoek: The Namibia Foundation, 1991), p. 19.

18. *Namibia Report*, p. 5.

19. U.S. Bureau of Mines, *Minerals Yearbook, Volume I: Metals, Minerals and Fuels* (Washington, D.C.: Bureau of Mines, various years).

20. Interview with H.A.R. Meiring, January 1990.

21. Namibia Ministry of Finance, *Statistical/Economic Review*, p. 16.

22. UNIDO, *Namibia: Industrial Development at Independence* (Vienna: UNIDO, 1990), p. 13; and International Bank for Reconstruction and Development, *World Development Report 1989* (New York: Oxford University Press, 1989), p. 168.

23. Donald L. Sparks, "Namibia's Coastal and Marine Resources Potential," in *African Affairs, The Journal of the Royal African Society*, 334 (January 1985), p. 487; and C. S. Ahlgren, "The Namibian Fishing Industry: Africa's Cannery Row." U.S. State Department airgram from Pretoria Embassy (June 1982), p. 2.

24. First National Development Corporation, Windhoek, 1989; and UNIDO, *Namibia*, pp. 16–17.

25. United Nations Institute for Namibia, *Namibia*, pp. 113–115.

26. J. H. van der Merwe, ed., *National Atlas of South West Africa* (Stellenbosch: University of Stellenbosch, 1983), frame 55.

27. *Namibia Report*, I (5) (June 1990), p. 4. The chairman of the parastatal, First National Development Corporation, confirmed the plans and added that about four thousand jobs would be created and that Namibia would move to sugar self-sufficiency and could even become an exporter.

28. UNIDO, *Industrial Development Programme for an Independent Namibia* (Vienna: UNIDO, 1984), p. 58.

29. *Namibia Report* I (5) (June 1990), p. 4.

30. According to the Department of Water Affairs in Windhoek.

31. Sparks, "Namibia's Coastal and Marine Resources Potential," pp. 486–487.

32. United Nations Institute for Namibia, *Namibia*, pp. 211–215; 224–242.

33. The Territorial Sea and Exclusive Economic Zone Bill was introduced in the National Assembly on May 21, 1990, by Minister of Agriculture, Fisheries, Water, and Rural Development Gerhard Hanekom. The existing six-nautical-mile territorial waters and twelve-nautical-mile fishing zone are now extended to two hundred nautical miles in accordance with international law. See *Namibia Report*, I (5) (June 1990), p. 4.

34. *Namibia Report*, I (3) (April 1990), p. 6.

35. *Namibia Report*, I (7) (August 1990), p. 4.

36. van der Merwe, *National Atlas of South West Africa*, frame 74; and UNIDO, *Namibia*, p. 39.

37. United Nations Institute for Namibia, *Namibia*, pp. 371–372; 375–377.

38. Interview with Professor Fanuel Tjingaete, chairman, Department of Economics, University of Namibia, Windhoek, January 1989.

39. United Nations Institute for Namibia, *Namibia*, pp. 374–375; and UNIDO, *Namibia*, p. 40.

40. Department of Water Affairs, Windhoek; and UNIDO, *Namibia*, p. 40.

41. Interview with H.A.R. Meiring, January 1990.

42. United Nations Institute for Namibia, *Namibia*, pp. 391–396; and UNIDO, p. 40.

43. United Nations Institute for Namibia, *Namibia*, p. 396; and Joe Putz, Heidi von Egidy, and Perri Caplan, *Political Who's Who of Namibia* (Windhoek: Magus Company, 1987).

44. Sparks, "Namibia's Coastal and Marine Resources Potential," pp. 490–495.

45. van der Merwe, *National Atlas of South West Africa*, frame 51.

46. United Nations Institute for Namibia, *Namibia*, pp. 877–879.

47. *Namibia Report*, I (5) (June 1990), p. 3.

48. UNIDO, *Industrial Development Programme for an Independent Namibia*, pp. 15–16; 284–286.

49. Putz, von Egidy, and Caplan, *Political Who's Who of Namibia*, pp. 331–336.

50. *Namibia Report*, I (4) (May 1990), p. 3.

51. For details see United Nations Institute for Namibia, *Namibia*, pp. 700–703.

52. Interview with Dr. M. Hartman, chief, economic policy, Directorate of Fiscal & Monetary Policy, Department of Finance, Windhoek, January 1989.

53. United Nations Development Programme, *Report of the Reconnaissance Mission to Namibia* (New York: UNDP, June 1989), p. 15.

54. Interview with M. Hartman, January 1989.

55. Namibia Ministry of Finance, *Statistical/Economic Review*, p. 21.

56. Ibid., p. 19.

57. Interview with Fanuel Tjingaete, January 1989.

58. Economist Intelligence Unit, *Namibia, Botswana, Lesotho, Swaziland*, p. 21.

59. Overseas Development Institute, *Economic Prospects for Namibia*, Briefing Paper (London: ODI, August 1989).

60. Interview with Fanuel Tjingaete, January 1989. When asked specifically what is a negative, he replied that Namibia is a small member and that South Africa can do what it wants. Namibia could not gain more by collecting taxes alone but could increase revenues if the numbers (percentage of customs-equivalent returned by the South African treasury) were increased.

61. *Namibia Report*, I (4) (May 1990), p. 4.

62. Ibid.

63. Walvis Bay is being boosted militarily and economically in a low-key way and is becoming the area's "boom town." For example, according to Dr. Wolfgang H. Thomas, general manager, Small Business Development Corporation in Cape Town, his organization gets numerous applications for support to build

buildings in Walvis Bay. According to Thomas, the construction industry is booming because white businessmen are "hedging their bets . . . they don't want to leave Namibia because there is still good money to be made. They are certain that South Africa will not leave Walvis Bay." He suggests that some moderates in SWAPO are now fairly happy that South Africa will continue to have control over Walvis Bay. The results could be similar to those in the People's Republic of China and Hong Kong. Interview with Dr. Wolfgang H. Thomas, Cape Town, December 1989.

64. See *Namibia Report*, I (3) (April 1990), p. 2.

65. Donald L. Sparks had numerous discussions with academics, business people, and government officials right before the independence ceremonies on March 21, 1990, when this issue was discussed. See also *Namibia Report*, I (3) (April 1990), p. 1.

66. Sparks, "Namibia's Coastal and Marine Resources Potential," p. 495; and Donald L. Sparks, "Walvis Bay, Plumpudding and Penguin Islands: Their History and Economic Importance to Namibia." Paper presented to the 22nd annual meeting of the African Studies Association, Los Angeles, California, 1979.

67. The results of these studies can be found in UNIDO, *Namibia*, pp. 272–273.

68. *Namibia Report*, I (7) (August 1990), p. 4.

69. Interview with Fanuel Tjingaete, January 1989.

70. UNIDO, *Namibia*, p. 13.

71. UNIDO, *Industrial Development Programme for an Independent Namibia*, p. 224.

72. H.A.R. Metring, January 1990.

73. Overseas Development Institute, *Economic Prospects for Namibia*.

74. Economist Intelligence Unit, *Namibia, Botswana, Lesotho, Swaziland*, pp. 28–29.

75. *Namibia Report*, I (6) (June 1990), pp. 1–2.

76. Economist Intelligence Unit, *Namibia, Botswana, Lesotho, Swaziland*, p. 26.

77. *Namibia Report*, I (1) (February 1990), p. 4.

78. According to a U.S. Embassy spokesman in Windhoek, March 22, 1990.

79. *Namibia Report*, I (4) (May 1990), p. 2.

80. Economist Intelligence Unit, *Namibia, Botswana, Lesotho, Swaziland*, p. 21.

81. Namibia Ministry of Finance, *Statistical/Economic Review*, pp. 2–4.

82. Economist Intelligence Unit, *Namibia, Botswana, Lesotho, Swaziland*, p. 22.

83. This was declared "an economic policy position document of the Political Bureau of the Central Committee of SWAPO," issued November 28, 1988, in Luanda, Angola.

84. Good sources used for the preindependence period are United Nations Institute for Namibia, *Namibia: Perspectives for National Reconstruction and De-*

velopment (Lusaka: UNIN, 1986); and Harbans S. Aulakh and Wilfred W. Asombang, *Economic Development Strategies for Independent Namibia* (Lusaka: UNIN, 1985).

85. Paper delivered by Hage Geingob, SWAPO Politburo, to the Business International Conference, *Southern Africa: What Namibian Independence Will Mean for Business,* London, April 21, 1989.

86. *Namibia Brief,* no. 13 p. 1.

87. Geingob, *Southern Africa;* and Economist Intelligence Unit, *Namibia, Botswana, Lesotho, Swaziland,* p. 18.

88. *The Namibian* (July 16, 1990), p. 1.

89. SWAPO, *SWAPO Policy Paper,* No. 13 (Lusaka, Zambia: SWAPO, 1980), p. 16.

90. *The Namibian* (April 2, 1990), p. 5.

91. SWAPO, *Political Program* (Lusaka: SWAPO, 1976), p. 12.

92. Geingob, *Southern Africa,* p. 14.

93. *SWAPO Policy Paper* p. 3.

94. Geingob, *Southern Africa,* p. 5.

95. *Namibia Brief,* no. 13, p. 7.

96. *Namibia Report,* I (1) (February 199u), p. 4. Hanekom, a South African white, has lived in Namibia for thirty years. He is one of several whites to have a key role in the independent government.

97. Interview with M. Hartman, January 1989.

98. UNIDO, *Namibia,* p. 36.

99. Ibid., pp. 37; 44–45.

100. *Namibia Report,* I (5) (June 1990), p. 4.

4

Society and Culture

Although it is a small country, Namibia has a rich cultural heritage. It has a strong mix of peoples, languages, religions, and education. South Africa's colonial policies, especially in education and to a lesser extent in religion, have greatly influenced this heritage. As Namibia moves away from its colonial past, its society and culture will undergo major changes. Important changes have already taken place or are about to take place in the schools and in the workplace.

PEOPLES AND DEMOGRAPHICS

Peoples

Namibia contains a vast range of peoples (see Table 4.1). These groups arrived in Namibia at different times. Although it is impossible to establish an exact date of human immigration to the area, the San—a society based on hunting and gathering—are widely recognized as Namibia's oldest inhabitants. The San came to the area from central Africa (as did later groups), between 8000 B.C. and A.D. 1300. They are a patrilocal people who live in small, autonomous communities.[1] Due to population pressures and colonial land policies, the San have been pushed increasingly to the most marginal zones of Namibia—on the north bank of the Orange River, to the edge of the Namib, and into the Kalahari Desert. Historians suggest that the San's isolation should not be overstated. The San became involved in working for the Khoi and other groups in the seventeenth and eighteenth centuries as herders, hunters, and client-soldiers. They traded honey, ostrich shell beads, and game for pottery, grain, and metal pieces.[2] The San lived in hunting bands, or groups of thirty to fifty. They valued working as a collectivity, never having sought any centralized form of authority for themselves or domination over other groups. Rather, the political culture of the San was based on authority held by the small group, which was often represented by a senior member selected through common consent. The

131

TABLE 4.1 Namibia's Population Groups

Group	Population Size (percent of total population)	
	1983	1989
Ovambo	49	50
Kavango	8	9
Herero	8	7
Damara	7	7
White	7	5
Nama	5	5
Coloured	5	4
Caprivi	4	4
Bushman	3	3
Baster	2	3
Tswana	1	0.6
Other	1	2.4

Sources: J. H. van der Merwe, ed., National Atlas of South West Africa (Namibia) (Goodwood, Cape: National Book Printers, 1983); Robert S. Jaster, "The 1988 Peace Accords and the Future of South-western Africa," Adelphi Papers 253 (Autumn 1990), p. 6.

San today number between 35,000 and 55,000. They have maintained their cultural integrity and system of organization with relatively minor external influence.[3]

Namibia's largest ethnic group is the Ovambo. This group originally settled, probably with the Hereros, in what is now southern Angola and northern Namibia, where most still live today. The Hereros continued south into the interior of Namibia; each group then developed into a distinct society. The various kingdoms that made up the Ovambo were known for their relative prosperity. This wealth was based on effective use of a favorable environment with rich soils. Sedentary agriculture and pastoralism were centered around the kraal, which included the home of an extended family (often polygamous) and the lands it cultivated. There was no private ownership of land; rather, all land was held communally and was parceled out by the political leadership for individual use. In addition to their activities as agriculturalists, the Ovambo were also active participants in trade. Although it is uncertain when basketry, pottery, and the metal working industries developed, the highly spe-

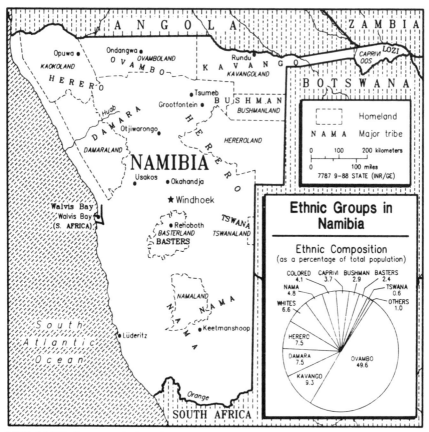

MAP 4.1 Ethnic groups in Namibia.

cialized metal workers of Ovambo had long been manufacturing axes, hoe blades, needles, and arrows when Europeans first reported on the area from their travels in the early nineteenth century.[4] The success of this industry contributed to the development of a long-distance trade based on Ovambo-controlled caravans that linked the Ovambo to the south and the interior of Namibia, to the north, and far into Angola and the Kalahari. These caravans were eventually the first contacts with Europeans seeking game and ornaments. We must emphasize that long before the Europeans began to mine (an activity that dominates Namibia's economy today), Africans such as the Ovambo mined and controlled the trade in important commodities such as copper, iron ore, and salt.

The political organization of the Ovambo revolved around a system of centralized authority based on hereditary succession. There were eight

Ovambo women in Oshakati celebrating independence. (Courtesy Edzard Ellerkmann)

recognized clans, or kingdoms, and the leader of each had significant political, economic, and religious powers. With advice from a powerful coterie of councillors and headmen working within a federal system, power was delegated by the leader of each kingdom. Ultimate power was held by a king or queen. The Ovambo practice of tracing descent matrilineally made female leadership a possibility, although it was rare.

The Okavango, who settled in the northern Namibian swamplands that share their name, are divided into four clans. Traditional economic production centers on sedentary agriculture, pastoralism, and fishing. Like the Ovambo, the Okavango trace their descent matrilineally, but the Okavango society is patrilocal and is based on small kingdoms. The current population is approximately seventy thousand. The Okavango are distinguished by their more common acceptance of women in positions of leadership and by the broad individual freedoms granted by their system. Although the Okavango traditionally yield legislative, executive, and judicial powers to the king, the individual is guaranteed a great deal of independence. The Okavango developed a complex system for the resolution of disputes that is based on conciliation rather than coercive sanctions. Great personal freedom appears to have been the norm in Okavango society, and only in a crisis did the leader intervene and make full use of his or her power.[5]

The Caprivi are divided into six clans of different sizes; the two largest control 85 percent of Caprivi territory. Caprivi homesteads have traditionally included approximately thirty members who are involved in a variety of forms of production on land that is communally held. Today's population is estimated at forty thousand. The government is modeled on the Bulozi system also found in Angola, Zambia, and Zimbabwe. Basically consisting of a leader and his or her council, this democratic system allows the population to suggest candidates for the council, and the leader is appointed by the council.

The Hereros, the Damara, the Nama, and the Rehoboth Basters are the major ethnic groups that inhabited central Namibia in the precolonial period. Herero is a name perhaps most easily recognized by non-Namibians; the Hereros (and others) were the targets of German genocide in the early twentieth century. Yet contrary to the image created by Europeans, the Hereros had lived in relative peace in Namibia for hundreds of years before coming into conflict with the Germans.

As they crossed into Namibia some five hundred years ago and moved south, they split into two major clans. One clan remained in present-day Kaokoland and is known as the Himba. The Himba, who live in a very demanding and isolated environment, have maintained a great measure of independence from European influence. The larger group, known as the Herero, moved into the central regions of Namibia. There they lived patrilocally as seminomads and identified themselves by a complex system based on the principle of double descent (each member belonged to one each of twenty patrilineages and six matrilineages). As was the case with many other ethnic groups in Namibia, land was communally owned. The homestead, composed of an extended family, was the basis of Herero society. The head of the homestead played a key role as its political and religious leader, and the heads of each homestead in turn paid homage to the senior man from their shared patrilineage. These senior men had religious and political authority to settle disputes, although that authority was not autocratic. Whereas day-to-day matters internal to the homestead were resolved by the head of the homestead, external matters were the province of the senior man.

Historians disagree about the origins of the Damara. Some treat them as a society distinct from its neighbors, and others suggest that the Damara are actually cousins of the Nama.[6] The Damara are sometimes divided into two groups, the cattle Dama and the Berg (mountain) Dama. The former have clearer ties to the Nama and share the Nama language, although they consider themselves distinct from the Nama and the Hereros. They are scattered throughout the southern areas of Namibia but are concentrated in the Auas Mountains and near the Swakop River. Their history has not been documented. Oral history suggests that the

Herero woman in traditional dress.

ancestors of the Damara lived in southern Namibia before the Hereros or the Nama and that they were some of the original inhabitants of Namibia. The Damara were distinguished by their highly effective hunting techniques, copper mining and smithing, and cultivation of large fields of tobacco and marijuana. Not surprisingly, then, the Damara were instrumental in the long-distance trade that flourished in Namibia well before the Europeans arrived. Yet by the mid-nineteenth century, the Damara faced persecution by other African groups because of their economic success and had taken refuge in the mountains. They organized themselves politically into several ministates based on extended families of ten to thirty members. There was no single source of authority; rather, each ministate was an autonomous unit governed by its elders. It is difficult to find published information on the Damara, especially on their legal or religious systems.[7]

The Nama lived in southern and central Namibia and were eventually drawn into land disputes with the Hereros and the Europeans. Nama is very inclusive as an ethnic identification and is composed of several groups such as the Khoi (it eventually included the Oorlams and the Bondleswaarts). The Nama numbered over forty-five thousand at their peak in the nineteenth century, about the same number as today. Archaeologists suggest that the Khoi may have migrated to this area of Africa more than two thousand years ago.[8] It is believed that by the beginning of the Christian era, people living along the coast between present-day Swakopmund and the Cape (probably the Khoi) were involved in a lively pottery and textile industry.[9] Whether hunter-gatherers, gatherers of shellfish, or pastoralists, the many groups that made up the Nama (including the Khoi) were referred to derogatorily by Europeans as "Hottentots." The Nama were probably the first Namibians to develop regular contacts with Europeans. The political organization of the Nama centered on a loose alliance, or federation, of several groups.[10] Each group had a leader who worked in concert with a council of elders and was assisted by a magistrate. This system of government was distinguished by its flexibility; government intervention was very low-key in periods of peace but could become autocratic when deemed necessary in times of war.

The Nama and Oorlam societies eventually became integrated (so much so that some analysts do not distinguish between them), and it is useful to briefly examine how this relationship developed. Compared to the populations discussed thus far, the Oorlams came to Namibia in relatively recent times. Large numbers of people who had been integrated on a marginal basis into the European system dominated by the Cape called themselves Oorlams. Their situation in the Cape became increasingly marginalized, and in the early nineteenth century the Oorlams moved north in large numbers toward the Orange River and lands populated by the Nama. By 1835, the Oorlam presence had dramatically altered the sociopolitical and economic scene in the territory. The Oorlams were of Khoi and European heritage, spoke Africaans, and had adopted Christianity. They were unique because of their formation of "commandos," or posses, of ten to fifty men who were armed and on horseback. These commandos quickly became renowned for their prowess in a number of activities such as hunting, trading, and raiding cattle. Their successes in southern and central Namibia were based on organization, mobility, and superior firepower.[11]

The Basters, who chose this name for themselves (which is still in use today), are descendants of mostly Afrikaner fathers and Khoi mothers who moved from the northern Cape and since the late nineteenth century have settled mostly in the area south of Windhoek, especially at Rehoboth. They compose much of the Coloured community in Namibia; they are Christian and speak Afrikaans. They were well-armed, and led by Captain Hermanus Van Wyk, they won control of the Rehoboth area from Jan Jonker and the Oorlams in the 1870s. The Basters prize their autonomy. An independent Baster republic organized through elected councils was established with its own constitution shortly after they took Rehoboth.

Demographics

Namibia has a population of 1.2–1.6 million people (the exact population is not known because of irregularities during the last South African census, which was taken in 1981). Namibia has one of the world's sparsest patterns of human settlement, with a density of perhaps 1.5 people per square kilometer. However, its annual birth rate of approximately 3.4 percent is one of the region's highest. From 1970 to 1981 the total population increased by 35 percent. Approximately 26 percent of the state's population is urbanized, and the rate of urbanization has increased since the 1960s. Windhoek, the capital, is the largest urban center, with a population of about 300,000—or nearly 20 percent of the total population and perhaps half of the total urban population.[12] The country's dependency ratio (the total percentage of the population under eighteen years old) is 49.4 percent. This ratio is higher in the communal areas, particularly in the north. The "economically active" (which excludes retirees, housewives, the jobless, subsistence farmers, preschool children, and students) constitute somewhat less than 20 percent of the total population. Such a classification tends to discount the economic contributions made by the informal sector of the economy.

RELIGION

Western religion was introduced primarily by the Germans, Finns, British, and later by the South Africans. Religious associations were especially important in Namibia for coalescing dissatisfaction with colonial policies. Religion and politics are clearly connected in Namibia. Although by the early twentieth century perhaps two-thirds of the Namibian population was Christian, few missions spoke out against the German genocidal policy. Over time the white churches were considered by increasing numbers of blacks to be racist.[13] There is good reason for this: Going back to the first years of European penetration, but especially since 1924, most white churches in Namibia had worked with the administration and supported government policy. This was part of the missions' legacy in Namibia; through their sermons and in their schools blacks were encouraged to accept contracts and were taught loyalty to the administration and to traditional authority. Because of this, in the 1920s several black congregations broke away from white churches and formed their own congregations.

> There is no doubt that the Lutheran and Catholic missionaries from Germany were the forerunners and willing supporters of the colonial system which in Namibia—as in South Africa—included from the beginning a hidden, but very effective racism. Letters, reports, statements of missionaries from Namibia clearly betray uncritically the Eurocentric Christian superiority over the "heathens." The division of the human species into masters and servants, civilized and savages, whites and blacks, Christians and pagans was easily accepted by traders, soldiers and missionaries. In conflict situations, the European missionaries were naturally on the side of the European conqueror.[14]

There was some friction between some missions and the government and settlers, even in early colonial times. Missionaries, for example, called on masters not to mistreat their servants or misuse their power. Although the administration (first German, then South African) provided for white education and other social services, black education and health care were left to the missions. The church also took over black land. For example, just after the Herero and Nama wars, both Lutheran and Catholic churches confiscated farms in the conquered German "crown land." Missions also used migratory labor and generally supported the colonial socio-economic system.

African and European members of the churches (especially Anglicans) became prominent international spokespersons calling for change in Namibia. In addition to providing the traditional services, the Anglican, Catholic, and other churches became extremely important places for the articulation and aggregation of nationalist sentiment. At least part of the reason religion became a crucial part of activism in Namibia was that the church was virtually the only assembly point for Africans that was allowed by the South African administration. The African Methodist Episcopal (AME) church was established relatively late in Namibia, yet by the mid-1940s it was growing very rapidly. Part of its appeal was the AME's clear political agenda. Oruuano, another religious movement with specific political goals, came to the fore in the 1950s. A Herero-dominated association, Oruuano was distinguished by a prophet who called for a return to precolonial status and the reallocation of land to Africans.[15]

In 1947, the Reverend Michael Scott was the first to petition the United Nations on behalf of Namibia. Anglican Reverend Theophilus Hamutumpangela was also known for his activism and letter-writing campaigns. Because of their active role in the anticolonial movement and their criticism of apartheid, the churches soon became targets for intimidation and harassment. Church printing presses were destroyed, and leaders were deported, denied passports and visas, or banned.[16] In the face of this repression, the churches unified to push for peaceful change.

In the early 1960s, the German and Finnish Lutheran churches became independent, and this signaled a turning point in their attitudes toward liberation. In 1971, following the International Court of Justice ruling on Namibia, the black Lutheran church sent an open letter endorsing the court's ruling that South African occupation was illegal. It called for the government to grant independence to Namibia and offered to act as a conduit for talks. Black churches, then, took a lead in advocating change.

> The main contribution of the Black Namibian churches on the operational level toward a new and free Namibia is their total identification with the oppressed and suffering people: they do not talk to political prisoners; . . . their workers, their pastors are among the detainees, among those who are held, tortured, condemned, or shot. . . . These Black Namibian Christians pay their share in the bloody struggle for liberation. Here, then, lies an ultimate difference with the "European" churches.[17]

The Council of Churches of Namibia was established in 1978 and includes all the major denominations with the exception of the (white) Dutch Reformed church. One feature of the resistance led by the churches was the anticonscription campaign, in which the two black Lutheran churches have been especially prominent. The churches supported many other aspects of the liberation movement. Overall, however, the position of the church was guarded on the issue of armed struggle. For many years the churches were strictly opposed to the concept of violent change; however, as South African violence continued unabated, some church people began to accept violence as part of a larger effort for change. Some church leaders openly advocated liberation theology, maintaining that it is the right of the oppressed to fight for their liberation. Consequently, SWAPO attracted some religious leaders as members. However, the sentiment among most church activists in Namibia clearly preferred nonviolent solutions. The church has thus sought to play a mediating role in Namibia. By the early 1980s, the Council of Churches of Namibia began to help shape international opinion about Namibia's future. It began to meet regularly with the Contact Group and the administrator-general to press for progress toward implementing UN Resolution 435.

Using South African terminology, Namibia has three types of churches: Afrikaner, European (Lutheran, Anglican, and Roman Catholic), and African. There are around seven thousand church bodies. The Afrikaner churches are all white, but they have black "daughter churches." The European churches are officially mixed; because of the past urban settlement laws, most in fact are either entirely white or black. The major churches in Namibia today include the African Methodist Episcopal church, the Church of the Province of Southern Africa, Deutsche Evangelische Lutherische Kirche, the Evangelical Lutheran church, Methodist Church of Southern Africa, the Roman Catholic church, and the United Congregational Church of Southern Africa.[18]

ROLE OF WOMEN

Although there is disagreement about the status of women in the societies of precolonial Namibia, women clearly suffered discrimination under German and South African law. Women have been active to varying degrees in the movement against apartheid. Yet the record gives the impression that women were only sporadically involved in protest. Some examples of women's activism are the Herero women's response to German genocidal policies, women's participation in the defiance of Pass Laws, and the leading role women took in the 1959 demonstrations at the Old Location.

Yet on closer observation one finds that women have been active in the resistance on a number of levels. A leading organization that represents women in Namibia is the SWAPO Women's Council. Created in 1976, the Women's Council has coordinated women's participation as soldiers, managers, workers, teachers, and politicians. It was through SWAPO and the resistance that women adopted a number of unconventional, traditionally male roles. Women proved their importance to the movement both from inside Namibia and from exile. In neighboring African states such as Angola, Tanzania, and Zambia, thousands of women supported SWAPO. Women regularly assumed leadership roles in planning and implementing diverse community programs such as food production and cottage industries, literacy, math, and political study programs. Although there was some resistance, there was a blurring of the traditional sexual division of labor for SWAPO supporters and refugees in exile. For example, 90 percent of the transportation system was run by women as drivers and mechanics. Other programs such as a literacy campaign, training in various trades, and the provision of child care were extremely effective. The highly celebrated kindergarten system operated in many camps from 8 A.M. to 5 P.M. to allow mothers to study or work. Such programs were considered pilots for independent Namibia.[19]

Activism by women inside Namibia was indispensable to the liberation movement. Women, especially in the north, played crucial roles in harboring SWAPO members and fighters, providing intelligence, and assisting with the storage and movement of weaponry around the country. According to SWAPO, several thousand women left the country after the crackdowns in the early 1970s, and many of these women joined the People's Liberation Army of Namibia as soldiers. Refugees and volunteers came to SWAPO camps over the years, and although it was common for women to be delegated to noncombatant roles, Namibian women did participate in confrontations and sabotage activities. According to the SWAPO Women's Council, this policy was questioned by men at first; however, women were eventually accepted in the role of soldier, and some women have risen to high rank in the military. Yet because the 1989 SWAPO manifesto mentions conscription only for men, it appears that this role for women was considered extraordinary and that it will be limited now that Namibia is independent. In addition, house-to-house meetings often led by women were important in politicizing and maintaining support for the resistance.

Women both within and outside Namibia accepted roles as political officers for SWAPO. Many of these women were also members of the SWAPO Women's Council, which has coordinated policy on issues especially important to women. For many years it worked to mobilize the population, and it played an important part in organization during the elections. Women are well represented at the lower and middle levels of the party, and there are a few highly visible women near the top of the party hierarchy. Gertrude Kikumbi was the first woman elected to the Central Committee. Other prominent women in SWAPO are Pendukeni Kaulinge, current secretary of the Women's Council, and Dr. Libertine Amathila, former head of SWAPO's Department of Health. Both women have been named to ministerial positions in the new government.

Many believe that women's full participation in independent Namibia is possible because of their activism and acceptance of unconventional roles during the long struggle. The large number of female-headed households consequent to the contract system placed many women in situations where they had to assume burdens traditionally undertaken by men. A 1988 SWAPO paper considered whether after independence women would want to relinquish the power they had taken into their own hands.[20]

The changes expected in independent Namibia will include on some level changes in the status of women. SWAPO offered a comprehensive set of proposals for the reform of gender-discriminatory policies. Many of the reforms are adapted from the governments of other recently liberated countries, and they cover issues of production and reproduction. SWAPO's clearest statement of intent is included in the constitution of the Women's Council. (See Appendix H.)

A major area for reform involves issues of employment. In colonial Namibia, women were simply restricted from certain kinds of jobs (such as working underground in the mines). In general, women were not hired for jobs in which labor was organized. With the exceptions of nursing or teaching, few women work in the professions. Of the black women who participate in the cash economy, over 60 percent work as domestic laborers. These women are not covered even by the weak Labor Relations Act. Therefore, they have virtually no rights as laborers; there is no minimum wage or standards for conditions of work. The hours are long and pay is low (on average, a domestic servant who does not "live in" works from 6 A.M. to 10 P.M. and takes home as little as R 15 a month).[21] Furthermore, the employer is not required to offer paid holidays, sick leave, or pension. The worker can be fired without notice and can easily be replaced. Although much less information has been collected on the status of rural women, most accurate accounts suggest that their situation is even more dire. The developmental neglect of rural areas of Namibia is notorious. Whether they live in overcrowded or environmentally marginal reserves or work on white farms, these women have even less autonomy than women working as domestic laborers.

SWAPO has intervened on behalf of women on issues of divorce and property rights. According to colonial and traditional laws, in the event of a divorce a woman has no right to the couple's property. Widows face similar difficulties. In addition, municipal regulations such as those for Katutura allow for a divorced woman to be expelled from her home regardless of whether she has custody of the couple's children.[22] Given the experience of other reform-minded governments, it is understandable that there is debate inside Namibia as to how easily changes will be made.

At least on paper, the status of women has changed radically. Women's rights are recognized in the constitution. At age eighteen all persons are to be considered equal before the law. One chapter of the constitution, which is on human rights, specifically mentions women's unique problems. The terms *he* and *she* are employed throughout the document. Men married to Namibian women will be eligible for citizenship, a policy that is unusual in the region.

Much, however, remains to be done. The Constituent Assembly refused to fully accept the 1981 UN Convention on the Elimination of All Forms of Discrimination Against Women (although a similar convention on children's rights was accepted). The legislature must now pass long-promised reforms such as provisions for paid maternity leave and equal pay for equal work. Interestingly, the female members of the Constituent Assembly were paid 10 percent less than their male counterparts.[23]

Considering the record of neighboring states with similar histories, it is clear that despite grand plans and the keenest intent, there are no guarantees of sweeping changes beneficial to women in postindependent Namibia. These plans might be subverted in a number of ways, including by problems of communication and administration. The new government will encounter problems in setting priorities. There will be many demands from diverse interest groups, and even with the initial outpouring of assistance expected from the international community, the government's resources will be limited.

Most difficult, however, may be resistance by traditional European and African elements. Although the political changes of 1989 were dramatic, there has been no displacement of the ideologies that subordinate women to men. The shift to democracy may make it more, not less, difficult to initiate change in gender-based relations. Whenever it is necessary to place a priority on maintaining popular support and building legitimacy, the prospects of challenging traditional values and mores concerning women are risky at best. Although analysts disagree about the status of women in precolonial Namibia, there is little reason to believe that the sexism produced by a long history of colonial chauvinism will be any easier to deal with in Namibia than has been the case elsewhere.

EDUCATION

Relative to the white population, education for the majority of Namibians has been poor, although today about 75 percent of all Namibians are literate.[24] By 1981 about one percent of Namibian blacks had completed secondary school. Over the years, Namibia's educational system has been closely intertwined with that of South Africa. Initially, education for blacks was provided by missionaries, but after 1948 education for blacks was taken over by the Department of Bantu Education and by the Department for Coloured Affairs for Namibia's Coloureds. In the 1970s, South Africa introduced its nonracial syllabus from Cape

Province, which was quickly adopted by the white schools. However, because the new system required new textbooks and teacher training, change was slow to come to black schools. Additionally, in 1980 the government established ten Educational Authorities along racial lines that were not conducive to developing a common educational system. Black children have been taught in traditional languages and in Afrikaans. To indicate the magnitude of the differences between white and black education, in FY 1986–1987 the Ovambo Educational Authority spent R 70.9 million to educate 188,552 pupils in its system (or R 377 per capita), and the White Educational Authority spent R 64.6 million for 16,292 students (or R 3,966 per capita).[25] Finally, although there were twenty-one secondary schools for whites (who make up around 10 percent of the population) at independence, there were also only twenty-one secondary schools for blacks (who make up around 90 percent of the total population).

Namibia's previously racist educational system has resulted in low skill levels for many blacks. Whites were also disadvantaged. The Christian National Education (CNE) institution gave a Christian and Calvinist justification for separate development in South African–controlled Namibia. The CNE was the dominant philosophy for white education in Namibia. Although originating in South Africa in the 1940s, CNE was transplanted almost directly to Namibia. According to one education expert, it had "a devastating effect on the minds of the white youth. In short, it created racist and fascist attitudes and values."[26]

Because of the need for poorer children to perform a variety of duties at home, the drop-out rate for black pupils is extremely high. Secondary education is scant; only five schools offer vocational training to blacks. Until recently, all instruction was either in a local language or in Afrikaans. English is now both the national language and the language of instruction, although Afrikaans will still be taught for the medium term because of the strong historical linkages with South Africa and the lack of trained English-speaking teachers.

The educational system has changed, and in May 1989 the administrator-general (under pressure from the UN special representative) repealed the educational responsibilities of the second-tier authorities and put education under the national administration. Education is also considered a top priority by the SWAPO Women's Council.[27] Formal education was available to a small percentage of blacks in colonial Namibia. The Bantu education that was offered taught white stereotypes and apartheid-sanctioned roles for blacks and women. In 1980, only 7 percent of all black Namibian children were in a secondary or vocational school, and not one young black woman was registered as a student in any technical field in Namibia. Although girls outnumbered boys at the

TABLE 4.2   Formal Education/Training Estimates for the Labor Force

Level[a]	Whites	Coloureds	Blacks	Total
University or equivalent	5,000	25	10	5,035
Other tertiary	5,000	12	10	5,022
Secondary or equivalent	10,000	3,000	200	13,200
Other post primary	12,500	7,500	3,000	23,000
Complete primary	9,000	24,000	19,000	52,000
Substantial primary	negligible	9,500	110,000	119,500
Negligible or nil	negligible	9,500	300,000	309,500
Total	41,500	53,537	432,220	527,257

[a]These data are nearly a decade old, but they represent the most recent estimates available.

Sources: United Nations Institute for Namibia, Namibia: Perspectives for National Reconstruction and Development (Lusaka: UNIN, 1986); and the Institute for International Education's conference, Education for Namibians, New York, New York, 1989.

primary school level, the number of girls fell off dramatically and disproportionately at the secondary level.[28]

To remedy this situation, the Women's Council has planned progressive reforms of curricula and an aggressive policy of "positive discrimination" favoring women. Such programs were experimented with in camps during exile. In many of these camps the illiteracy rate was 90 percent. With the provision of child care to allow women the time to study, the rate quickly decreased by 35 percent. At higher levels of education, the UN Institute for Namibia trained Namibian men and women as administrators and professionals. As an example of the positive discrimination practiced there, approximately 65 percent of the scholarships were granted to women. Further, women are consciously encouraged to enter fields traditionally dominated by men.[29]

The shortcomings of Namibia's educational system can be summarized as follows. Of the nearly twenty thousand students who left school in Namibia in 1981, 33 percent were functionally illiterate; 45 percent could proceed only to unskilled jobs; 17 percent could be trained as skilled workers; and only 5 percent could proceed to advanced training.[30] Formal education-training estimates of the major ethnic groups are given in Table 4.2.

Many Namibians—principally exiles—have taken advanced training overseas under the auspices of the United Nations High Commission for Refugees (UNHCR), UNIDO, the Commonwealth Namibia Programme, and bilateral agreements between SWAPO and a number of governments and private foundations. Two UN bodies have provided considerable training for Namibians: The United Nations Institute for Namibia, founded in Lusaka in 1976, has trained over one thousand Namibians for jobs primarily in government, but the quality of their education has been uneven; and the UN Vocational Training Centre for Namibia, founded in Angola in 1983, provided courses in technical training. Namibia's post-secondary education now basically consists of the Academy, which is composed of a College for Out-of-School Training, a technical school (Technikon), and an autonomous University of Namibia. There are attempts to incorporate UNIN with the University of Namibia, although no specific plans have been announced.

Most Namibians will need significant training in virtually all areas if the new state is to achieve economic and social development. In fact, training and education are major priorities for the new government. Minister of Education, Culture, and Sport Nahas Angula has indicated that the government wants to unify and decentralize the educational system and create an educational council to introduce a new school system for the country. The government does not intend to try to equalize education by taking funding from formerly well-endowed schools and giving it to poorer schools. The education minister reassured middle-class black parents, whose children are in reasonably well-furnished schools, that "it would not be wise or productive to deprive the functioning schools of resources in order to alleviate the situation of dysfunctional schools."[31] In January 1991 the Education Ministry helped establish the Windhoek International School, which opened with 127 students from 23 countries.

Each ethnic group described in the first section of this chapter generally uses its own language plus, for those with some education, Afrikaans and possibly some English. Because Afrikaans has been regarded as the language of the oppressor, English has been designated the official language of Namibia. Full use of English will be difficult to achieve until the educational system, which has been overwhelming Afrikaans-based until now, is changed. The use of English will prove beneficial economically because most of Namibia's neighbors and trade partners are English-speaking countries.

HEALTH

It is difficult to make any precise statements about health care in Namibia, partly because the statistics provided by the South African administration have been unrepresentative. According to Tim Lobstein, who has written widely on this topic, there are no national statistics for mortality in Namibia. In fact, there has been no legal requirement to register births and deaths.[32] Traditionally, the only time an official record has been kept of blacks has been when black men sign a contract to sell their labor.[33] However, some conclusions can be drawn about health problems in Namibia. There are many problems, and they are widespread, especially for a country that is potentially as wealthy as Namibia. Just as income is shared unequally in Namibia, so is the impact of disease. Although most of the health problems confronting Namibia are directly linked to poverty, the diseases most problematic in Namibia are linked to the environment to some degree. For example, among the poor in the drier areas of the south, respiratory diseases such as bronchitis and tuberculosis (TB) are major contributors to morbidity. In 1980 in some areas of the south, an estimated 25 percent of the population suffered from TB. It is also estimated that a black Namibian is three times more likely to have TB than his or her white counterpart.[34]

In the wetter northern regions of Ovambo and Kavango, tropical diseases such as malaria and bilharzia are more common. Another threat to health in the north has been its situation as the theater of war. These two major threats to health are interlinked in a number of ways. For example, Lobstein reports that the intensification of the war disrupted mosquito control programs (only 20 percent of the necessary area was being sprayed). Consequently, by 1982 malaria was more prevalent in the north than at any time in twenty years. So many people sought medical care for malaria that the skeletal health services were flooded. It is reported that noncerebral cases were turned away due to a shortage of space and supplies.[35] Similarly, epidemics of typhoid and the bubonic plague hit the north in the 1980s; in 1983, 548 cases of the plague were confirmed. Analysts have linked the outbreak of this and similar highly contagious diseases to the overcrowding in squatter camps created during the war.[36] If the war were not a direct contributor to such threats, the destabilization caused by war has long been recognized as a contributor to conditions for epidemics.

Besides regional distinctions, other generalizations can be made about health in Namibia. Crowded black townships surrounding the urban areas have unusually high rates of cancer and other problems, such as hypertension and strokes, usually only found in developed countries. An estimated one out of every six deaths among black adults in the townships is due to cancer. This rate is twice as high as that of South Africa.[37] The widespread use of unsealed asbestos in houses (some of which shelter as many as fifteen people per two-bedroom house) may explain part of the problem. Other health problems reported to be common in the townships involve various forms of substance abuse. Alcoholism is said to be high in black and colored townships; Lobstein contends that approximately half of the adult population may suffer from its effects. Similar problems are reported with abuse of tranquilizers, especially among mineworkers.[38]

Because of administrative suppression of trade activism, unions have encountered difficulties in pressing for health and safety regulations. There has generally been little legislation to protect worker health; employers prefer to draw from the pool of labor rather than to keep the workers they employ healthy. A common practice of many mining employers has been to break the contract of sick workers and rather than treat them, send them back to the reserves.[39] Provision of adequate health care and improvement of working conditions have become major demands of the twelve thousand–member Mineworkers Union of Namibia (MUN).[40]

The uranium mines run by Rössing have been a point of contention in the past. Rössing maintains that in the absence of specific national legislation, it has developed a comprehensive occupational health management program and has been publicly commended for its employee health care by President Nujoma. Further, Rössing has a comprehensive radiation protection program based on international standards and audited by international experts. There has never been an incident of cancer among Rössing employees that was attributable to occupational exposure.[41] Nonetheless, in July 1990 Deputy Minister of Mines Helmuth Angula asked the International Atomic Energy Commission to test radiation levels at Rössing.[42] Although Rössing takes every precaution in the protection of its workers (including applying strict hygiene standards and using air conditioned equipment and respirators), uranium mining can pose potential hazards. Radon molecules are present in radon gas released during mining and processing uranium ore. Persons working with radium and its compounds are exposed to these molecules. Even with the strictest precautions, tailings or radon molecules are impossible to remove; they are odorless and invisible. They are absorbed as dust, which may enter the body by inhalation or ingestion. Poisoning, which may be acute or chronic, attacks several areas of the body and endangers cardiovascular, urinary, reproductive, and nervous systems. According to Rössing officials, no case of radiation poisoning has occurred at Rössing, and no incidents of internal organ damage through radiation exposure have occurred because of the low-grade ore present and the company's radiation control program.[43] Uranium miners in other parts of the world experience high rates of kidney damage and lung cancer, the latter probably associated with another danger of mining—silicosis.[44]

Another segment of the Namibian population considered at risk for many ailments are infants and children. Again, statistics are unreliable, but we can break down infant mortality rates by color for Windhoek in the early 1980s. The white infant mortality rate is relatively high but is comparable to that of developed countries at 21 per 1,000 live births. However, the rates for Coloured and black infant mortality are high even compared to the poorest countries: 145 and 165 per 1,000 live births, respectively.[45] According to Dr. Soloman Amadhila, a pediatrician at Oshakati Hospital, no nationwide survey has ever been carried out to determine the health status of black children.[46] However, from his experience gastroenteritis is clearly a major killer of infants. Because so little of the black population receives full immunization, childhood diseases such as measles are far more deadly than in the developed world.

Because of the high rates of infant and child morbidity and mortality among blacks in Namibia, the subject of population control or family planning is very controversial. The former administration pointed to the population growth rate (over 3 percent) and took what might be called a two-track policy. It urged white women to "have one for SWA," but various forms of coercion were used to persuade black women to accept birth control. The most notorious of these abuses was the use of the drug Depo-Provera, an injectible that offers several months of sterility but that has been banned in the United States and European countries because of severe side effects and possible links to cancer. Although there has been no official investigation of the charges, stories of abuse abound, and they come from several different sources. For example, health workers maintain that Depo-Provera was routinely administered to black women after childbirth without their consent. The previous administration's position was that actions are taken to "solve" problems of housing shortages, unemployment, and the like. Others accused the official health services of administering the drug to young girls at the onset of menstruation ostensibly to "cut down" on teenage pregnancy. Such allegations are so widespread that they have caused an uproar; according to Lindy Kazombaue and Nashilongo Elago, the issue of population control was considered so sensitive that anyone raising it could be accused of agitating against the state.[47]

In the face of mounting health problems, the South African administration took little action. The health service was segregated, as were most other aspects of life in Namibia. In the 1980s, under the three-tiered system of Turnhalle the provision of health care was left to the ten ethnic administrations. The central government paid a certain amount per capita to supplement these services, but the ethnic administrations had to raise the bulk of their own revenues through taxes.

Thus, all the taxes raised from whites were spent on services only open to whites, and so forth. Consequently, the situation was one of "separate and unequal." The breakdown of health spending per capita for 1980–1981 was R 233.70 for whites compared with a range of only R 4.70 to R 56.84 for blacks and coloreds, depending on the specific reserve.[48]

In addition to the services provided by the ethnic administrations, other providers of care were the churches, (in some cases) the mines, and the SADF. As part of the campaign to "win hearts and minds," the SADF gradually took control over the medical services in the war zones. As the large military presence and destabilization caused by the war contributed to a deteriorating health situation, both SADF and SWAPO became involved in the provision of some level of care. The superintendent of the large Oshakati hospital was a commandant in the Permanent Forces. In 1983, the chief of staff of SWATF announced that of fifty-eight physicians in Kaokoland, forty-eight were soldiers.[49]

Much like the efforts of the Council of Churches of Namibia to set up clinics and hospitals that concentrate on preventive health, SWAPO piloted several programs from exile. In the refugee camps, in addition to basic services and a training program for health care workers, SWAPO established rehabilitation programs for those wounded or disabled by the war. These programs had some success. For example, in some areas infant mortality dropped from more than one hundred per one thousand live births to forty-one per one thousand.[50] Another potential health legacy of the war may be AIDS. Although little information is available on the extent of AIDS within Namibia, its prevalence was expected to be low, but the disruptions of the war in Angola may contribute to increasing rates.[51]

It is likely that as the new government continues to dismantle apartheid, the current health care system will be replaced. Although some inequality in terms of access to care will probably continue for some time, Namibia is expected to turn away from a high-tech, curative program responsive only to a tiny minority and move toward more cost-effective, preventive methods as espoused by the World Health Organization (WHO). The WHO strategy (adopted by ever-increasing numbers of the world's states and long sanctioned by SWAPO) seeks to make primary health care available to all people.

LITERATURE

Namibia's society, like its economy, can almost be characterized by dualism: a white culture based on European and South African values alongside a black one based more on African values. White Namibians share much with their counterparts in South Africa: their literature, their

Windhoek retains much of its German colonial architectural heritage. (Photo by Donald L. Sparks)

religion, and even their education. Namibia's best-known author is probably Cosmo Pieterse, who was educated in South Africa. He has written numerous scripts, plays, and poems, and his writings have been political, expressing a pro-liberation point of view. Black Namibians, especially those in the north and in other more isolated areas, lead their lives along traditional lines and have a rich oral history. Stories were passed down from generation to generation. Although many such stories were about the natural world—hunting, rains, grazing, and similar topics—many were about the people's history. In the 1970s and 1980s, literate black Namibians contributed to what has been termed "liberation literature."[52]

SPORTS

Perhaps the most unifying aspect of Namibia's social life in the future will be sports. Before independence, organized sports were played predominantly by whites, who enjoyed first-class facilities and sponsorship. For example, private companies supported teams, and white students' schools generally have had excellent equipment, facilities (swimming pools, tracks, tennis courts), and coaches. Such sports were linked with South Africa, however; for example, Namibia was not allowed to play in many international sporting events because sanctions against South Africa also applied to Namibia. With independence Namibia suspended its sporting links with South Africa and will now be able to compete internationally in a variety of sports including track, rugby, soccer, cricket, swimming, field hockey, golf, squash, cycling, lawn bowling, and fistball.[53]

NOTES

1. Laurens van der Post, *The Lost World of the Kalahari* (New York: William Morrow and Company, 1988), p. 24.

2. Richard Gray, ed., *The Cambridge History of Africa, Volume 4* (Cambridge: Cambridge University Press, 1975), p. 420.

3. Helmut Angula, "Tracing the History of the San," in *Namibia: 1884–1984; Readings on Namibian History and Society*, Brian Wood, ed. (London: Namibia Support Committee and NUNIN, 1988), p. 114.

4. Gervase Clarence-Smith and Richard Moorsam, "Underdevelopment and Class Formation in Ovamboland, 1844–1917," in Ibid., pp. 97–100.

5. Gordon D. Gibson and T. J. Larson, et al., *The Kavango People* (Weisbaden: Frantz Steiner Verlag, 1981), p. 32; and Winifred Hoernle, *The Social Organization of the Nama* (Johannesburg: Witwatersrand University Press, 1985), p. 20.

6. Gray, *The Cambridge History of Africa*, pp. 423–424.

7. One source is South African Department of Foreign Affairs, *SWA Survey 1967* (Pretoria: Cape and Transvaal Printers, Ltd., 1967).

8. J. D. Fage, ed., *The Cambridge History of Africa, Volume 2* (Cambridge: Cambridge University Press, 1986), p. 375.

9. Roland Oliver, ed., *The Cambridge History of Africa, Volume 3* (Cambridge: Cambridge Unitersity Press, 1977), pp. 618–620.

10. Gray, *The Cambridge History of Africa*, p. 424.

11. Brigitte Lau, "'Pre-colonial' Namibian Historiography: What Is to Be Done?" in *Namibia: 1884–1984*, ed. Brian Wood, p. 188.

12. J. H. van der Merew, ed., *National Atlas of South West Africa (Namibia)* (Goodwood, Cape: National Book Printers, 1983), frames 42–51.

13. Peter Katjavivi, *A History of Resistance in Namibia* (London: James Curry Ltd., 1988), p. 36.

14. Heinz Hunke, "The Role of European Missionaries in Namibia," in *Namibia: 1884–1984*, ed. Brian Wood, p. 628.

15. Katjavivi, *A History of Resistance in Namibia*, p. 87.

16. Andre du Pisani, *SWA/Namibia: The Politics of Continuity and Change* (Johannesburg: J. Ball Publishers, 1985), p. 130.

17. Hunke, "The Role of European Missionaries in Namibia," in *Namibia: 1884–1984*, ed. Brian Wood, p. 634. See also Catholic Institute for International Relations, *Namibia in the 1980s* (London: British Council of Churches, 1981), pp. 58–59.

18. Joe Putz, Heidi von Egidy, and Perri Caplan, *Political Who's Who of Namibia* (Windhoek: Magus Company, 1987), pp. 361–368.

19. Patricia McFadden, "Forms and Spheres of Anti-Colonial Resistance with Special Reference to Namibia," in *Namibia: 1884–1984*, ed. Brian Wood, p. 623.

20. SWAPO Women's Solidarity Campaign, "Women in Production and Reproduction," in *Namibia: 1884–1984*, ed. Brian Wood, pp. 351–357.

21. *The Namibian* (April 8, 1989), p. 11; and L. Kazombaue and N. Elago, "The Exploited Women in Namibia: A Testimony," in Gerhard Totemeyer and Vezera Kandetu, et al., *Namibia in Perspective* (Windhoek: Council of Churches of Namibia, 1987), pp. 199–200.

22. "Katutura Revisited, 1986: Essays on a Black Namibian Apartheid Suburb," *Series of Social Research Number 1* (Windhoek: Angelus Publishing Company, 1986), p. 47.

23. Colleen Lowe Morna, "No Place At Home," *Africa Report* 35 (6) (November-December 1990), p. 60.

24. Putz, von Egidy, and Caplan, *Political Who's Who of Namibia*. For a recent report on education and returning exiles, see *Africa Report* 35 (6) (November-December 1990), pp. 59–65.

25. From "Education for Namibians: A Workship," Institute for International Education, New York, NY, January 27, 1989.

26. Nghidi Ndilula, "Namibian Education and Culture," in *Namibia: 1884–1984*, ed. Brian Wood, p. 392.

27. Maria Kapere, interviewed by December Green, August 9, 1989, SWAPO Campaign Headquarters, Windhoek.

28. SWAPO Women's Council, "Namibian Women in Production," in *Namibia: 1884–1984*, ed. Brian Wood, p. 616.

29. *The Namibian* (May 20, 1989), p. 20.

30. UNIDO. *Industrial Development Programme for an Independent Namibia* (Vienna: UNIDO, 1984), p. 161; and Justin Ellis, *Education, Repression and Liberation: Namibia* (London: CIIR, 1984), pp. 8; 34–41.

31. *Namibia Report*, I (4) (May 1990), p. 4.

32. Tim Lobstein, et al., *Namibia: Reclaiming the People's Health* (London: Namibia Support Committee, 1988), p. 10.

33. Susanna Smith, *Namibia: A Violation of Trust* (Oxford: Oxfam, 1986), p. 9.

34. Lobstein, *Namibia: Reclaiming the People's Health*, p. 9.

35. Ibid., p. 10.

36. Tony Weaver, "Namibian Review," *South African Review* 2 (1984), p. 219.

37. Lobstein, *Namibia: Reclaiming the People's Health*, p. 12.

38. Ibid., p. 10.

39. Ibid., p. 12.

40. Ibid., p. 11.

41. Communications with the director of corporate affairs, Rössing Uranium, Ltd., June 25, 1990. Anderson and Marks maintain that as of 1980, no black worker in Namibia had ever been compensated for occupational cancer. For details, see Neil Anderson and Shula Marks, "Work and Health in Namibia: Preliminary Notes," *Journal of Southern African Studies* 13 (1987), p. 281.

42. *The Namibian* (February 3, 1989), p. 5.

43. Communications with the director of corporate affairs, Rössing Uranium, Ltd., June 25, 1990; and interviews by Don Sparks with the general manager of Rössing, March 20, 1990. According to the company, Rössing has one of the most comprehensive health care systems in Namibia. For example, all employees who are ill and unable to work are given full medical care, and in the case of full disability the employee receives 75 percent of his or her salary until retirement and then receives a full pension. Employees who are injured on the job and cannot work on the mine but seek alternative work (and are judged fit to do so by a medical board on which a MUN doctor sits) are assisted by a six-month salary, relocation expenses, and a full pension refund. The employee can also remain a member of the Rössing Medical Benefit Society if he or she continues to pay the contribution.

Rössing has an impressive safety record. It holds the National Occupational Safety Association record for the highest number of fatality-free man-hours worked at any mine in Namibia. In 1988 and 1989, Rössing was awarded the British Safety Council's Sword of Honour as one of the thirty safest organizations worldwide.

44. Luigi Parmeggiani, *Encyclopedia of Occupational Health and Safety* (Geneva: ILO, 1986), pp. 2,238–2,239; 1,896–1,897. See also Anderson and Marks, "Work and Health in Namibia: Preliminary Notes," p. 281.

45. Kazombaue and Elago, "The Exploited Women in Namibia: A Testimony," in Totemeyer and Kandetu, *Namibia in Perspective*, pp. 20–23.

46. Lobstein, p. 26.

47. Kazombaue and Elago, "The Exploited Women in Namibia: A Testimony," in Totemeyer and Kandetu, *Namibia in Perspective*, pp. 20–23.

48. Lobstein, *Namibia: Reclaiming the People's Health*, p. 1.

49. *The Namibian* (March 24, 1989), p. 5.

50. Kazombaue and Elago, "The Exploited Women in Namibia: A Testimony," in Totemeyer and Kandetu, *Namibia in Perspective*, pp. 20–23.

51. Norman Miller and Richard C. Rockwall, *AIDS in Africa* (Lewiston: Edwin Mellen Press, 1988).

52. For details, see Wood, *Namibia: 1884–1984*, pp. 383–494.

53. *Windhoek Observer* (March 17, 1990), p. 85. Interestingly, the Namibian Fistball Association, formed in 1966, has been allowed to compete internationally, as South Africa does not have an organized fistball association.

Conclusion

The constitution developed by Namibia's first freely elected Constituent Assembly gives the country a strong basis for democratic government. The system creates a separation of powers between the executive and legislative branches, and it also establishes the framework for an independent judiciary. Guarantees of individual liberties are set down in a Bill of Rights.

The multiparty elections in November 1989 resulted in a system in which one party does carry a majority, but the majority is sufficiently weak to necessitate coalition politics. This situation in itself countervails against the abuses of power so often demonstrated in other African countries with systems clearly dominated by one party. Yet coalition governments also have their weaknesses, inertia being perhaps the most important of these. However, so far this has not been a problem in Namibia, which is quite remarkable given that within the period of only a year, groups that were often involved in violent competition have become contending political parties in a parliamentary setting. Even more remarkably the leaders of these parties have made substantial compromises to ensure that all interests are represented.

Although the conciliatory spirit demonstrated by Namibian politicians in the Constituent Assembly has been widely applauded and Namibia may well provide a model for power sharing for South Africa, Namibia's new government will likely be confronted with various challenges. First, as long as South Africa dominates the economy, the government's independence will be constrained. Another challenge will be meeting the expectations raised by independence and satisfying demands that were ignored by the colonial administrations. For example, for years SWAPO promised a redirection of development assistance to Ovambo, its base of support and an area considered by colonial administrations to be only a labor reservoir. However, as much as the SWAPO-led government may want to fulfill its promise, any new government in its position is likely to be overwhelmed with demands, as will be discussed below. With Namibia's limited resources, the new government will have a difficult time satisfying all interests.

In an attempt to satisfy all interests, it is likely that there will be some shuffling of parties and interests in the near future. As one example, there is some indication that former SWAPO supporters view what some consider pragmatism as co-optation. It has already been suggested that union leaders and the Left inside SWAPO are concerned about the party's willingness to forget the past and to make amends with former enemies. Similar splits are likely within other parties as well.

Yet these are heady times for Namibia and for the new government. New parties and alignments will likely develop in the coming years. However, the framework of the system constructed since independence does provide a strong basis for a democratic government that is capable of surviving party formation and reformation. Namibia's economic situation will be *a*, if not *the*, determining factor in the system's resilience.

The new government will have little leverage in radically changing its economic policies in the short term. Nevertheless, Namibia will want to expand health, education, and housing services, especially in Ovamboland—an area long neglected by the South African regime. There are perhaps 750,000 people in the north who currently have few human services. Programs to change this will be expensive, and they could take the majority of the new government's budget. The new government will also be pressured to offer jobs to its political supporters. Given the current unemployment rate of perhaps 15–30 percent (in the formal sector), Namibia will need to create perhaps 50,000 jobs over the next five years.

Namibia will not achieve all of its economic and social development goals in the short term or perhaps even during the next generation. However, in many ways Namibia's chances of achieving many of these goals are good.[1] Namibia's resource-based industries will be the cornerstone for long-term economic expansion and will be geared primarily toward the export market. The domestic market will remain small, but some internal demand should increase due to income redistribution, although employment potential will not dramatically increase. General economic expansion, particularly in the resources-based industries, will also be limited because of the lack of trained manpower.

A number of major issues must be considered for Namibia's future. Given the historical constraints, in actual practice Namibia will have little latitude in establishing new—especially radical—economic policies. Any Namibian government at independence would have found itself constrained due to historical economic linkages over which it would have limited control. SWAPO has realized this and has drawn back from some of its previous policy positions. Although there may be some harsh rhetoric by many in the new government, there will be little immediate change. Eventually, Namibia will lessen its financial ties with South Africa by establishing its own currency and possibly withdrawing from the Custom Union. Thus, the SWAPO government will not be able to make immediate radical changes if it wants to maintain a viable economy.

By the mid-1990s, Namibia will probably have an economy based somewhat more on state participation, but a strong private sector will be allowed. Although it will probably never nationalize the mines, Namibia will likely press for increased black presence in senior management positions, change the tax codes, and take control of marginal areas. It will probably form an umbrella state organization to engage in mineral marketing and exploration. It may also establish large parastatals in the fisheries area, but it will have to rely on the private sector's capital-intensive fleets to bring in the large catches it will need for a viable processing industry. Given recent policy statements made by the new government and a general mood across Africa (indeed, worldwide), it is highly unlikely that Namibia will emerge as a centrally planned economy, although the government will no doubt develop annual national economic development plans, which are necessary for foreign economic assistance.

Direct foreign investment will be particularly important for the new nation. Namibia does not have the domestic savings resources necessary to support capital-intensive extraction industries. As the economy will be resources-based for the foreseeable future (that is, it cannot soon industrialize or create a major manufacturing sector), it will need increased levels of investment. If the political relations with South Africa are at least nonconfrontational (from South Africa's perspective), private investment will likely proceed. If Namibia is able to achieve political stability early on, it can expect sufficient amounts of foreign investment. Some believe that the new government may go overboard to gain domestic and foreign business confidence. The reason for this, according to Wolfgang Thomas, is that it has "learned from the rest of Africa."[2] On the other hand, if it is seen to be politically unstable, such investment will be scant. The government launched an investment code, according to Minister of Trade and Industry Ben Amathila, that "does not . . . suggest any restrictions on the range of activities in which foreign investors may engage."[3] In addition, in July 1990 the Trade and Industry Ministry announced plans to establish an investment center to give potential investors information about the country.

Another important problem is how Namibia can satisfy the pent-up desires of the majority, especially in terms of employment, housing, and education. Despite its best efforts, the new government will not be able to meet the staggering needs of Namibia's majority. Namibia's population has been growing at a rate of over 3 percent annually—about three times faster than the economy has grown—since 1980. The urbanization rate is likely to get higher in the future. According to a recent study by the state housing corporation (National Building and Investment Corporation), 27 percent of the Namibian population in 1982 was urbanized; by 1985 that figure had risen to 28 percent. By the year 2000 it is expected that nearly 40 percent of the total population will be urbanized. This raises problems with employment possibilities. Namibian economist Fanuel Tjingaete cites the 7 percent unemployment rate in 1980; he feels that in 1986 some 23 percent were unemployed and estimates that by 1994 there will be a 44 percent unemployment rate. He warned, "You can imagine the social problems associated with those rates."[4]

According to the National Building and Investment Corporation (NBIC), there is a critical need for at least ten thousand new homes.[5] Minister of Housing Dr. Libertine Amathila announced plans for a national housing policy to help with what is estimated as a twenty thousand low-income housing shortfall. Housing needs are desperate in Windhoek's Katutura township, where perhaps seven thousand people do not have homes. Additionally, literally hundreds of makeshift houses have been built by returning exiles and people moving down from the north. The problem has been compounded by a nationwide mortgage repayment boycott, which prompted the NBIC to warn owners that it might have to issue eviction orders.[6] To meet this pressing housing need, Namibia will have to invest over R 15 million annually, which does not include housing requirements for the returning refugees.

Income redistribution pressures will be a problem. For example, "trade unionists are getting more powerful . . . and they will exert pressures, as well as . . . civil servants . . . but the SWAPO government will have the same relationship with their trade unionists in Namibia as other African governments have . . . that is, as soon as they are in power they have to look at the balances of their budgets."[7] Currently the Mineworkers Union of Namibia (MUN) is trying to establish conciliation boards as a standard feature of the labor scene instead of functioning ad hoc as they are now.

Health services will have to be expanded, as recent studies show that incidences of tuberculosis and malnutrition have not decreased. Additionally, the number of school children increased by nearly 20 percent between 1983 and 1987 (from 297,837 to 364,404), and the government's education budget more than doubled (from R 132 million to R 278 million). Namibia launched a universal and mandatory educational system at independence, which will be even more expensive and difficult to finance. Minister of Education, Culture, and Sports Nahas Angula indicated that government expenditures on education would have to increase to R 800 million annually if Namibia is to maintain a compulsory universal schooling system.[8]

The economic choices the SWAPO government has made since independence have immediate and important short- and long-term economic consequences for Namibia. In outlining the government's needs at independence, Finance Minister Otto Herrigel reiterated his position that "nationalisation does not form a part of government strategy" and expressed his belief that "business is the partner" of government in economic success. He suggested that Namibia will have a mixed-market economy "based on social responsibility," with a "dynamic role" envisoned for the private sector.[9]

The period of political independence has been accompanied by social and political upheaval as Namibia has left a century-old colonial heritage. Institutions will change, society is changing, and ultimately the economy will change. The last vestiges of apartheid are being removed, and Namibia's society is more open to change of all sorts. For example, Namibians now live and work without legal restrictions (although there will be social, traditional, and economic "restrictions" for some time) and have more flexibility in the type of jobs to which they can aspire. This opens up the economy to greater participation—especially among the informal sector—which had been discouraged by South Africa because it competed with South African and white commercial interests. Change will be most pronounced in the far north, which was woefully neglected by the South Africans. The population there is typical of subsistence communities elsewhere in sub-Saharan Africa with a rural, agricultural-based economy and limited contact with the "modern" sector. Small changes (such as a village water bore well or the introduction of electricity) can make big differences in the way of life. Small improvements may ultimately lead to increased demands for other changes in the communities (such as more and better jobs and better education).

Thousands of refugees returned from Angola and Zambia under UNHCR auspices just prior to independence. Because of the loss of incomes due to the SADF withdrawal combined with the demands of these refugees, around sixty thousand people are looking for new employment, no more than one-third of which can be absorbed by the modern sector. Additionally, there is little prospect of integrating these people into the traditional rural economy in the short term.

The SWAPO government runs the risk of continually raising expectations past the point of no delivery. These services and demands must be met, and soon. Nevertheless, as eloquently stated by the late

Anton T.A.W. Lubowski, "Relative to the population of 1.5 to 2 million, we're talking about a wealthy country comparative to the population, [although] not in the international sense a rich country. Still, no one can tell me that there should be so much poverty here in this country if it's run properly."[10]

Nonetheless, if independence in other countries (such as Kenya, Zimbabwe, or the Ivory Coast) serves as an example, the white population may see few economic changes that affect it, certainly over the short term. Those whites who can accommodate political change may find their lifestyles essentially unchanged. For Namibia, the difference will be seen by the many South African public sector employees and their families, many of whom will return to South Africa and be replaced by black Namibians.

Namibia has certain advantages over other countries in the region at their respective times of independence. Namibia anticipated and planned for independence for a dozen years. As Lubowski suggested, "One of the advantages of being the last colony is that we've learned a lot from other independent countries, and this is an advantage of the returning exiles."[11] For the 1990s, the general worldwide move is toward more economic openness and creativity and less state involvement. Much depends on how effectively Namibia will attract foreign private investment (which declined by over 30 percent in the 1980s). The trend since independence has been promising. There have been substantial offers of official development assistance from countries such as the United States, the Federal Republic of Germany, and the United Kingdom as well as promises of priority support from the secretary-general of the United Nations and promises of a number of multi-million dollar private-sector projects by overseas investors. If it maintains the momentum and pursues a course of orderly economic growth combined with a maturing political system, Namibia has the potential to develop into one of the most successful and progressive democracies and economies in Africa.

NOTES

1. See United Nations Institute for Namibia, *Namibia: Perspectives for National Reconstruction and Development* (Lusaka: UNIN, 1986); UNIDO, *Industrial Development Programme for an Independent Namibia* (Vienna: UNIDO, 1984); and Harbans S. Aulakh and Wilfred W. Asombang, *Economic Development Strategies for Independent Namibia* (Lusaka: United Nations Institute for Namibia, 1985).

2. Interview with Dr. Wolfgang H. Thomas, general manager, Small Business Development Corporation, Cape Town, December 1988.

3. *Namibia Report*, I (7) (August 1990), p. 4.

4. Interview with Professor Fanuel Tjingaete, chairman, Department of Economics, University of Namibia, Windhoek, January 1989.

5. National Building and Investment Corporation, unpublished document, Windhoek.

6. See *Namibia Report*, I (3) (April 1990), p. 5.

7. Interview with Wolfgang Thomas, December 1988.

8. See *Namibia Report*, I (3) (April 1990), p. 6.

9. Economist Intelligence Unit, *Namibia, Botswana, Lesotho, Swaziland: Country Report*, 3 (London: EIU, 1990), p. 22.

10. Interview with Anton T.A.W. Lubowski, unofficial spokesman for SWAPO, Windhoek, January 1989.

11. Ibid.

Appendix A: The Mandate for South West Africa of the League of Nations

The Council of the League of Nations

Whereas in Article 119 of the Treaty of Peace with Germany signed at Versailles on June 28th, 1919, Germany renounced in favour of the Principal Allied and Associated Powers all her rights over her overseas possessions, including therein German South-West Africa; and

Whereas the Principal Allied and Associated Powers agreed that, in accordance with Article 22, Par 1 (Covenant of the League of Nations) of the said Treaty, a Mandate should be conferred upon His Britannic Majesty to be exercised on his behalf by the Government of the Union of South Africa to administer the territory aforementioned, and have proposed that the Mandate should be formulated in the following terms; and

Whereas His Britannic Majesty, for and on behalf of the Government of the Union of South Africa, has agreed to accept the Mandate in respect of the said territory and has undertaken to exercise it on behalf of the League of Nations in accordance with the following provisions; and

Whereas, by the aforementioned Article 22, paragraph 8, it is provided that the degree of authority, control or administration to be exercised by the Mandatory, not having been previously agreed upon by the Members of the League, shall be explicitly defined by the Council of the League of Nations:

Confirming the said mandate, defines its terms as follows:

Article 1. The Territory over which a mandate is conferred upon His Britannic Majesty for and on behalf of the Government of the Union of South Africa (hereinafter called the Mandatory) comprises the territory which formerly constituted the German Protectorate of South-West Africa.

Article 2. The Mandatory shall have full power of administration and legislation over the territory subject to the present Mandate as an integral portion

163

of the Union of South Africa, and may apply the laws of the Union of South Africa to the territory subject to such local modifications as circumstances may require. The Mandatory shall promote to the utmost the material and moral well-being and the social progress of the inhabitants of the territory subject to the present Mandate.

Article 3. The Mandatory shall see that the slave trade is prohibited, and that no forced labour is permitted, except for essential public works and services, and then only for adequate remuneration. The Mandatory shall also see that the traffic in arms and ammunition is controlled in accordance with principles analogous to those laid down in the Convention relating to the control of the arms trade, signed on September 10th, 1919, or in any Convention amending the same. The supply of intoxicating spirits and beverages to the natives shall be prohibited.

Article 4. The military training of the natives, otherwise than for purposes of internal police and the local defence of the territory, shall be prohibited. Furthermore, no military or naval bases shall be established or fortifications erected in the territory.

Article 5. Subject to the provisions of any local law for the maintenance of public order and public morals, the Mandatory shall ensure in the territory freedom of conscience and the free exercise of all forms of worship, and shall allow all missionaries, nationals of any State Member of the League of Nations, to enter into, travel and reside in the territory for the purpose of prosecuting their calling.

Article 6. The Mandatory shall make to the Council of the League of Nations an annual report to the satisfaction of the Council, containing full information with regard to the territory, and indicating the measures taken to carry out the obligations assumed under Articles 2, 3, 4 and 5.

Article 7. The consent of the Council of the League of Nations is required for any modification of the terms of the present Mandate. The Mandatory agrees that, if any dispute whatever should arise between the Mandatory and another Member of the League of Nations relating to the interpretation or the application of the provisions of the Mandate, such dispute, if it cannot be settled by negotiation, shall be submitted to the Permanent Council of International Justice provided for by Article 14 of the Covenant of the League of Nations.

The present Declaration shall be deposited in the archives of the League of Nations. Certified copies shall be forwarded by the Secretary-General of the League of Nations to all Powers Signatories of the Treaty of Peace with Germany.

Made at Geneva the 17th day of December, 1920.

Appendix B: Chronology of International Efforts

1920: South Africa is granted the mandate from the League of Nations. South West Africa is to be administered by South Africa on the behalf of the United Kingdom under Article 22 of the Covenant of the League of Nations as a "Class C" mandate.

1946: All mandatory powers are invited to transfer their mandates to trusteeship under the United Nations system. South Africa alone refuses.

1950: The International Court of Justice (ICJ) finds that South Africa has no legal obligation to place South West Africa under trusteeship but that the mandate is still in force.

1956: The ICJ confirms the General Assembly's right to adopt resolutions and hear petitions concerning South West Africa.

1960: Liberia and Ethiopia challenge South Africa's mandate.

1966: By one vote, the ICJ denies the right of Liberia and Ethiopia to bring the case to court.

1966: The General Assembly passes UN Resolution 2145, which terminates the mandate over South West Africa.

1967: The UN Council for South West Africa is created to administer the territory. It is refused landing rights in South West Africa.

1968: The United Nations recognizes the change of name from South West Africa to Namibia.

1969: The Security Council recognizes the General Assembly's right to revoke the mandate and requests that South Africa end its administration immediately.

1971: The ICJ declares the mandate lawfully terminated and calls the continued presence of South Africa in Namibia illegal.

1976: The Security Council unanimously passes UN Resolution 385, calling for South Africa to transfer power to the people of Namibia through free elections.

1977: Contact Group negotiations begin.

1978: UN Resolution 435 is adopted, calling for internationally supervised elections. It is supplemented in 1982, adding provisions for a Bill of Rights, a multiparty democracy, and an independent judiciary.

August 1988: Geneva Protocol sets Nov. 1, 1988, as date of implementation of UN Resolution 435. Angola and Cuba agree to Cuban withdrawal from Angola.

August 1988: SWAPO and South Africa agree to cease-fire. South Africa completes withdrawal of troops from Angola.

August–December 1988: Negotiations mediated by the United States at Brazzaville, the Congo.

December 1988: Brazzaville Protocol and Tripartite Agreement are signed. New date of UN Resolution 435 implementation set for April 1, 1989.

April 1, 1989: Implementation of UN 435 begins.

November 1, 1989: Elections for Constituent Assembly under UN supervision.

February 1990: Constituent Assembly unanimously adopts constitution.

March 21, 1990: Independence.

Appendix C: UN Security Council Resolution 435

Adopted by the Security Council on 29 September 1978

The Security Council Recalling its resolutions 385 (1976) and 431 (1978) and 432 (1978),

Having considered the report submitted by the Secretary-General pursuant to paragraph 20 resolution 431 (1978) (S/12827) and his explanatory statement made in the Security Council on 29 September 1978 (S/12869),

Taking note also of the letter dated 8 September 1978 from the President of the South West Africa People's Organization (SWAPO) addressed to the Secretary-General (5/12841),

Reaffirming the legal responsibility of the United Nations over Namibia,

1. *Approves* the report of the Secretary-General (S/12827) for the implementation of the proposal for a settlement of the Namibian situation (S/12636) and his explanatory statement (S/12869);

2. *Reinterates* that its objective is the withdrawal of South Africa's illegal administration of Namibia and the transfer of power to the people of Namibia with assistance of the United Nations in accordance with resolution 385 (1976);

3. *Decides* to establish under its authority a United Nations Transition Assistance Group (UNTAG) in accordance with the above-mentioned report of the Secretary-General for a period of up to 12 months in order to assist his Special Representative to carry out the mandate conferred upon him by paragraph 10~ Security Council resolution 431 (1978), namely, to ensure the early independence of Namibia through free and fair elections under the supervision and control of the United Nations;

4. *Welcomes* SWAPO's preparedness to co-operate in the implementation of the Secretary-General's report, including its expressed readiness to sign and observe the cease-fire provisions as manifested in the letter from the President of SWAPO dated 8 September 1978 (5/12841);

5. *Calls* on South Africa forthwith to co-operate with the Secretary-General, in the implementation of this resolution;

6. *Declares* that all unilateral measures taken by the illegal Administration in Namibia in relation to the electoral process, including unilateral registration of voters, or transfer power, in contravention of Security Council resolutions 385 (1976), 431 (1978) and this resolution are *null* and *void;*

7. *Requests* the Secretary-General to report to the Security Council not later than 28 October 1978 on the implementation of this resolution.

Appendix D:
UN Security Council
Resolution 435 as Supplemented

Letter dated 12 July 1982 from the Representatives of Canada, France, Germany, Federal Republic of, the United Kingdom of Great Britain and Northern Ireland and the United States of America, Addressed to the Secretary-General

On Instructions from our Governments we have the honour to transmit to you the text of Principles concerning the Constituent Assembly and the Constitution for an Independent Namibia put forward by our Governments to the parties concerned in the negotiations for the implementation of the proposal for a settlement of the Namibian situation (S/12636) in accordance with Security Council resolution 435 (1978) adopted on 29 September 1978.

We have pleasure in informing you that all parties to the negotiations now accept these Principles. Our Governments believe that a decision on the method to be employed to elect the Constituent Assembly should be made in accordance with the provision of Security Council Resolution 435 (1978).

All parties are agreed that this issue must be settled in accordance with the terms of Security Council resolution 435 (1978) and that the issue must not cause delay in the implementation of 435 (1978). In this regard, our Governments are in consultation with all parties.

Principles concerning the Constituent Assembly and the Constitution for an independent Namibia (S/15287)

CONSTITUENT ASSEMBLY

In accordance with United Nations Security Council Resolution 435 (1978), elections will be held to select a Constituent Assembly which will adopt a Constitution for an independent Namibia. The Constitution will determine the organization and powers of all levels of government.

- Every adult Namibian will be eligible, without discrimination or fear of intimidation from any source, to vote, campaign and stand for election to the Constituent Assembly.
- Voting will be by secret ballot, with provisions made for those who cannot read or write.
- The date for the beginning of the electoral campaign, the date of elections, the electoral system, the preparation of voters' rolls and the respective electoral procedures will be promptly decided upon so as to give all political parties and interested persons, without regard to their political views, a full and fair opportunity to organize and participate in the electoral process.
- Full freedom of speech, assembly, movement and press shall be guaranteed.
- The electoral system will seek to ensure fair representation in the Constituent Assembly to different political parties which gain substantial support in the election.

The Constituent Assembly will formulate the Constitution for an independent Namibia in accordance with the principles in Part B below and will adopt the Constitution as a whole by a two-thirds majority of its total membership.

Appendix E:
Protocol of Geneva

Delegations representing the Governments of the People's Republic of Angola, Republic of Cuba, and the Republic of South Africa, meeting in Geneva, Switzerland, 2–5 August 1988, with the mediation of Dr. Chester A. Crocker, Assistant Secretary of State for African Affairs, United States of America, have agreed as follows:

1. Each side agrees to recommend to the Secretary-General of the United Nations that 1 November 1988 be established as the date for implementation of UNSCR 435.

2. Each side agrees to the establishment of a target date for signature of the tripartite agreement among Angola, South Africa and Cuba not later than 10 September 1988.

3. Each side agrees that a schedule acceptable to all parties for the redeployment toward the North and the staged and total withdrawal of Cuban troops from Angola must be established by Angola and Cuba, who will request on-site verificatioin by the Security Council of the United Nations. The parties accept 1 September 1988 as the target date for reaching agreement on that schedule and all related matters.

4. The complete withdrawal of South African forces from Angola shall begin not later than 10 August 1988 and be completed not later than 1 September 1988.

5. The parties undertake to adopt the necessary measures of restraint in order to maintain the existing de facto cessation of hostilities. South Africa states its willingness to convey this commitment in writing to the Secretary-General of the United Nations. Angola and Cuba shall urge SWAPO to proceed likewise as a step prior to the cease-fire contemplated in Resolution 435 which will be established prior to 1 November 1988. Angola and Cuba shall use their good offices so that, once the total withdrawal of South African troops from Angola is completed, and within the context also of the cessation of hostilities in Namibia, SWAPO's forces will be deployed to the north of the 16th parallel. The parties deemed it appropriate that, during the period before 1 November

1988, a representative of the United Nations Secretary-General be present in Luanda to take cognizance of any disputes relative to the cessation of hostilities and agreed that the combined military committee contemplated in paragraph 9 can be an appropriate venue for reviewing complaints of this nature that may arise.

6. As of 10 August 1988, no Cuban troops will deploy or be south of the line Chitado-Ruacana Calueque-Nauliia-Cuamato-N'Giva. Cuba furthermore stated that upon completion of the withdrawal of the South African troops from Angola not later than 1 September 1988 and the restoration by the People's Republic of Angola of its sovereignty over its international boundaries, the Cuban troops will not take part in the offensive operations in the territory that lies east of meridian 17 and south of parallel 15 degrees, 30 minutes, provided that they are not subject to harassment.

7. Following the complete withdrawal of South African forces from Angola, the Government of Angola shall guarantee measures for the provision of water and power supply to Namibia.

8. With a view toward minimizing the risk of battlefield incidents and facillitating exchange of technical information related to implementation of the agreements reached, direct communications shall be established not later than 20 August 1988 between the respective military commanders at appropriate headquarters along the Angola-Namibia border.

9. Each side recognizes that the period from 1 September 1988, by which time South African forces will have completed their withdrawal from Angola, and the date established for implementation of UNSCR 435, is a period of particular sensitivity, for which specific guidelines for military activities are presently lacking. In the interest of maintaining the cease-fire and maximizing the conditions for the orderly introduction of UNTAG, the sides agree to establish a combined military committee to develop additional practical measures to build confidence and reduce the risk of unintended incidents. They invite United States membership on the committee.

10. Each side will act in accordance with the Governor's Island principles, including paragraph E (non-interference in the internal affairs of states) and paragraph G (the acceptance of the responsibility of states not to allow their territory to be used for acts of war, aggression, or violence against other states).

Signed at Geneva on 5 August 1988.

Appendix F:
Tripartite Agreement

Agreement among the People's Republic of Angola, the Republic of Cuba and the Republic of South Africa

The governments of the People's Republic of Angola, the Republic of Cuba and the Republic of South Africa, hereinafter designated as the Parties,

Taking into account the Principles for a Peaceful Settlement in Southwestern Africa, approved by the parties on 20 July 1988, and the subsequent negotiations with respect to the implementation of these Principles, each of which is indispensable to a comprehensive settlement,

Considering the acceptance by the Parties of the Implementation of United Nations Security Council Resolution 435 (1978), adopted on 29 September 1978, hereinafter designated as UNSCR 435,

Considering the conclusion of the bilateral agreement between the People's Republic of Angola and the Republic of Cuba providing for the redeployment toward the North and the staged and total withdrawal of Cuban troops from the territory of the People's Republic of Angola,

Recognizing the role of the United Nations Security Council in implementing UNSCR 435/78 and in support of the implementation of the present agreement,

Affirming the sovereighty, sovereign equality, and independence of all states of southwestern Africa,

Affirming the principle of non-interference in the internal affairs of states,

Affirming the principle of abstention from the threat or use of force against the territorial integrity or political independence of states,

Reaffirming the right of the peoples of the southwestern region of Africa to self-determination, independence, and equality of rights, and of the states of southwestern Africa to peace, development, and social progress,

Urging African and international co-operation for the settlement of the problems of the development of the southwestern region of Africa,

Expressing their appreciation for the mediating role of the Government of the United States of America, desiring to contribute to the establishment of peace and security in southwestern Africa,

Agree to the provisions set forth below.

1. The Parties shall immediately request the Secretary-General of the United Nations to seek authority from the Security Council to commence implementation of UNSCR 435 on 1 April 1989.

2. All military forces of the Republic of South Africa shall depart Namibia in accordance with UNSCR 435/78.

3. Consistent with the provisions of UNSCR 435, the Republic of South Africa and the People's Republic of Angola shall co-operate with the Secretary-General to ensure the independence of Namibia through free and fair elections and shall abstain from any action that could prevent the execution of UNSCR 435/78. The Parties shall respect the territorial integrity and inviolability of borders of Namibia and shall ensure that their territories are not used by any state, organization, or person in connection with acts of war, aggression, or violence against the territorial integrity or inviolability of borders of Namibia or any other action which could prevent the execution of UNSCR 435.

4. The People's Republic of Angola and the Republic of Cuba shall implement the bilateral agreement, signed on the date of signature of this agreement, providing for the redeployment toward the North and the staged and total withdrawal of Cuban troops from the territory of the People's Republic of Angola, and the arrangements made with the Security Council of the United Nations of the on-site verification of that withdrawal.

5. Consistent with their obligations under the Charter of the United Nations, the Parties shall refrain from the threat or use of force, and shall ensure that their respective territories are not used by any state, organization, or person in connection with any acts of war, aggression, or violence against the territorial integrity, inviolability of orders, or independence of any state of southwestern Africa.

6. The Parties shall respect the principle of non-interference in the internal affairs of the states of southwestern Africa.

7. The Parties shall comply in good faith with all obligations undertaken in this agreement and shall resolve through negotiation and in a spirit of cooperation any disputes with respect to the interpretation or implementation thereof.

8. This agreement shall enter into force upon signature.

Signed at New York in triplicate in the Portuguese, Spanish, and English versions, each version being equally authentic, this 22nd day of December 1988.

Appendix G: The Government at Independence

President	Sam Shafiishuna Nujoma
Prime minister in charge of public service personnel	Hage Gottifried Geingob

Ministers

Foreign Affairs	Theo-Ben Gurirab
Defense	Peter Mueshihange
Finance	Otto Herrigel
Information and Broadcasting	Hidipo Hamutenya
Home Affairs	Hifikepunye Pohamba
Trade and Industry	Ben Amathila
Mines and Energy	Andimba Toivo ya Toivo
Works, Transport, and Communications	Richard Kapelwa
Labour, Public Service, and Manpower Development	Hendrik Witbooi
Agriculture, Fisheries, Water, and Rural Development	Gerhard Hanekom
Wildlife, Conservation, and Tourism	Nico Bessinger

175

Education, Culture, and Sport   Nahas Angula

Health and Social Services   Nicky Iyambo

Local Government and Housing   Libertine Amathila

Lands, Resettlement, and Rehabilitation   Marco Hausiku

Justice   Ngarukutuke Tjiriange

Appendix H: Goals of the SWAPO Women's Council

1. To achieve equality for women as well as their full participation in the struggle for national and social liberation;

2. To develop and deepen political consciousness and revolutionary militancy among the Namibian women;

3. To bring about women's full participation in productive work, in public administration, in education, and in the cultural creativity of Namibian society;

4. To prepare the thousands of female workers, now engaged in domestic work in Namibia, for productive jobs;

5. To campaign for the creation of sufficient nursery schools and day boarding schools in a liberated Namibia as to facilitate women's full participation in productive work;

6. To inculcate in the Namibian child a sense of justice and revolutionary respect for women; and,

7. To develop an internationalist spirit in the Namibian woman by enabling her to work in solidarity with all militant and progressive female movements thereby strengthening the worldwide anti-imperialist, and anti-colonialist fronts.

Source: Constitution of the SWAPO Women's Council.

Selected Bibliography

Africa Confidential. April 14, 1989.

Africa Today. "Namibia and the West: Multinational Corporations and International Law." Denver: University of Denver, 1983, 123 pp.

African-American Scholars Council, Inc. *Zimbabwe, Namibia. Anticipation of Economic and Humanitarian Needs: Transition Problems in Developing Nations in Southern Africa.* Washington, DC: United States Agency for International Development, 1977.

Allison, Caroline. "Women in Waged Employment: Some Basic Information and Questions of Relevance to a Future Independent Namibia." In *Namibia: 1884–1984; Readings on Namibian History and Society,* ed. Brian Wood. London: Namibia Support Committee, 1988, pp. 358–362.

Anderson, Neil, and Shula Marks. "Work and Health in Namibia: Preliminary Notes." *Journal of Southern African Studies* 13 (1987), pp. 274–292.

Angula, Helmut. "Tracing the History of the San." In *Namibia: 1884–1984; Readings on Namibian History and Society,* ed. Brian Wood. London: Namibia Support Committee, 1988, pp. 102–114.

Asombang, Wilfred W. *Trade Policy Options for Independent Namibia.* Lusaka: United Nations Institute for Namibia, 1982.

Aulakh, Harbans S. and Wilfred W. Asombang. *Mineral Development Strategy Options for Independent Namibia.* Lusaka: United Nations Institute for Namibia, 1982.

———. *Economic Development Strategies for Independent Namibia.* Lusaka: United Nations Institute for Namibia, 1985.

Bley, Helmut. *South-West Africa Under German Rule, 1894–1914.* Evanston: Northwestern University Press, 1971.

Business International Conference. "Southern Africa: What Namibian Independence Will Mean for Business: Summary of Proceedings and Conclusions." London, April 1989.

Calvert, Albert F. *South West Africa During the German Occupation, 1884–1914.* New York: Negro University Press, 1915.

Catholic Institute for International Relations. "South African Occupation and the Namibian Economy." London: CIIR, 1984, 11 pp.

178

————. *Namibia in the 1980s*. London: British Council of Churches, 1981.

Clarence-Smith, Gervase. "The Angolan Connection in Namibian History." In *Namibia: 1884–1984; Readings on Namibian History and Society*, ed. Brian Wood. London: Namibia Support Committee, 1988.

Clarence-Smith, Gervase, and Richard Moorsam. "Underdevelopment and Class Formation in Ovamboland, 1844–1917." In *Namibia: 1884–1984; Readings on Namibia's History and Society*, ed. Brian Wood. London: Namibia Support Committee, 1988, pp. 175–189

Clark, J. Desmond, ed. *The Cambridge History of Africa, Volume I*. Cambridge: Cambridge University Press, 1987.

Collett, Sue. "Small and Medium-Sized Enterprises in Southwest Africa/Namibia." *South African Journal of Economics* 48 (3) (1980), pp. 276–287.

Cooper, Allan D. *U.S. Economic Power and Political Influence in Namibia, 1700–1982*. Boulder: Westview Press, 1982.

————. *Allies in Apartheid: Western Capital in Occupied Namibia*. London: Macmillan, 1988.

Dale, Richard. "The Armed Forces as an Instrument of South African Policy in Namibia." *Journal of Modern African Studies* 18 (1980), pp. 57–71.

Douwes-Dekker, Loet, et al. "Case Studies in African Labour Action in South Africa and Namibia." In *The Development of an African Working Class*, ed. Richard Sandbrook and Robin Cohen. Toronto: University of Toronto Press, 1975.

Drechsler, Horst. *The Struggle of the Herero and Nama Against German Imperialism, 1884–1915*. London: Zed Press, 1980.

Dugard, John. "Legal Aspects of Investment in Namibia." In John Dugard, *The Role of Foreign Firms in Namibia*. London: Study Project on External Investment in South Africa and Namibia, 1974, pp. 183–216.

du Pisani, Andre. *SWA/Namibia: The Politics of Continuity and Change*. Johannesburg: J. Ball Publishers, 1985.

————. "History and Politics in Namibia: The Historical Legacy." In *Namibia in Perspective*, ed. Gerhard Totemeyer, Vezera Kandetu, and Wolfgang Werner. Windhoek: Council of Churches of Namibia, 1987, pp. 13–26.

Economic Commission for Africa. *Transport Survey for Namibia: Report of a Multidisciplinary Team of Experts*. Addis Ababa: ECA, n.d.

Economist Intelligence Unit. *Namibia, Botswana, Lesotho, and Swaziland: Country Report*. London: EIU, various years.

Ellis, Justin. *Education, Repression and Liberation*. London: Catholic Institute for International Relations, 1984.

Emmett, Tony. "Popular Resistance in Namibia, 1920–5." In *Resistance and Ideology in Settler Societies*, ed. Tom Lodge. Johannesburg: Ravan, 1986.

ENOK/First National Development Corporation. "Information for Investors." Windhoek: ENOK, 1984, 24 pp.

Evenson, John A. "The Transition Timetable." *Africa Report* (March–April 1989).

Fage, J. D., ed. *The Cambridge History of Africa, Volume 2*. Cambridge: Cambridge University Press, 1986.

Fage, J. D., and Roland Oliver, eds. *The Cambridge History of Africa, Volume 6*. Cambridge: Cambridge University Press, 1985.

Falk, Pamela. "Cuba in Africa." *Foreign Affairs* 65 (1987).

Financial Mail. "Namibia: A Survey." Johannesburg, 40 pp. (a supplement to the *Financial Mail* July 2, 1983).

First, Ruth. *South West Africa.* Baltimore: Penguin Books, 1963.

Flint, John E., ed. *The Cambridge History of Africa, Volume 5.* Cambridge: Cambridge University Press, 1976.

Food and Agriculture Organization of the United Nations. *Namibia: Prospects for Future Development.* Rome: FAO, 1977.

German Development Institute. *Perspectives of Independent Development in Southern Africa: The Cases of Zimbabwe and Namibia.* Berlin: GDI, 1980.

Gervasi, Sean. "The South West African Economy." In *South West Africa: A Travesty of Trust,* ed. Ronald Segal and Ruth First. London: Deutsch, 1967, pp. 128–150.

Gibson, Gordon D., Thomas J. Larson, and Cecilia R. McGurk. *The Kavango People.* Wiesbaden: Frantz Steiner Verlag, 1981.

Ginwala, Frene. "Women's Oppression and National Liberation from Apartheid." In *Namibia: 1884–1984; Readings on Namibian History and Society,* ed. Brian Wood. London: Namibia Support Committee, 1988, pp. 49–52.

Goldblatt, Israel. *The Mandated Territory of South West Africa in Relation to the United Nations.* Cape Town: C. Struik, 1961.

————. *History of South West Africa.* Cape Town: Juta and Company, 1971.

Gordon, Robert J. *Mines, Masters and Migrants: Life in a Namibian Compound.* Johannesburg: Raven Press, 1977.

Gottschalk, Keith. "Restructuring the Colonial State: Pretoria's Strategy in Namibia." In *Namibia in Perspective,* ed. Gerhard Totemeyer, Vezera Kandetu, and Wolfgang Werner. Windhoek: Council of Churches of Namibia, 1987, pp. 27–35.

Gray, Richard. *The Cambridge History of Africa, Volume 4.* Cambridge: Cambridge University Press, 1975.

Green, Reginald H. *Manpower Estimates and Development Implications for Namibia.* Lusaka: United Nations Institute for Namibia, 1978.

————. *Namibia: A Political Economic Survey.* Sussex: University of Sussex, 1979, 123 pp. (Institute of Development Studies Discussion Paper No. 144).

————. "The Unforgiving Land: Basis for a Post-Independence Liberation Programme in Namibia." *IDS Bulletin* 11 (1980), pp. 70–76.

————. "Transition to What? Some Issues of Freedom and Necessity in Namibia." *Development and Change* 11 (3) (July 1980), pp. 419–453.

————. *From Sudwestafrika to Namibia: The Political Economy of Transition.* Uppsala: Scandinavian Institute of African Studies, 1981.

————. "One Namibia, One Nation: The Political Economy of Transition." In Reginald H. Green, *Changing Realities in Southern Africa.* Berkeley: Institute of International Studies, 1982, pp. 92–122.

Green, Reginald H., M. Kiljunen, and K. Kiljunen, eds. *Namibia: The Last Colony.* London: Longman, 1981.

Hamutenya, Hidipo L., and Gotfried H. Geingob. "African Nationalism in Namibia." In *Southern Africa in Perspective,* ed. Christian P. Potholm and Richard Dale. New York: The Free Press, 1972.

Hartman, P. W. "SWA/Namibia: Some Economic Problems and Prospects." *Bulletin of the Africa Institute of South Africa* 24 (5) (1984), pp. 51–53.

Heinz, Hunke. "The Role of European Missionaries in Namibia." In *Namibia: 1884–1984; Readings on Namibian History and Society*, ed. Brian Wood. London: Namibia Support Committee, 1988, pp. 627–634.

Hishongwa, Ndeutala Selma. *Women of Namibia*. Stockholm: By and Bygd, 1983.

Hoernle, Winifred. *The Social Organization of the Nama*. Johannesburg: Witwatersrand University Press, 1985.

Jaster, Robert S. "The 1988 Peace Accords and the Future of South-western Africa." Adelphi Papers No. 253 (London: IISS, 1990).

Katjavivi, Peter. *A History of Resistance in Namibia*. London: James Curry, Ltd., 1988.

"Katutura Revisited, 1986: Essays on a Black Namibian Apartheid Suburb." *Series of Social Research, No. 1*. Windhoek: Angelus Publishing Co., 1986.

Kazombaue, Lindy, and Nashilongo Elago. "The Exploited Women in Namibia: A Testimony." In *Namibia in Perspective*, ed. Gerhard Totemeyer, Vezera Kandetu, and Wolfgang Werner. Windhoek: Council of Churches of Namibia, 1987, pp. 196–204.

Kok, Leon. "The Namibian Economy." *Rossing* (February 1979), pp. 12–15.

Lau, Brigitte. *Southern and Central Namibia in Jonker Afrikaner's Time*. Windhoek: National Archives, 1987.

———. "'Pre-colonial' Namibian Historiography: What Is to Be Done?" In *Namibia: 1884–1984; Readings on Namibian History and Society*, ed. Brian Wood. London: Namibia Support Committee, 1988, pp. 90–101.

Leistner, G.M.E. "Public Finance in South West Africa 1945/6 to 1969/70." *South African Journal of Economics* (1) (1972), pp. 1–32.

———. "Is South Africa Exploiting SWA/Namibia Economically?" *Africa Insight* 11 (1) (1981), pp. 23–24.

———. "SWA/Namibia's Economic Problems Viewed in an African Context." *Africa Institute of South Africa Bulletin* 21 (11–12) (1981), pp. 81–86.

Leistner, G.M.E., P. Esterhuysen, and T. Malan. *Namibia/SWA Prospectus*. Pretoria: Africa Institute of South Africa, 1980.

Lobstein, Tim, and the Namibia Support Committee Health Collective, eds. *Namibia: Reclaiming the People's Health*. London: Namibia Support Committee, 1988.

Loomis-Price, Lynne. *Education for Namibians: A Workshop Report*. New York: Institute of International Education, 1989.

McFadden, Patricia. "Forms and Spheres of Anti-Colonial Resistance with Special Reference to Namibia." In *Namibia: 1884–1984; Readings on Namibian History and Society*, ed. Brian Wood. London: Namibia Support Committee, 1988, pp. 622–626.

Mensah, J. H. "Review of the Economic Conditions in Namibia and South Africa: Part I: Namibia." Geneva: UNCTAD, 1981, 49 pp.

Moleah, Alfred T. *Namibia: The Struggle for Liberation*. Wilmington, DE: Disa Press, 1983.

Moorsom, Richard. "Underdevelopment, Contract Labor and Worker Consciousness in Namibia, 1915–72." *Journal of Southern African Studies* 17 (October 1977), pp. 71–82.

————. *Walvis Bay: Namibia's Port.* London: International Defense and Aid Fund for Southern Africa, 1984.

Morna, Colleen Lowe. "The Development Challenge." *Africa Report* 35 (2) (March/April 1990).

Murray, Roger. *The Mineral Industry of Namibia: Perspectives for Independence.* London: Commonwealth Secretariat, 1978.

Murray, Roger, John Dugard, and Neville Rubin. *The Role of Foreign Firms in Namibia: Studies on External Investment and Black Workers' Conditions in Namibia.* London: Study Project on External Investment in South Africa and Namibia, 1974.

Murray-Hudson, Anne. "SWAPO: Solidarity with Our Sisters." In *Namibia: 1884–1984; Readings on Namibian History and Society*, ed. Brian Wood. London: Namibia Support Committee, 1988, pp. 616–621.

Namibia Report 1, February 1990; June 1990; July 1990.

Oliver, Roland, ed. *The Cambridge History of Africa, Volume 3.* Cambridge: Cambridge University Press, 1977.

Overseas Development Institute. *Economic Prospects for Namibia.* Briefing Paper. London: ODI, August 1989.

Putz, Joe, Heidi von Egidy, and Perri Caplan. *Namibia Handbook and Political Who's Who of Namibia.* Windhoek: Magus Company, 1990.

Republic of South Africa. *Industrial Strategy for SWA/Namibia.* Windhoek: ENOK, 1987.

————. *The National Development Strategy of South West Africa.* Windhoek: Department of Governmental Affairs, 1987.

Rogers, Barbara. *Foreign Investment in Namibia.* New York: UN Council for Namibia, 1975.

Rotberg, Robert I., ed. *Namibia: Political and Economic Prospects.* Lexington: Lexington Books, 1983.

————. "Namibia and the Crisis of Constructive Engagement." In *African Crisis Areas*, ed. Bender and Coleman. Berkeley: University of California Press, 1985.

Ruppel, Hartmut. "Namibia: Security and Its Consequences." In *Namibia in Perspective*, ed. Gerhard Totemeyer, Vezera Kandetu, and Wolfgang Werner. Windhoek: Council of Churches of Namibia, 1987, pp. 227–238.

Sano, H. O., and J. Koponen, et al. *Namibia and the Nordic Countries.* Uppsala: Scandinavian Institute of African Studies, 1981.

Savosnick, Kurt. *Economics of the Namibian Diamond Industry.* Geneva: UNCTAD, 1978.

Schneider-Barthold, Wolfgang. *Namibia's Economic Potential and Existing Ties with the Republic of South Africa.* Berlin: German Development Institute, 1977.

————. "The Phenomenon of External and Internal Dependence in the Namibian Manufacturing Industry and Prospects of Overcoming It." In Hartmut Brandt, et al., *Perspectives of Independent Development in Southern Africa.* Berlin: German Development Institute, 1980, pp. 100–127.

Schrank, Gilbert I. *German SWA: Social and Economic Aspects of Its History, 1884–1915.* Ph.D. dissertation, New York University, 1974.

Segal, Ronald, and Ruth First. *SWA: Travesty of Trust.* London: Andre Deutsch, 1967.

Seiler, John. "South Africa in Namibia: Persistence, Misperception, and Ultimate Failure." *Journal of Modern African Studies* 20 (1982), pp. 689–712.

Simon, David. "Decolonisation and Local Government in Namibia: The Neo-Apartheid Plan, 1977–83." *Journal of Modern African Studies* 23 (1985), pp. 507–526.

Smith, Susanna. *Namibia: A Violation of Trust.* Oxford: Oxfam, 1986.

Soggot, David. *Namibia: The Violent Heritage.* New York: St. Martin's Press, 1986.

South African Department of Foreign Affairs. *SWA Survey, 1967.* Pretoria: Cape and Transvaal Printers, Ltd., 1967.

Southern African Development Coordination Conference. *Namibia.* Arusha: SADCC Secretariat, 1979.

South West Africa Administration. *The Economy of SWA/Namibia: Problems, Future Prospects and Required Policy Measures.* Windhoek: Department of Finance, 1978.

Sparks, Donald L. "Walvis Bay, Plumpudding and Penguin Islands: Their History and Economic Importance to Namibia." Paper presented to the 22nd annual meeting of the African Studies Association, Los Angeles, 1979.

––––––. "Namibia's Future: Prospects for the Economy and Foreign Involvement." *Multinational Business* 1 (1983), pp. 11–21.

––––––. "Namibia's Coastal and Marine Resources Potential." *African Affairs, The Journal of the Royal African Society,* 334 (January 1985), pp. 477–496.

Sparks, Donald L., and Roger Murray. *Namibia's Future: The Economy at Independence.* (EIU Special Report No. 197). London: The Economist Intelligence Unit, 1985.

SWAPO Department of Information and Publicity. *To Be Born a Nation: The Liberation Struggle for Namibia.* London: Zed Press, 1981.

SWAPO Women's Council. *Namibian Women's Struggle and Solidarity in Britain.* London: SWAPO Women's Solidarity Campaign, 1981.

––––––. "Namibian Women in Production." In *Namibia: 1884–1984; Readings on Namibian History and Society,* ed. Brian Wood. London: Namibia Support Committee, 1988, pp. 347–350.

SWAPO Women's Solidarity Campaign. "Education for Subservience and Liberation: Another Perspective." In *Namibia: 1884–1984; Readings on Namibian History and Society,* ed. Brian Wood. London: Namibia Support Committee, 1988, pp. 425–430.

––––––. "Women in Production and Reproduction." In *Namibia: 1884–1984; Readings on Namibian History and Society,* ed. Brian Wood. London: Namibia Support Committee, 1988, pp. 351–357.

Thomas, Wolfgang H. *Economic Development in Namibia: Toward Acceptable Development Strategies for an Independent Namibia.* Munich: Kaiser, 1978.

––––––. *Employment Generation in the Context of a Basic Needs-Oriented Development Strategy for Namibia.* Windhoek: Private Sector Foundation, 1982.

——. "The Economy in Transition to Independence." In Robert I. Rotberg, *Namibia: Political and Economic Prospects.* London: D. C. Heath & Co., 1983, pp. 41–91.

Tostensen, Arne. "Independent Namibia in the Southern African Region." Paper presented to the Conference on Research Priorities in Namibia, Institute of Commonwealth Studies, University of London, London, 1984.

Totemeyer, Gerhard. *Namibia Old and New.* London: C. Hurst, 1978.

Totemeyer, Gerhard, Vezera Kandetu, and Wolfgang Werner. eds. *Namibia in Perspective.* Windhoek: Council of Churches of Namibia, 1987.

Tuupainen, Maija. *Marriage in a Matrilineal African Tribe: A Social Anthropological Study of Marriage in the Ondonga Tribe in Ovamboland.* Helsinki: Academic Bookstore, 1970.

United Nations Centre on Transnational Corporations. *Role of Transnational Corporations in Namibia.* New York: UNCTC, 1982 (draft).

United Nations Council for Namibia. "Activities of Foreign Economic Interests Operating in Namibia." Paper presented to the International Conference in Support for the Struggle of the Namibian People for Independence, Paris, 1983.

United Nations Development Programme. *Report of the Reconnaissance Mission to Namibia.* New York: UNDP, June 1989.

United Nations Industrial Development Organization. *Industrial Development Programme for an Independent Namibia.* Vienna: UNIDO, 1984.

——. *Namibia: Industrial Development at Independence.* Vienna: UNIDO, 1990.

United Nations Institute for Namibia. "Planning for Namibian Independence: Manpower Development Strategies." New York: United Nations, 1983.

——. "Brainstorming Meeting on the Comprehensive Study: *Namibia: Perspectives for National Reconstruction and Development.*" Lusaka: UNIN, 1986.

——. *Namibia: Perspectives for National Reconstruction and Development.* Lusaka: UNIN, 1986.

United States Agency for International Development. *A Report to the Congress on Development Needs and Opportunities for Cooperation in Southern Africa. Annex A: Namibia.* Washington, DC: USAID, 1979.

University of Stellenbosch Transport Research Centre. *Report on an Investigation into the Potential Development at Walvis Bay.* Stellenbosch: USTRC, 1977.

Unterhalter, Elaine. "White Supremacy, the Colonial State, and the Subordination of Women: Some Notes and Questions." In *Namibia: 1884–1984; Readings on Namibian History and Society,* ed. Brian Wood. London: Namibia Support Committee, 1988, pp. 547–550.

van der Merew, J. H., ed. *National Atlas of South West Africa.* Goodwood, Cape: National Book Printers, 1983.

Vedder, Heinrich. *South West Africa in Early Times.* New York: Barnes and Noble, 1966.

Wallenkampf, Arnold Valentin. *The Herero Rebellion in SWA, 1904–1906: A Study of German Colonialism.* Ph.D. dissertation, University of California, Los Angeles, 1969.

Weaver, Tony. "Namibian Review." *South African Review* 2 (1984), pp. 211–227.

Wood, Brian, ed. *Namibia: 1884–1984; Readings on Namibian History and Society.* London: Namibia Support Committee and United Nations Institute for Namibia, 1988.

Wright, Quincy. *Mandates Under the League of Nations.* Chicago: University of Chicago Press, 1930.

Zorn, Stephen. *The Mineral Sector in Namibia and Strategic Options for an Independent Government.* New York: Office of Technical Cooperation, 1978.

Interviews

Dr. M. Hartman, chief, economic policy, Directorate of Fiscal & Monetary Policy, Department of Finance, Windhoek. Interviewed by Donald L. Sparks in Windhoek, January 1989 and March 1990.

Brett Hone, superintendent industrial and public relations, Rössing Uranium. Interviewed by Donald L. Sparks in Arandis, March 21, 1990.

Maria Kapere, deputy director of information and publicity, SWAPO. Interviewed by December Green, SWAPO Campaign Headquarters, Windhoek, August 9, 1989.

Nelago Kasuto, lawyer. Interviewed by December Green, Private Office, Windhoek, August 3, 1989.

Steve Kessler, general manager, Rössing Uranium. Interviewed by Donald L. Sparks in Arandis, March 21, 1990.

Anton T.A.W. Lubowski, unofficial spokesman for SWAPO. Interviewed by Donald L. Sparks in Windhoek, January 1989.

Mr. H.A.R. Meiring, former chairman, Namibian Chamber of Mines (former executive director of Tsumeb Corp., Ltd.). Interviewed by Donald L. Sparks in Swakopmund, January 1989.

Dr. Wolfgang H. Thomas, general manager, Small Business Development Corporation, Ltd., Cape Town (formerly professor, University of Cape Town). Interviewed by Donald L. Sparks in Cape Town, December 1988.

Dr. Fanuel Tjingaete, chairman, Department of Economics, University of Namibia, Windhoek. Interviewed by Donald L. Sparks in Windhoek, January 1989 and March 1990.

About the Book and Authors

Namibia, formerly South West Africa, is a vast, sparsely populated country the size of France. The last African colony to achieve independence, it represents a watershed in the African political experience. Namibia faces formidable political and economic challenges; constraints to growth and development include a lack of skilled workers, a low capital formation base, small internal markets, poor prospects for import substitution, and a potentially uneasy relationship with South Africa, its economically powerful neighbor to the south. Nevertheless, Namibia has some of the world's largest deposits of yellow cake uranium and diamonds. Its location could prove attractive for mineral exports to the North American and Western European markets.

This introduction to Namibia surveys the contemporary trends in the country's political, social, and economic development. The authors examine the lessons Namibia—which had over a decade to plan for independence—has learned from the experience of its neighbors concerning the workings of the international economic system and the subtleties of relations with South Africa. They conclude that the independent, SWAPO-led government must find a pragmatic path to develop an economy with the potential to be one of southern Africa's strongest.

Donald L. Sparks is associate professor of economics at the Citadel; he was formerly regional economist for Africa, Office of Economic Analysis, U.S. Department of State. **December Green** is assistant professor of politics and director of non-Western studies at the Citadel; she formerly worked for the Commission on Security and Cooperation in Europe.

Index

ACP. *See* African, Caribbean, and Pacific States

Action Christian National Party, 5, 54, 58

Activists, 24, 33, 140

Adimishin, Anatoly, 67–68

Affirmative action, 99

African, Caribbean, and Pacific States (ACP), EEC and, 111

African Development Bank, 113

African Methodist Episcopal (AME) church, 25, 141
  political agenda of, 139–140

African National Congress (ANC), 63, 67
  guerrilla training for, 66
  SWAPO and, 65–66

Afrikaans, 2, 137, 138
  teaching in, 145, 147

Afrikaner, Jager, 9

Afrikaner, Jonker, 9

Afrikaners, 138
  emigration of, 11, 17

Agriculture, 1
  aid in, 114
  capital-intensive, 89
  employment in, 98
  foreign investment in, 90
  growth of, 123, 124
  role of, 89–91
  subsistence, 5, 73, 89, 90, 98, 132, 134

See also Farms

Agro-industry, 91, 123

Ahtisaari, Martti, 54, 67

AIDS, extent of, 151

Alcoholism, 149

Amadhila, Soloman: on health issues, 150

Amathila, Ben, 104, 158, 175

Amathila, Libertine, 59, 142, 159, 176

AME church. *See* African Methodist Episcopal church

Amnesty International, investigation by, 53

ANC. *See* African National Congress

Andersson, Charles, 8

Anglican church, 139, 141

Anglo American Corp., 80

Angola
  Cuban withdrawal from, 49
  mediation by, 64
  South African activity in, 35
  trade with, 108

Angula, Helmuth, 149

Angula, Nahas, 57, 147, 160, 176

Antiapartheid movements, 65–66

Anticonscription campaign, 34
  Lutheran church and, 140

Apartheid, 3, 16, 19, 20, 27, 29, 30, 38, 61, 63, 140
  contract labor and, 18
  education and, 24–25, 145
  health care and, 151

opposition to, 27, 40, 43, 65–66, 69
petty, 42
women and, 141
See also Racism
Arandis, 86
Artisan workshops, 99
Assassinations, 52–53
Augustineum College, blacks at, 26
Automobile and Metal Workers Union, 100

Baker, James, 67
Bank of Botswana, 102
Bantustan system, 19–20, 29, 38, 98, 145
Barclays Bank, 103
Base minerals, 76
  lower demand for, 115
  prices for, 87
  production of, 86–87
  See also Minerals; Various minerals by name
Basters, 24, 42, 135, 138
Beef processing, 89, 113, 123
Bender, Gerald: on Constructive Engagement, 47
Benguela (research vessel), 94
Benguela Current, fishing in, 92
Bessinger, Nico, 175
Bill of Rights, 3, 61, 156, 166
Biological and Toxic Weapons Convention, 34
Birth rate, 138, 148
Black majority rule, 39
Bondelswaarts, 12, 137
Bondelswaarts Rebellion of 1922, 24
Botha, Louis, 14
Botha, Pik, 12, 45, 54
Botswana, 66
  joint venture with, 81, 84
  Lome IV and, 114
  PTA and, 109
  rail link through, 110
  trade with, 108
Boundaries, establishing, 8–9
Boycotts, 26, 47. *See also* Strikes

Brazzaville Accord, 48, 49, 166
Budget deficits, 104, 119
Bulozi system, 135
Bush, George, 115
Bushman Alliance, 42
Business International, 119

Cabinet ministers, appointment of, 56–57, 59
Cadmium, 76
Canada, relations with, 67
Cancer, 149, 150, 153(n41)
  deaths from, 148
CANU. *See* Caprivi African National Union
Cape Cross, port at, 107
Capital punishment, abolition of, 61
Caprivi, 1, 2, 33
  clans of, 135
  guerrilla warfare in, 31
  population of, 135
Caprivi African National Union (CANU), 56
Caprivi Alliance Party, 42
Carter, Jimmy: Constructive Engagement and, 44–45
Castro, Fidel, 48
CDA. *See* Christian Democratic Action for Social Justice
CDM. *See* Consolidated Diamond Mines
Cease-fire, 48–49
Central bank, establishing, 120
Central planning, 158. *See also* Socialism
Central Selling Organization (CSO), 82, 110
Chemical warfare, 34
Child care, 142
Child mortality, 150
Children, rights of, 144
Christian Democratic Action for Social Justice (CDA), 58
Christianity, 137, 138, 139
Christian National Education (CNE), 145

Churches
  apartheid and, 140
  black, 139, 140, 141
  health care and, 151
  nationalism and, 139–140
  types of, 141
  white, 139
  See also Religion
Church of the Province of Southern
  Africa, 141
Clans, 5–6, 134–135
Climate, 1–2
CNE. *See* Christian National Education
Coal, developing, 110
Coalition politics, 55–56, 156. *See also*
  Parties
Cold war, 48, 67, 70–71(n28)
College for Out-of-School Training,
  147
Colonialism, 7, 10, 144
  break from, 15, 62
  German, 11–14
  resistance to, 23, 32
  South African, 14–20
  See also Decolonization
Commerce, employment in, 98
Commission for the Prevention and
  Combatting of Intimidation and
  Election Malpractices (O'Linn
  Commission), 52
Common Currency Area, 101, 102
Commonwealth, membership in, 68–
  69
Commonwealth Namibia Programme,
  147
Communications, 74
  cooperation in, 109
  employment in, 98
Concessional status, gaining, 113
Conciliation boards, MUN and, 159
Conference of Berlin, 8, 11
Consolidated Diamond Mines (CDM),
  76, 80, 101, 124
  employment by, 82
  overmining by, 81
  production by, 84
  profit by, 82

  transfer pricing by, 81
Constituent Assembly, 56, 70(n20)
  constitution by, 156
  elections for, 166
  powers of, 60
  UN and, 169–170
  women's issues and, 144
  See also National Assembly
Constitution, 59
  adoption of, 156, 170
  changing, 60
  SWAPO and, 52, 55
  UN and, 169
  whites and, 38
Construction, 129(n63)
  employment in, 98
  growth of, 117–118
Constructive Engagement, 47, 48
  Carter and, 44–45
  Contact Group and, 46
Contact Group, 40, 41, 43, 48, 106, 141,
  166
  Constructive Engagement and, 46
  members of, 39
  South Africa and, 44
Contract labor system, 18, 97–98
  reform of, 100
  See also Labor
Convention on the Elimination of All
  Forms of Discrimination Against
  Women (UN), Constituent
  Assembly and, 144
Cooptation, 59, 157
Copper, 76
  export of, 106
  production of, 77, 87
  reserves of, 124
Cottage workshops, 99
Council for Namibia (UN), 37, 68
Council of Churches of Namibia, 140
  health care and, 151
  Resolution 435 and, 141
Council of Traditional Leaders, powers
  of, 61
Crocker, Chester A., 44–45, 46, 47,
  71(n30)
  mediation by, 171

Crops, 123–124
    diversification of, 114
CSO. *See* Central Selling Organization
Cubans, 45
    in Angola, 33, 47, 71(n29), 71(n30)
    withdrawal of, 48, 49, 71(n30), 166,
        171, 172
Cuito Cuanavale, 48, 71(n30)
    battle at, 32, 35, 47
Currency, establishing, 102, 120, 158

Dama, 135
Damara, 8
    origins of, 135–137
DeBeers Consolidated Mines, 76, 80,
        82, 84
    transfer pricing by, 81
Debswana diamond project, 81, 84
Debt, 10, 103–104
Decolonization, 23, 28. *See also*
        Colonialism
Defense spending, reducing, 119
Defiance Campaign, 65
Deficits
    budget, 104, 119
    trade, 110, 115, 117
Deforestation, 94
de Klerk, F. W., 63(photo), 106
Delimitation Commission, powers of,
        60
Demand deposits, increase in, 103
Democracy, 3, 16
    threats to, 64
    transition to, 67, 161
Democratic Turnhalle Alliance (DTA),
        42, 46, 56, 58, 70(n21)
    international recognition of, 44
    as loyal opposition, 61
    self-portrayal of, 43
    SWAPO and, 43, 44, 49, 50, 52, 54-
        55
Democratic Turnhalle Party of
        Namibia, 42
Demographics, 131–138. *See also*
        Population; Urbanization
Denmark, relations with, 67

Department of Economic Affairs, 76
Dependency ratio, 97, 138
Dependency syndrome, 115
Depo-Provera, 150
Deutsche Evangelische Lutherische
        Kirche. *See* Lutheran church
Development, foreign aid for, 113–115,
        161
Development brigade, 62
Diamond Board of South West Africa,
        81
Diamond processing, 124
Diamond Producer's Association, 82
Diamonds, 3, 8, 73, 76
    export of, 79
    production of, 77, 82–84
    taxation of, 81
Diamond Trading Company, 82
Diplomatic relations, 40, 62–69, 109–
        110
Discrimination, 17, 61, 97–98
    economic, 25
    positive, 146
Diseases, 149, 150, 159
    impact of, 148
Disposable income, growth of, 118
Diversification, 75, 88–89, 91, 111, 114
Dobra Teachers Training School, blacks
        at, 26
Dog tax, rebellion against, 24
Domestic services, employment in, 98
Drivers, Transport, and Allied Workers
        Union, 100
Drought, 89, 91
DTA. *See* Democratic Turnhalle
        Alliance
Dutch East India Company, 7
Dutch Reformed church, 140

ECA. *See* Economic Commission for
        Africa (UN)
Economic Commission for Africa (UN)
        (ECA), 107
Economic growth, 115, 117–119, 123,
        157
    limits on, 108, 109

negative, 117–118
Economic relations, international, 108, 110–113
Economic sectors, 74–97
Economy
  foreign involvement in, 9, 19, 65, 122
  prospects for, 119–120, 122, 123
  resources-based, 123
Education, 131, 152, 159–160
  aid in, 114, 118
  apartheid and, 24–25, 145
  for blacks, 139, 144
  post-secondary, 147
  problems in, 26, 144–147, 158–159
  resistance and, 24–25
  secondary, 145
  for whites, 139
  women and, 145–146
Educational Authorities, 145
EEC. See European Economic Community
EEZ. See Exclusive economic zone
Elago, Nashilongo, 150
Elections, 45, 49–51, 61, 166, 170, 174
  call for, 29
  debate about, 40–41
  fraud in, 53–54
  participants in, 42, 54–55, 156
  See also Voting
Electricity, 94–95, 160
Elizabeth Bay, mine at, 82
Emigration, 7, 8–9, 11, 17
Employment, 97–98
  creating, 75, 123, 157
  problems in, 158–159
  refugees and, 160
  See also Unemployment
Energy, increased use of, 94–95, 125–126
English
  as official language, 2, 61, 145
  teaching in, 145, 147
ENOK. See First National Development Corporation
Ethnicity, 20–21(n1), 131–138
  management by, 20
  segregation by, 27

Etosha Game Reserve, 125
Etosha Petroleum Company, 95
European Economic Community (EEC), 111
European settlers, immigration of, 7, 17
Evangelical Lutheran church. See Lutheran church
Exchange rate, 102, 126(n1)
Exclusive economic zone (EEZ), 101, 106–108, 121
  monitoring, 92–93
Exiles, 31, 32, 53. See also Refugees
Exports, 108, 110, 111
  beef, 113
  new markets for, 75, 123, 124
  problems with, 115
  to South Africa, 105
Extermination campaign. See Genocide

Farms
  nationalization of, 121
  redistribution of, 89
  subsistence, 90, 125
  See also Agriculture
FCN. See Federal Convention of Namibia
Federal Convention of Namibia (FCN), 58
Fields, Kimberley, 82
Finance, 103–104
  employment in, 98
Finland, relations with, 67
First National Bank, 103
First National Development Corporation (ENOK), 89
Fisheries, 97
  managing, 92–93
  SWAPO and, 121
  USSR and, 114–115
Fishing, 125
  employment in, 98
  growth of, 117
  migrant workers and, 99
  problems with, 115
Fish processing, 93, 123

problems for, 89
USSR and, 125
Food and Agriculture Organization
    (UN), 91, 94
Food processing, 93, 123, 125
    fluctuations in, 88–89
    opportunities in, 123–124
Food Products and Associated Workers
    Union, 100
Foodstuffs, importing, 123
Foreign aid, 113–115, 158, 161. *See also*
    Official development assistance
Foreign investment, 73, 78, 120, 161
    in agriculture, 90
Foreign Investment Act of 1990, 122
Foreign relations. *See* Diplomatic
    relations
Fouche, Piet, 59
Freehold property, blacks and, 39
Fruit production, 91
Fund for Namibia (UN), 37

GATT. *See* General Agreement on
    Tariffs and Trade
GDP. *See* Gross Domestic Product
Geingob, Hage Gottifried, 57, 99, 119,
    175
Gender-based relations
    changes in, 141–144
    See also Women
General Agreement on Tariffs and
    Trade (GATT), 111, 115
Generalized System of Preferences
    (GSP), 111, 115
Geneva Protocol (1988), 48
    text of, 171–172
Genocide, 12–14, 135, 138
    women and, 141
    See also Massacres
Germany
    aid from, 114, 161
    control by, 1, 3, 10–14
    emigration from, 7, 11
    genocide by, 12, 135, 138
    relations with, 67
    trade with, 110

Gold Fields Namibia, Ltd., 76, 80, 86
Gold Fields of South Africa, 76, 80, 86
Gorbachev, Mikhail, 67
Goringstrasse (Windhoek), 64(photo)
Government
    affirmative action in, 99
    employment in, 98
Government Staff Association, 100
Great Britain
    aid from, 161
    class "C" mandate for, 15
    emigration from, 7
    relations with, 67
Grootfontein, guerrilla warfare in, 31,
    32
Gross Domestic Product (GDP), 73, 76,
    82, 115, 117
    agriculture's part of, 89–90
    imports/exports and, 110
    manufacturing's part of, 88
    mining's part of, 78
    South Africa and, 101
    structure of, 74
Group Areas Act (1923), 20
GSP. *See* Generalized System of
    Preferences
Guerrilla warfare, 3, 29–32
    training for, 66
Guest workers. *See* Migrant labor
Gurirab, Theo-Ben, 57, 66, 175

Hahn, Hugo, 7
Halbscheid agreement (1923), 81
Hamutenya, Hidipo, 59, 99, 175
Hamutumpangela, Theophilus, 140
Hanekom, Gerhard, 92, 94, 123,
    127(n33), 130(n96), 175
Hausiku, Marco, 121, 176
Health care, 154(n43), 159–160
    for blacks, 139
    churches and, 151
    providing, 147–151
    spending for, 118, 151
Henties Bay, port at, 107
Herero (language), 2
Herero Council, 26, 29

Herero-German War, 11, 139
  atrocities of, 12–13
  See also Genocide
Herero Rebellion of 1904, 12–13, 24
Hereros, 6, 9, 42, 132–133, 135–137
  as cabinet ministers, 56
  clans of, 135
  genocide of, 12–13, 14, 135
  protection for, 10
Herrigel, Otto, 102, 114, 115, 119, 160,
    175
Himba, 135
Homelands. *See* Reserves
Housing, problems in, 158–159
Human rights violations, 50, 53

ICJ. *See* International Court of Justice
ICSEAF. *See* International Commission
    for Southeast Atlantic Fisheries
IMF. *See* International Monetary Fund
Immigration, 7, 8–9, 11, 17
Immorality and Mixed Marriages Act,
    43
Imports, 111, 123
  GDP and, 110
  South African, 101, 105
  via South Africa, 101
Income, redistribution of, 157
Independence, 14, 39, 46–47, 49, 69,
    119, 161, 166
  black churches and, 140
  celebration of, 62
  peaceful transition to, 40
  regional political relations and, 62–
    66
  struggle for, 1, 23, 36
  UN and, 3, 23, 37–38, 68
  U.S. and, 45, 48, 115
  women and, 142–143
Independent Mineworkers Union, 100
Industrial and Commercial Union of
    Africa, 100
Industrialization, 108, 111, 120
  coal and, 110
  problems with, 73, 75
Industry
  categories of, 99

diversification of, 88–89, 111, 123
  foreign-dominated, 19
  resources-based, 123, 157
  textile, 124
  training for, 114
  See also Manufacturing
Infant mortality rates, 150
Inflation, 115, 117, 118, 119
Infrastructure. *See* Transportation
International Commission for
    Southeast Atlantic Fisheries
    (ICSEAF), 93
International community, pressure by,
    27–28, 40
International Court of Justice (ICJ), 30,
    37, 140, 164, 165
  SWA and, 27–28, 36
International Monetary Fund (IMF),
    102, 103, 104
Irrigation, 94, 114
Iscor, 80
Ivory, 8, 10
Iyambo, Nicky, 176

Japan
  relations with, 67
  trade with, 110
Jaster, Robert S., 64
Jobs, creating, 75, 123, 157
Jonker, Jan, 138

Kaiserstrasse (Windhoek), 64(photo)
Kalahari Desert, 2, 5, 131
  coal deposits in, 110
Kaokoland, guerrilla warfare in, 31
Kapelwa, Richard, 175
Kapuuo, Clemens, 29–30
Karakul pelts, export of, 91
Kassinga massacre, 32, 41, 47
Katutura, 100
  housing shortage in, 159
  resettlement in, 27
Kaulinge, Pendukeni, 142
Kavango Alliance Party, 42
Kazombaue, Lindy, 150
Kenya, independence for, 23

Khoi, 131, 137, 138
Kikumbi, Gertrude, 142
Koevoet, 35(photo)
   development brigade and, 62
   intimidation by, 34, 53
Kombat Mine, 80
Kudu offshore gas field, 81–82
Kwanyama (language), 2

Labor, 97–98
   control of, 13–14, 17–18
   education of, 146
   prison, 17–18
   resistance and, 25–27
   wage, 13
   women and, 143
   See also Contract labor system;
      Migrant labor
Labor Code (1907), 13
Labor leaders, harassment of, 26
Labor Relations Act, women and, 143
Labour Party of SWA, 42
Lagos Plan of Action (OAU), 109
Land
   nationalization of, 121
   need for, 13–14
   reallocation of, 89, 91, 140
   settlement of, 17, 121
Languages, 2, 61, 131
LDCs. See Less Developed Countries
Lead
   production of, 77, 87
   reserves of, 124
League of Nations, 15, 16, 27, 28
   mandate by, 106, 163–164
Least developed country (LLDC)
   status, 113, 114
Leather products, manufacturing, 125
Less Developed Countries (LDCs),
   manufacturing in, 88
Leutwein, Theodore, 12
Liberation Committee (OAU), 68
Liberation literature, 152
Liberation movements, 32
   women and, 142
Liberation theology, advocacy of, 140

Literacy campaign, 142
Literacy rate, 144, 146
Literature, 151–152
Lithium, 76
Livestock, 124–125
LLDC. See Least developed country
   status
Lobstein, Tim, 148, 149
Lome IV, 111, 114
London Missionary Society, 7
Lonhro, 90–91, 110
Lubowski, Anton T.A.W., 52, 161
Luderitz, 2
   port at, 97, 107
   strike at, 25
Luderitz, F.A.E., 8
Lutheran church, 141
   anticonscription campaign and, 140
   liberation and, 140
   mediation by, 140–141
   missionaries from, 139

McHenry, Donald, 40
Maharero, 12
Malnutrition, 159
Mandate
   class "C," 15, 106, 165
   responsibilities of, 28
   revocation of, 36–37, 165
   text of, 163–164
   See also Trusteeship
Mandela, Nelson, 26
Manufacturing, 74–75, 87, 88–89, 123–
   125
   colonial policies and, 88
   employment in, 89, 98
   energy consumption by, 94
   garment, 124
   growth and, 109
   informal, 89
   migrant workers and, 99
   See also Industry
Manufacturing firms, location of, 89,
   90
Markets, diversity in, 91
Massacres, 32, 41, 47, 66

radicalizing effect of, 27
See also Genocide
Master and Servant Proclamation of
    1920, 18
Mediation, 36, 64
    Lutheran church and, 140–141
    U.S., 48, 68
Merchants, arrival of, 7–8
Metal and Allied Namibian Workers
    Union, 100
Metall Mining Corp., 80
Methane gas, discovery of, 95
Methodist Church of Southern Africa,
    141
Meyer, Willie, 59
MFN. *See* Most Favored Nation status
Migrant labor, 9, 13–14, 20, 27, 98
    importance of, 18
    occupations for, 99
    See also Labor
Migration, forced, 26–27
Minerals, 75, 76–87, 124
    dependence on, 73
    exploration for, 76
    export of, 76, 79
    investment in, 76
    ownership of, 121
    production of, 77, 87
    taxes from, 76
    See also Base minerals; Various
        minerals by name
Miners, death of, 78
Mines, list of, 80
Mines, Works, and Minerals Act
    (1969), 87
Mines, Works, and Minerals Ordinance
    of 1968, 78
Mineworkers Union of Namibia
    (MUN), 86, 100, 101, 154(n43)
    health issues and, 149
    pressure from, 159
Mining, 7–8, 76–87
    employment in, 98
    government monitoring of, 78
    growth of, 117
    migrant workers and, 99
    revenues from, 78, 81

SWAPO and, 121
taxation of, 81
transportation and, 96–97
water and, 95
Ministry of Mines and Energy, 81
Missionaries, 21(n1), 139, 144
Missions
    establishment of, 7
    reservation system and, 11
Mixed economy, 120, 122, 160
Moly Copper, 80
Mortality rates, 148, 150
Mosquito control programs, disruption
    of, 148
Most Favored Nation (MFN) status,
    109
Mowe Bay, port at, 107
MPLA. *See* Popular Movement for the
    Independence of Angola
Mueshihange, Peter, 57, 175
Multiparty system, guaranteeing, 59
MUN. *See* Mineworkers Union of
    Namibia
Muyongo, Mishake, 55

NAM. *See* Nonaligned Movement
Nama, 6, 7, 12, 13, 135, 137
    dispute with, 9
    protection for, 10
    trade with, 10
    war against, 11, 139
Nama (language), 2, 135
Namib Air, 97
Namib Desert, 2, 95
Namibia Building Workers Union, 100
Namibia National Democratic Party
    (NNDP), 58
Namibia National Front (NNF), 56, 58
Namibian Food and Allied Workers
    Union, 101
Namibian National Teachers Union,
    101
Namibian Transport and Allied
    Workers Union, 101
Namibia Patriotic Front (NPF), 56

Namibia: Perspectives for National Reconstruction and Development (UNIN), 119
Namibia Wholesale and Retail Workers Union, 101
Namib-Naukluft Park, 125
Namutoni, German fort at, 8
National Assembly
    election of, 59
    powers of, 60
    See also Constituent Assembly
National Building and Investment Corporation (NBIC), 159
National Convention of South West Africa, 29–30
National Council, powers of, 60
National Democratic Party, 42
Nationalism, 3, 24, 36, 37
    churches and, 139–140
Nationalist party (SA), SWA and, 19
Nationalization, 78, 119, 120, 122
    opposition to, 61, 81, 160
    SWAPO and, 87, 121
National Patriotic Front (NPF), 58
National Union for the Total Independence of Angola (UNITA), 35, 46, 48, 49, 62
    aid to, 71(n28), 71(n31)
    attacks by, 34
    SWAPO and, 33
National Union of Namibian Workers (NUNW), 101
Navachab Gold Mine, 80
NBIC. *See* National Building and Investment Corporation
NNDP. *See* Namibia National Democratic Party
NNF. *See* Namibia National Front
Nonaligned Movement (NAM), 68
Nontariff barriers, 109
Norway
    aid from, 114
    relations with, 67
NPF. *See* Namibia Patriotic Front; National Patriotic Front
Nuclear Energy Act of 1982, 84

Nujoma, Sam Shafiishuna, 63(photo), 65, 66, 106, 114, 115, 175
    cabinet ministers of, 56–57, 59
    death threats for, 52
    health issues and, 149
    land issue and, 121
    swearing in of, 62
NUNW. *See* National Union of Namibian Workers

OAU. *See* Organization of African Unity
ODA. *See* Official development assistance
Odendaal Commission Report of 1964, 19, 20
Official development assistance, 113. *See also* Foreign aid
Off-shore islands, 106–108
Offshore oil exploration, 81–82, 95
Okavango, 33
    clans of, 134
    guerrilla warfare in, 31
Old Location
    demonstrations at, 141
    removal from, 26–27
O'Linn Commission. *See* Commission for the Prevention and Combatting of Intimidation and Election Malpractices
Ondongas, domination by, 6
Oorlams, 9, 137
    protection for, 10
    trade with, 10
OPC. *See* Ovambo People's Congress
OPIC. *See* Overseas Private Investment Corporation
OPO. *See* Ovamboland People's Organization
Orchards, 91
Organization of African Unity (OAU), 29, 68, 106, 109
Oruuano, 139–140
Otijibingue, importance of, 7
Otjhase Mining Company, 80
Otjiwarongo, guerrilla warfare in, 32

Ovambo, 8, 13, 17, 29, 30, 33
  decline of, 9
  development aid to, 156
  precolonial history of, 5–6
  resistance by, 9, 24
  SADF control of, 34
  SWAPO and, 52
  trading by, 132–134
Ovambo Educational Authority, 145
Ovamboland, 8, 9, 14, 33
  drought in, 91
  guerrilla warfare in, 30
  services for, 122, 157
Ovamboland People's Organization
    (OPO), 25, 29, 59, 65, 100
  See also South West Africa People's
    Organization
Ovambo People's Congress (OPC), 57,
    100
Overfishing, 89, 92
Overmining, 81
Overseas Business Corporation, 108
Overseas Development Institute, 104
Overseas Petroleum Investment
    Corporation, 95
Overseas Private Investment
    Corporation (OPIC), 115

Pan-Africanist Conference, 66
Parastatals, 74, 82, 88, 95–97, 120, 121
Parent's Committee, SWAPO and, 53
Parties
  description of, 3–4
  splits in, 157
  See also Coalition politics
Passive resistance, 26, 65
Pass Law of 1922, 18
Pass Laws, 18, 99
  demonstrations against, 141
  modification of, 43
Pastoralism, 132, 134, 137
  precolonial, 5, 6
Peace Corps, 115
People's Liberation Army of Namibia
    (PLAN), 49, 51, 54, 66
  development brigade and, 62

Koevoet and, 34
offensive by, 30–32
South African response to, 32–35
women and, 142
Peralin, 80
Perez de Cuellar, Javier, 46
Permanent Mandates Commission
    (League of Nations), 15
Pescanova Industries, investment by,
    125
Piennar, Louis, 42(photo)
Pieterse, Cosmo, 152
PLAN. See People's Liberation Army of
    Namibia
Pohamba, Hifikepunye, 59, 175
Police force, training, 62
Police violence, 25–26
Popular Movement for the
    Independence of Angola (MPLA),
    35, 49, 65, 67, 71(n28)
Population
  control, 150
  density, 138
  groups, 132
  See also Demographics; Urbanization
Ports, 110
  alternative, 107
  description of, 97
Portugal
  emigration from, 8–9
  problems with, 23
Posh Pinah Mine, 80
Positive discrimination, policy of, 146
Positive Engagement (Great Britain),
    46
Precolonial era, history of, 5–11
Preferential Trade Area for Eastern and
    Southern African States (PTA),
    109
President
  election of, 59
  powers of, 60
Private property, 120, 132
  acceptance of, 10
  SWAPO and, 52
Private sector, 74, 78
  development of, 118, 158

role of, 160
SWAPO and, 120–121
Private Sector Investor Conference, 120
Private voluntary organizations (PVOs), 113
Processing industries
food, 88–89, 123–124, 125
potential for, 87
PTA. *See* Preferential Trade Area for Eastern and Southern African States
Public sector, 115, 122
Public Service Commission Bill, 99
PVOs. *See* Private voluntary organizations

Racism, 3, 12, 138, 139
educational system and, 145
institutionalized, 19
opposition to, 24
See also Apartheid
Radiation control program, 149
Railroads, 110
mining and, 96
Rainfall, 1, 2, 73
Rand
dominance of, 102
exchange rate for, 126(n1)
Rand Monetary Zone, SWAPO and, 120
Reagan, Ronald, 47
sanctions and, 46
South Africa and, 44, 45
SWA and, 45–46
Red Cross, investigation by, 53
Refugees
demands of, 160
health care for, 151
return of, 53
See also Exiles
Regional cooperation. *See* Diplomatic relations
Rehoboth Baster Association, 42
Rehoboth Basters, 24, 135, 138
Religion, 131, 138–141. *See also* Churches

Religious associations, importance of, 138
Rembrandt Group, 87
Republican Party, 42
Mudge and, 70(n21)
Republic of South Africa. *See* South Africa
Reserves, 3, 16, 70(n16), 98
dismantling, 61
missions and, 11
use of, 17, 19–20, 38, 39
Resettlement, 26–27
Resistance
education and, 24–25
external, 27–29
internal, 24–27
labor and, 25–27
passive, 26
quasi-legal status of, 29
violent, 23
Resolution 385 (UN), 40, 41, 166
ignoring, 46
Resolution 432 (UN), 122
Resolution 435 (UN), 40, 41, 43–46, 70(n20), 106, 141, 166, 171–174
ignoring, 46
implementation of, 46–50, 52, 53
supplement to, 169–170
text of, 167–168
Resolution 2145 (UN), 165
Resources, 3
depletion of, 10, 81, 89, 92
economic, 74–97
management of, 92
marine, 92–93
Rhenish Mission Society, 7
Rio Tinto Zinc Corp. (RTZ), 76, 80, 84
earnings of, 85
Rivers, description of, 1
Roads, 108, 110
mining and, 96–97
Robinson, Randall, 49
Roman Catholic church, 139, 141
"Ro-ro" (roll-on, roll-off) services, 97, 107
Rössing Uranium, Ltd. (RUL), 76, 80, 84, 101

earnings of, 85–86
health issues and, 149, 154(n43)
water for, 95
RTZ. *See* Rio Tinto Zinc Corp.
Ruacana station, 94–95
RUL. *See* Rössing Uranium, Ltd.
Rural electrification, priority of, 94–95

SACU. *See* Southern African Customs
    Union
SADCC. *See* Southern African
    Development Coordination
    Conference
SADF. *See* South African Defense
    Force
Salt, production of, 124
Salt Company (mine), 80
San
    arrival of, 131–132
    manipulation of, 34
    population of, 132
    trading by, 131
Sanctions, 37, 41, 43, 111
    adopting, 40
    effect of, 36
    elimination of, 91
    mandatory, 36, 45
    U.S. and, 46, 47
    vetoing, 45
Satyagraha. See Passive resistance
Schools
    black, 145
    compulsory, 159–160
    white, 145
    See also Education
Scott, Michael, 140
Security Council (UN), 37, 39, 71(n31),
    166
    resolutions by, 40, 49
    sanctions and, 36
Segregation, 20, 27, 43, 150–151
Self-determination, 39, 44
Sexism, dealing with, 141–144
Sharpville massacre, 66
    radicalizing effect of, 27
Skeleton Coast Park, 125

Slaves, 8
Smuts, Jan, 14
Socialism, 119
    SWAPO and, 120, 122
    See also Central planning
Social services, 75, 157
    spending for, 118
    for whites, 139
Solar energy, 125
Sonangol, 82
South Africa
    control by, 1, 3, 14–20, 17, 63, 73,
        101
    economic links with, 22(n20), 101–
        108, 110, 158
    mandate for, 15, 165
    pressure on, 27–28, 40, 43, 47
    sporting links with, 153
    SWAPO and, 120
    UN and, 35–37
South African Airways, 97
South African Defense Force (SADF),
    32, 47, 50, 71(n30)
    goals of, 33, 34
    medical services from, 151
    withdrawal of, 41, 49, 117, 160, 166,
        171, 172
South African Electricity Supply
    Commission, 94
South African Land Ordinances of
    1903 and 1912, 17
South African Railway, 96
South African Railways & Harbour
    Corporation, 88
South African Reserve Bank, 102
South African Transport Services, 97
"Southern Africa: What Namibian
    Independence Will Mean for
    Business" (Business International),
    119
Southern African Customs Union
    (SACU), 101
    revenue sharing by, 104–105, 119
    SWAPO and, 120
    withdrawing from, 158

Southern African Development
    Coordination Conference
    (SADCC), 65, 68, 69, 109
Southern Oil Exploration Corporation,
    95
South West Africa National Union
    (SWANU), 26, 29
    exclusion of, 38
    split of, 56
South West Africa Native Labor
    Association (SWANLA), 18
South West Africa People's
    Organization (SWAPO), 3–4, 26,
    40, 41, 51, 58, 59, 71(n30), 108,
    129(n63), 140, 167, 171
    ANC and, 65–66
    cooperation by, 48, 56, 166
    DTA and, 43, 44, 49, 50, 52, 54–55
    economic policies of, 119–120, 160
    exclusion of, 38, 39, 42
    guerrilla warfare by, 29, 32
    Koevoet and, 53
    NAM and, 68
    Ovambo and, 52, 156
    policy positions of, 87, 157–158
    problems for, 30, 34
    South Africa and, 32–35, 120
    training and, 31, 147
    UN and, 37–38, 46, 50, 53
    UNITA and, 33
    USSR and, 67–68
    women and, 142–143
    See also Ovamboland People's
       Organization
South West African People's
    Organization Democrats
    (SWAPO/D), 58, 69(n6)
South West African People's
    Organization Women's Council,
    141, 142
    constitution of, 143
    education and, 145–146
    goals of, 177
Southwest African Progressive
    Association (SWAPA), 25, 26
South West African Territorial Forces
    (SWATF), 151

development brigade and, 62
    recruiting for, 34
South West Africa Water and
    Electricity Commission, 94
Special Committee for Southwest
    Africa (UN), 36
Special Forces, fear of, 34, 35
Sports, 152–153
Standard Bank, 103
Strikes, 18–19, 25, 78, 87, 99–100. See
    also Boycotts
Suppression of Communism Act of
    1950, 33
Supreme Court, powers of, 61
Swakopmund, 1, 2
    guerrilla warfare in, 32
    port at, 107
SWAKOR, 82
SWA Lithium Mines, 80
SWA Mineworkers Union, 101
SWA Municipal Staff Association, 101
SWANLA. See South West Africa
    Native Labor Association
SWANU. See South West Africa
    National Union
SWAPA. See Southwest African
    Progressive Association
SWA People's Democratic United
    Front, 42
SWAPO. See South West Africa
    People's Organization
SWAPO/D. See South West Africa
    People's Organization Democrats
SWATF. See South West African
    Territorial Forces
Swaziland, 66
Sweden, relations with, 67
Switzerland, trade with, 110

Tanzania, 108
Tariffs, eliminating, 109
Taxes, 39, 119, 128(n60)
    from minerals, 76
TB. See Tuberculosis
TCL. See Tsumeb Corporation Limited
Technikon, 147

Technology, 109, 114
Terrorism Act of 1967, 32–33
  enforcing, 25–26
Textile industry, 124
Thatcher, Margaret: South Africa and, 44
Thirion Commission, establishment of, 78, 81
32 Battalion, 33
Thomas, Wolfgang H., 128–129(n63), 158
Tin, 76
Tjingaete, Fanuel, 128(n60), 159
Tjiriange, Ngarukutuke, 176
Toivo, Andimba Toivo ya, 81, 82, 175
  imprisonment of, 26
Toivo, Herman Toivo ya, 100
Total strategy, 33–34
Tourism, future of, 108, 125
Trade, 21(n1), 40, 63, 68, 104–105
  balance, 110, 112
  control of, 8–9, 105
  cooperation in, 109
  deficits, 110
  direction of, 113
  international, 110–113
  long-distance, 133, 136
  precolonial, 5, 6
  Southern African, 108
  surplus in, 115
Trade unions. See Unions
Trading companies, 7
Training, 121, 146, 147
Transfer pricing, 81
Transition, 67, 161
  concept of, 39
  peaceful, 40
Transnamib Limited, 96
Transportation, 73, 74, 104–105, 110
  advancements in, 96–97
  air, 97
  control of, 105, 107
  cooperation in, 108
  employment in, 98
  public, 97
  women and, 141

Transport Corporation Workers Union of Namibia, 101
Tripartite Agreement, 166
  text of, 173–174
Trusteeship, 15–16, 28, 165. See also Mandate
Trusteeship Commission, 15
Trusteeship Committee, 16
Trusteeship Council (UN), 15
Tsumeb, 6
  guerrilla warfare in, 32
Tsumeb Corporation Limited (TCL), 76, 80, 86
  criticism of, 101
  sales by, 87
Tswana Alliance, 42
Tuberculosis (TB), 148, 159
Turnhalle Conference, 38–39, 42
Twelve Principles to Promote and Maintain the Welfare of the People, 61

UDF. See United Democratic Front
Uis Tin Mine, 80
Umkhonto we Sizwe, 66
UN. See United Nations
UNDP. See United Nations Development Programme
Unemployment, 157, 159. See also Employment
UNHCR. See United Nations High Commission for Refugees
UNIDO. See United Nations Industrial Development Organization
UNIN. See United Nations Institute for Namibia
Unions, 78, 86, 99–100, 154(n43)
  health issues and, 149
  legal recognition for, 25
  pressure from, 159
  quelling, 18–19
  registering of, 100–101
  SWAPO and, 100
  women and, 143
UNITA. See National Union for the Total Independence of Angola

United Congressional Church of
Southern Africa, 141
United Democratic Front (UDF), 54, 58
United Nations
criticism by, 35–36
independence and, 3, 23
LLDC status and, 114
mandate and, 15, 36–37, 165
recognition by, 165
South Africa and, 36–37
SWA and, 27–28
SWAPO and, 37–38, 46, 50, 53
training and, 147
United Nations Children's Fund, 91
United Nations Development
Programme (UNDP), 91, 102–103,
113, 117
United Nations High Commission for
Refugees (UNHCR), 147, 160
United Nations Industrial
Development Organization
(UNIDO), 91, 147
United Nations Institute for Namibia
(UNIN), 74, 92, 119, 147
United Nations Transitional Assistance
Group (UNTAG), 40, 50, 54, 67,
71(n31), 167, 172
Koevoet and, 53
withdrawal of, 117
United States
aid from, 115, 161
mediation by, 48, 68
relations with, 67
trade with, 110
Universal Negro Improvement
Association, 24
University of Namibia, 147
UNTAG. See United Nations
Transitional Assistance Group
Uranium, 3, 67, 73, 76
export of, 106
monitoring of, 84
production of, 77, 84–87
Uranium mining, 85(photo)
health concerns and, 149
Urbanization, 138, 159. See also
Demographics; Population

USSR, 47–48
fisheries and, 114–115
fish processing and, 125
support from, 29, 33
SWAPO and, 67–68

Vagrancy Law of 1920, 18
Van Wyk, Hermanus, 138
Vegetation, map of, 2
Vocational Training Centre for
Namibia, 147
von Trotha, Louis, 12–13
Vorster, John, 37
Voter registration, 50, 52
discouraging, 54
Voting, 56(photo), 57(photo)
fraud, 53–54
See also Elections

Wage and Industrial Conciliation
Ordinance, 100
Wage labor, forced, 13–14
Walvis Bay, 2, 7, 10, 106–108, 110,
128–129(n63)
alternatives to, 107
fishing at, 92, 94
as free port, 122
negotiations over, 41, 68
port at, 97
reintegration of, 106, 122
South African occupation of, 101,
106, 107
SWAPO and, 122
Water, 94–95, 160
increased use of, 125–126
mining and, 95
underground, 95
White Educational Authority, 145
White Wolves, vigilantism of, 52
WHO. See World Health Organization
Windhoek, 64(photo)
bombings in, 47
guerrilla warfare in, 32
population of, 138
Windhoek International School, 147
Windhoek Shootings, 66

radicalizing effect of, 27, 28–29
Witbooi, Hendrik, 175
Women
    education and, 145–146
    equality for, 177
    PLAN and, 142
    role of, 141–144
    SWAPO and, 142–143
    unions and, 143
World Bank, 108, 113
World Food Programme, 91
World Health Organization (WHO),
    151

World War, SWA and, 14, 16

Young, Andrew, 40

Zambia, trade with, 108
Zimbabwe
    independence for, 23
    PTA and, 109
Zinc, 76
    production of, 77
    reserves of, 124